One Year

with

Jesus

in the

Gospels

Yearly
DEVOTIONAL

**Daily readings based on excerpts from
The Life for Today
Study Bible and Commentary
Gospels Edition
by
Andrew Wommack**

Andrew Wommack Ministries
P.O. Box 3333
Colorado Springs, Colorado 80934

JANUARY 1
JESUS WAS GOD
LUKE 1:1-4; JOHN 1:1-18

John 1:1 "In the beginning was the Word, and the Word was with God, and the Word was God."

Jesus was not just a man sent from God, **He was God**.

This is the most important statement of the New Testament. On this truth hangs all other truths.

If Jesus was only a man, then regardless of how good He was, His life could only provide a substitute for one other man. But since He was God, His life was worth more than every human life since creation. Indeed it was worth more than the sum total of the universe that He created.

Any compromise on this point will negate the work of Christ in our lives. Jesus was God manifest in the flesh (1 Tim. 3:16)! Yet, this Almighty God came to dwell in a human body. He humbled Himself and took the form of a servant (Phil. 2:7).

Christ's humanity truly made Him one of us. He suffered the same temptations and pressures that we suffer (Heb. 4:15). It was His divinity, however, that gave Him the power to save us completely (Heb. 7:25). We must never let His humanity blind us to the truth that Almighty God Himself became our friend (Jn. 15:13-15). We must never let His divinity blind us to the truth that He knows exactly how we feel and cares for us.

Let the Holy Spirit give you a true revelation of the deity and humanity of our Lord Jesus Christ throughout this new year.

JANUARY 2
NOW, OR THEN?
JOHN 1:1-18

John 1:16 "And of his fulness have all we received, and grace for grace."

The Christian life is not like an insurance policy that only pays off when we die and go to heaven. **Every** believer has **now** received the grace of God and the fullness of God. We are **now** complete in Him (Col. 2:9-10).

When we receive Jesus as our Lord, we are instantly changed in our spirits (2 Cor. 5:17). Many Christians aren't aware of the change that takes place in their spirits. They continue to live within their physical and emotional realms and are oblivious to the new, born-again part of them that has received the fullness of God.

You can't see or feel your spirit. You just have to believe what the Word of God tells you because God's Word is spirit and life (Jn. 6:63). Your spiritual salvation is complete. Nothing can be added to it. In your spirit, you are right now as you will be throughout all eternity (1 Jn. 4:17). PRAISE THE LORD!

To the degree that we will renew our minds to these truths and believe them, we will experience this fullness in this life; "*for as a man thinketh in his heart, so [is] he*" (Pro. 23:7).

Pray the prayer of Ephesians 1:15-23 and let the Holy Spirit reveal "*Christ in you, the hope of glory*" (Col. 1:27).

JANUARY 3
ABOUT GENEOLOGIES
MATTHEW 1:1-17; LUKE 3:23-38

Luke 3:23 "And Jesus himself began to be about thirty years of age, being (as was supposed) the son of Joseph, which was the son of Heli."

Even the genealogies are inspired by God and profitable (2 Tim. 3:16). Matthew traces Jesus' genealogy through Joseph back to Solomon; however, there was a curse placed on one of Solomon's sons, Jechonias, (Jer. 22:24-30), which Jesus avoided by being born of a virgin.

Luke mentions Jesus as being the supposed son of Joseph who was the son of Heli. It was actually Mary who was the daughter of Heli. This was mentioned in other Old Testament instances (Num. 27:1-11; 36:12 and Ruth 4:6). Mary's genealogy was also from David, but was through Nathan, a half brother of Solomon. Thus the lineage was preserved, but the curse bypassed.

These genealogies show the infinite wisdom of God in fulfilling His promises despite the corruption of man. These genealogies are full of murderers, adulterers, and every sort of pervert known to man, yet these same people were used of God, not because of their actions, but in spite of them. That means there is still hope for us.

God has never had anyone working for Him who was qualified, and you won't be the first. The history of God's dealings with man reveals that He has always used less than perfect vessels. We can rejoice and take comfort because God uses us because of our faith, not our holiness.

JANUARY 4
CAN YOU BELIEVE IT?
LUKE 1:5-25

Luke 1:18 "And Zacharias said unto the angel, Whereby shall I know this? for I am an old man, and my wife well stricken in years."

Zacharias and Elisabeth were righteous people (v. 6) who prayed for a child for many years. They felt the same disappointments and frustrations that we would feel, but they kept believing God. The Lord finally answered their prayers and sent His angel to announce the good news.

What was Zacharias' reaction? **He couldn't believe it!** The very thing that he had been praying for was granted, and he doubted that it was true. In Zacharias' case he received his miracle anyway. Perhaps his wife's faith pulled him through.

Likewise, you may be praying for the right things. You may even be sincere and earnest, but would you be surprised if those prayers were suddenly answered today? Have you made preparations for your prayers to be answered?

Before the children of Israel were actually delivered from Egypt, they ate the passover meal by faith. Their bags were packed and ready to go. We need to anticipate our prayers being answered.

Right now, imagine how you would feel, or what you would do if the answer to your prayer was manifested this very minute. Then, as much as possible, begin to think and act that way. You'll find that your whole attitude will change as you focus on your answer instead of your problem.

JANUARY 5
KNOWING GOD'S WILL
IS NOT ENOUGH
LUKE 1:26-38

Luke 1:34 "Then said Mary unto the angel, How shall this be, seeing I know not a man?"

Contrast Mary's question and Gabriel's response with the question Zacharias asked Gabriel and the response that he received (Lk. 1:18-20). You will find that the questions are similar, but the responses are totally different.

Both Mary and Zacharias asked how these miracles would occur, but it is evident that Mary asked "how" in faith while Zacharias asked "how" in unbelief. It is a clear biblical teaching that unbelief doesn't please God (Heb. 11:6), but the Lord doesn't mind us questioning Him for the purpose of instruction, so we can cooperate with His will in our lives.

Abram knew that it was God's will for him to have a son, but Abram and Sarai came up with their own plan which caused them and the world much grief (Gen. 16:1-6). Abram would have avoided many problems if he had asked the Lord how He was going to accomplish this miraculous event.

If Mary had not questioned thisangel, she might have reasoned that Jesus would be born through the natural union of her and Joseph. This would have been a grave mistake. It would have disqualified her from being used.

It's not enough just to know God's will. We need to continue to seek the Lord until we know God's plan for accomplishing that will.

JANUARY 6
NOTHING IS IMPOSSIBLE
LUKE 1:26-38

Luke 1:37 "For with God nothing shall be impossible."

What a statement! If we just believed this, how different our lives would be!

From birth, we are trained to know our limitations. "You can't have this. Don't touch that. Don't put things in your mouth. You can't touch the fire." On and on the list goes.

As we grow up, it's actually a sign of maturity to recognize our limitations and learn to live within them. There are limits to everything. It's a fact of life.

God has no limits. When we enter into the realm of the supernatural, we have to take off the limits. We have to renew our minds with the truth that God is not like us. He can do anything.

We have an awesome God whose power is so great that we can't even comprehend it. He created the universe and it didn't even tax His ability. Yet many times we find ourselves wondering if our situation is too hard for the Lord. We can't see how even God can pull us through.

The Lord said to Jeremiah, *"Behold, I am the Lord, the God of all flesh: is there any thing too hard for me?"* (Jer. 32:27) The answer is a resounding **NO!** The only thing that limits God is our unbelief (Dt. 7:17). Today, let's honor God by believing that nothing is too difficult for Him.

JANUARY 7
THE POWER TO SERVE
LUKE 1:39-56

Luke 1:41 "And it came to pass, that, when Elisabeth heard the salutation of Mary, the babe leaped in her womb; and Elisabeth was filled with the Holy Ghost."

Upon hearing the greeting of Mary, John the Baptist leaped for joy inside his mother's womb (v. 44). A six-month-old fetus experienced unbridled emotion, voluntarily leaped for joy, and was actually filled with the Holy Spirit.

It is no coincidence that the man Jesus called the greatest of all Old Testament prophets, was the only man in the Bible to be filled with the Holy Ghost in his mother's womb (Lk. 7:28).

The anointing of God that breaks every yoke is simply the manifest presence and working of the Holy Spirit (Isa. 10:27). The Holy Spirit is the part of the Godhead that empowers us for service.

God is not asking us to live for Him. He is asking us to let Him live through us (Gal. 2:20). **The Christian life is not a changed life but an exchanged life.** This can only be accomplished when the Holy Spirit is leading and empowering us.

Even Jesus didn't begin His ministry until he was anointed with the Holy Spirit, and He was the sinless Son of God. How much more do we need to depend on the power of the Holy Spirit in our daily lives? Today, be conscious of the presence of the Holy Spirit in you and expect Him to supernaturally guide and empower you. If you ask, you will receive (Lk. 11:9-13).

JANUARY 8
BELIEVERS RECEIVE
LUKE 1:39-56

Luke 1:45 "And blessed [is] she that believed: for there shall be a performance of those things which were told her from the Lord."

There are many reasons why God's blessings don't always come to pass in people's lives, but the most frequent cause is their unbelief. There are no limitations on God. He is willing and able to do anything He has promised. The problem is with our unbelief.

The Lord has given every believer faith (Rom. 12:3). It was given to us at salvation through hearing the Word of God (Eph. 2:8; Rom. 10:17). It is a fruit of the Holy Spirit (Gal. 5:22). However, we must choose to exercise it.

Our faith is linked to our knowledge (2 Pet. 1:1-4). What we think on is how we will be (Pro. 23:7). It is not that we don't have enough faith; the problem is that we don't allow our faith to work because we don't keep our minds stayed on God's Word. Our faith is then choked by the cares of this life (Mk. 4:19).

Keeping our minds stayed on God's Word will release our faith and thereby release the power of God in our lives. Certainly, Mary must have been a person who put God's Word first in her life.

Mary saw a performance of what she believed. **We receive what we believe, not what we desire or even need.** Today, believe the word that the Lord has spoken to you.

JANUARY 9
CHOOSING JOY
LUKE 1:39-56

Luke 1:46-47 "And Mary said, My soul doth magnify the Lord, and my spirit hath rejoiced in God my Saviour."

Here, Mary makes a very clear distinction between her soul magnifying the Lord and her spirit rejoicing.

Our soul is the part of us that is considered to be our personality. It is our intellects, emotions and wills. Our spirits are the part of us that changes at salvation. Our spirits always operate in *"love, joy, peace, long-suffering, gentleness, goodness, faith, meekness, temperance"* (2 Cor. 5:17; Gal. 5:22-23). That's true whether our souls (feelings and emotions) feel it or not.

Many believers wait until their emotions feel like praising the Lord before they enter into worship. They think it's hypocritical to act like they are rejoicing in the Lord if they don't feel it. Our spirits are always rejoicing in the Lord. It's actually hypocritical to go by our feelings and not magnify the Lord with our souls, when our born-again spirits are already rejoicing.

Our born again spirits are always in tune with the Lord and walking in His joy. Our flesh is often dominated by what it sees and feels. Sometimes it doesn't feel like praising the Lord, but the choice rests with our souls. If we choose to praise the Lord, our emotions will follow.

The decision is yours (Dt. 30:19). Today, **choose** to walk in the joy of the Lord.

JANUARY 10
DESERT TRAINING
LUKE 1:57-80

Luke 1:80 "And the child grew, and waxed strong in spirit, and was in the deserts till the day of his shewing unto Israel."

John the Baptist had the most important job assignment ever given to any mortal in the history of the world. He was to prepare the way for the coming of the long awaited Messiah (v. 76).

How did the Lord prepare John for such an important task? What university could teach him all he needed to know? Who offered a course in becoming the greatest prophet who ever lived? (Mt. 11:11)

Of course, no one could prepare John for such an important position, so the Lord taught him personally. John was in the deserts until he was thirty years old. He was tutored directly by the Lord through the Holy Spirit.

The personal touch of the Lord became very obvious. Six months after John began his ministry, the whole nation of Israel experienced revival and anticipated the coming of the Christ. When Jesus came, the Jews wondered how He could know things He was never taught (Jn. 7:15).

This special knowledge that comes directly from the Lord through the Holy Spirit is now available to every believer. It's part of the new covenant (Heb. 8:11). The Holy Spirit was sent to be our teacher, but we have to show up for class and expect to receive (Jn. 14:26). He'll even show us things to come (Jn. 16:13).

JANUARY 11
JOSEPH WAS A MAN OF FAITH
MATTHEW 1:18-24

Matthew 1:24 "Then Joseph being raised from sleep did as the angel of the Lord had bidden him, and took unto him his wife."

Much attention is given to Mary and her piety, but Joseph was quite a man of faith too.

Verse 18 says that Mary was "found" with child, implying that the pregnancy was observed by Joseph, not explained to him by Mary. This was after Mary had been away visiting Elisabeth for three months! (Lk. 1:56) Certainly Joseph was tempted with the same thoughts that you or I would have been. How could Mary expect him to believe that this was a virgin birth?

As special as Mary was, she had an equally special young man for a fiance. How many men would have believed such an incredible story, even if an angel had told them in a dream? It took more faith on Joseph's part than it did on Mary's.

This is the way it always is. Those who hear of the vision or call of God secondhand have to exhibit greater faith than the person who received the word from the Lord directly.

The scriptures don't mention whether Mary ever attempted to convince Joseph of the truth. What would have been the use? Only God could make someone believe a story like that. It is to Mary's credit that she trusted God, and to Joseph's credit that he believed God. Today, do as the Lord bids you and trust God to take care of the rest.

JANUARY 12
GOD DESIRES FAITH
LUKE 2:1-7

Luke 2:7 "And she brought forth her firstborn son, and wrapped him in swaddling clothes, and laid him in a manger; because there was no room for them in the inn."

What an amazing account! God Almighty was born of a virgin and placed in a feeding trough in a stable. Who would ever expect the cCreator of the universe to make His entrance into the world in such a humble fashion?

Men always seek to proclaim their glory as far and wide as possible. Yet here is the only one who really has any glory to proclaim, and He comes humbly. It wasn't because He didn't have the power to do things otherwise.

He could have chosen to be born in a fashion that would have brought all creation to their knees in worship. He could have announced His birth to the most powerful and famous men of the day instead of to lowly shepherds. He could have had the most luxurious accommodations instead of a stable, but that is not the way of our God. It would not have taken any faith on the part of men if Jesus came in such a manner that His deity was obvious.

Likewise with us, the Lord could manifest Himself to us in such a way that we couldn't miss Him, but that wouldn't please Him. God desires faith and, "*without faith it is impossible to please Him*" (Heb. 11:6). Today, let's please our heavenly Father and acknowledge His presence in faith just because of His promise (Mt. 28:20; Heb. 13:5).

JANUARY 13
HE WAS BORN A SAVIOR
LUKE 2:8-20

Luke 2:11 "For unto you is born this day in the city of David a Saviour, which is Christ the Lord."

Jesus did not grow into being Lord and Saviour. He was born that way. Jesus was God manifest in the flesh (1 Tim. 3:16). What a great mystery!

How could Almighty God limit Himself to the form of a man? Even if He did, how could he possibly start as a baby? These questions defy mankind's ability to fully understand.

At the dedication of the first temple, Solomon said, *"But will God in very deed dwell with men on the earth? Behold, heaven and the heaven of heavens cannot contain thee; how much less this house which I have built!"* (2 Chr. 6:18) How much less the body of a little child!

Part of the answer is that God is a spirit (Jn. 4:24). Spirits are not limited by time and space. In Jesus' spirit, He was the eternal God who created the universe. The physical body of Jesus was just His earth suit that He used to manifest Himself to mankind. All of Jesus' deity could not fit inside that body.

Even though this is still hard to grasp, it helps us understand how Christ Himself can live in us as believers (Col. 1:27). If all the glory of God could fit inside the physical body of Jesus, then all the fullness of God can dwell in us too (Jn. 1:16). Believe that Christ is in you today.

JANUARY 14
PEACE WITH GOD
LUKE 2:8-20

Luke 2:14 "Glory to God in the highest, and on earth peace, good will toward men."

In another instance, Jesus said He did not come to send peace on the earth, but a sword. Then He prophesied that those who received Him would experience persecution, even from their own families (Mt. 10:34-36). How do these verses fit together?

The peace the angels were singing about was not a peace between men; they were rejoicing that there would be peace between God and man. When Jesus prophesied division and war in Matthew 10, he was speaking of relationships between men.

Through the Old Testament law, God released His wrath on man's sin (Rom. 4:15). It wasn't the wrath of Satan that Jesus suffered on the cross. He suffered the wrath of His Father (Isa. 53:10-12; 2 Cor. 5:21). The Father placed our punishment for our sins on Jesus. This ended the war between God and man. This is the peace that the angels were proclaiming.

As a result of men receiving this peace from God, there has also been reconciliation between men, but that is only an effect; not the actual peace. These effects are secondary.

Today, through Jesus, we now have peace with God (Rom. 5:1). God is not mad at us. He isn't even upset. We have been accepted through Jesus (Eph. 1:6). Believe the good news that through Jesus, the war between God and man is over.

JANUARY 15
GOD LOOKS FOR AVAILABILITY
LUKE 2:21-24

Luke 2:24 "And to offer a sacrifice according to that which is said in the law of the Lord, A pair of turtledoves, or two young pigeons."

The Old Testament passage being quoted is from Leviticus 12:6-8. There the Lord commanded a lamb, a young pigeon or a turtledove, as the prescribed sacrifice. If the woman was unable to offer a lamb, then two young pigeons or two turtledoves were acceptable. Mary would not have offered the lesser offering if it had been in her power to provide the lamb.

This reveals that Joseph and Mary were not well off financially, yet the Lord chose them to be the earthly parents of His only begotten Son.

The Lord doesn't choose the way man chooses. Man looks on the outward appearance, but God looks on the heart (1 Sam. 16:7).

Mary and Joseph were chosen when they were without: without fame, without position, without money. God entrusted the most precious gift He had, to a couple who would surely have been overlooked if men had been conducting the search.

God isn't looking for ability, but rather availability. D. L. Moody once heard a preacher say, "The world has never seen what God can do with one man who is totally yielded to Him." In response, D. L. said, "By the grace of God, I'll be that man." This uneducated man went on to shake three continents for God.

God will choose you too, if you'll make yourself available to Him (1 Cor. 1:26-28).

JANUARY 16
REVELATION KNOWLEDGE
LUKE 2:25-35

Luke 2:26 "And it was revealed unto him by the Holy Ghost, that he should not see death, before he had seen the Lord's Christ."

Simeon didn't receive this knowledge through the normal method of learning. This knowledge was revealed to him directly from the Holy Spirit.

This revelation knowledge that comes only from God, is distinctly different than knowledge acquired through study. Man's knowledge is based on observation. It cannot give perfect instruction about the future. God's knowledge can. Through the inspiration of the Holy Spirit we can know things to come (Jn. 16:13).

When dealing with God, revelation knowledge is essential. The Lord's ways are not always our ways (Isa. 55:8). A fear of trusting the intuitive knowledge that God gives us will cause us to miss many blessings of God.

If Simeon hadn't received the knowledge and anticipated its fulfillment, what a blessing he would have missed! He would not have been led into the temple at exactly the right moment to see the salvation of the Lord.

We need to ask for, and expect, to receive revelation knowledge from the Lord. God desires to impart it more than we desire to receive it. Great blessings await those who will not depend solely on their own understanding (Prov. 3:5).

JANUARY 17
GOD'S CHOICE
LUKE 2:36-40

Luke 2:37 "And she [was] a widow of about fourscore and four years, which departed not from the temple, but served [God] with fastings and prayers night and day."

Let's suppose that Anna was 14 years old when she married. Then would have been 98 years old at the writing of this passage. Yet she was still fasting and praying night and day!

Satan tries to convince us that God won't use us. He may cite things like age, lack of abilities, or failures we've had, but just like Anna, there are many scriptural examples of the Lord using those who would be considered unusable by worldly standards.

Moses was 80 before he began to fulfill God's plan for his life and he worked until he was 120. Abraham was in his 90's before he had the son that God had promised him.

Gideon was another one who looked unusable. He was hiding from the Midianites when an angel of God appeared and told him he was a mighty man of valor (Judg. 6:11-12). He couldn't believe it at first and had to have the Lord confirm it three times.

Truly, ". . . *God hath chosen the foolish things of the world to confound the wise; and God hath chosen the weak things of the world to confound the things which are mighty. . .*" (1 Cor. 1:27-28). If you feel foolish or weak, then you qualify. Let the Lord use you today.

JANUARY 18
BELIEVE THE WORD
MATTHEW 2:1-12

Matthew 2:1 "Now when Jesus was born in Bethlehem of Judaea in the days of Herod the king, behold, there came wise men from the east to Jerusalem."

How could this be? The greatest event in the history of God's dealings with mankind was taking place and the leaders of God's people didn't even know about it. Foreigners who were unfamiliar with the covenants of God perceived what God was doing more than His own chosen people! (Eph. 2:12)

The apparent answer to this question is that these Persian wise men were more in tune to the prophecies of scripture than the Jews were. Daniel had been promoted to be the head of all the wise men of Babylon (Dan. 2:48). While in Babylon, Daniel had come through the lions' den victoriously and had no doubt gained the reputation as the greatest wise man of all (Dan. 6).

It was during this time that Daniel wrote the prophecy of Daniel 9:24-27, that pinpoints the time of the Messiah's birth. No doubt, this provided the inspiration for these wise men. The star simply served as a sign that the prophesied event had come and directed them towards the place where the king was born.

The Jews had these same prophecies. They just weren't waiting in anticipation for the birth of the Messiah. The Word of God only profits us if we believe it (Heb. 4:2). Let's not make the same mistake the Jews did. Mix the truths that you know from God's Word with faith.

JANUARY 19
HEROD'S FOLLY
MATTHEW 2:13-15

Matthew 2:13 ". . . for Herod will seek the young child to destroy him."

Herod had been ruling over Judaea for nearly 43 years at the time of these events. He had the title of king conferred on him by the Roman senate at the recommendation of Antony and Octavius. His accomplishments included the building of the temple in Jerusalem, which was one of the most magnificent structures in the world. Most people would have thought that Herod had it made.

However, history reveals that Herod was extremely paranoid. He actually killed his wife and one of his sons because he feared they would take the kingdom from him. All his power and fame couldn't buy him the peace that the angels proclaimed (Lk. 2:8-14). His paranoia led him to kill the innocent children in Bethlehem. His insecurity was evident. He had everything, yet he had nothing.

In contrast, the king that Herod was trying to dispose of came humbly, not exalting Himself. He gained the acclaim of others by serving them, not oppressing them. The scepter of Jesus was righteousness—not tyranny. Jesus gave the ultimate sacrifice: Himself. He did this because of His great love for people.

Today, Herod's only claim to fame is that he was the man who tried in vain, to kill the King of Kings. Remember, it is worth nothing if you gain the whole world and lose your own soul (Mt. 16:26). Make today count for God.

JANUARY 20
SPIRITUAL WARFARE
MATTHEW 2:16-23

Matthew 2:16 "Then Herod, when he saw that he was mocked of the wise men, was exceeding wroth, and sent forth, and slew all the children that were in Bethlehem, and in all the coasts thereof, from two years old and under, according to the time which he had diligently enquired of the wise men."

Satan was the real motivator of Herod's actions. Ever since the Lord first prophesied that a man would bruise his head, Satan has been seeking out this "seed" of the woman (Gen. 3:15).

It appears that Satan is able to perceive when the Lord is making a major move in the earth. In the days of Moses, Satan moved Pharaoh to kill all the male children of the Israelite slaves, and here he motivates Herod to kill all the male children in Bethlehem. No doubt he was seeking to eliminate this "seed" who was going to bruise his head.

Once again, we see children being slaughtered today. This time it's through abortion. Our youth are also being attacked in unprecedented ways. Is it possible that Satan thinks this is the generation that is to bring in the second return of the Lord? Is he, in desperation, trying to put off his doom by destroying this generation?

We need to have enough spiritual perception to recognize that just as in the days of Moses and Jesus, the slaughter of the innocent children today, is an indication of an even more important struggle in the spiritual realm. We might be the generation that sees the Lord come back. Praise the Lord!

JANUARY 21
JESUS PREPARED HIMSELF
LUKE 2:41-51

Luke 2:46 "And it came to pass, that after three days they found him in the temple, sitting in the midst of the doctors, both hearing them, and asking them questions."

This is the only scriptural record of Jesus' childhood. Yet there is much that we can learn from this brief account.

At twelve years of age, Jesus' wisdom astounded the men who had spent a lifetime studying the scriptures (v. 47). Remember that Jesus did not have full-time access to a copy of the scriptures like we do today. He had to depend on His visits to the synagogue and the direct revelation knowledge from His heavenly Father.

He was also asking these scholars questions (v. 46). This is amazing when you realize that in Him are all the treasures of wisdom and knowledge! (Col. 2:3) Although He was God, He inhabited a physical human body that needed to be educated.

He also had a clear understanding at this young age of who His real Father was and exactly why He had come to the world (v. 49). We can only speculate how this must have influenced His childhood.

So we see that Jesus knew His call and purpose even in His early childhood. However, there is no record of miracles or ministry on His part until after His baptism by John, when He was 30. Preparing a body for God Almighty to manifest Himself through was no small task. Praise God for His great love that caused Him to sacrifice everything for us.

JANUARY 22
HE BECAME LIKE US
LUKE 2:52

Luke 2:52 "And Jesus increased in wisdom and stature, and in favour with God and man."

How could it be that Jesus, who was God (Jn. 1:1; 1 Tim. 3:16), and in whom are hidden all the treasures of wisdom and knowledge, increased in wisdom? (Col. 2:3)

God is a spirit (Jn. 4:24). Jesus, as God, had existed as a spirit forever. When He came to the earth as Jesus, He was Lord at birth, but that was in His spirit (Lk. 2:11). His spirit didn't have to grow or increase in wisdom, but His physical body did.

The Lord could have done things differently, but He didn't. Jesus came into this world in His physical body exactly as we did. He had to grow and learn.

He became just like us so that we could become just like Him (2 Cor. 5:21). This is the great exchange. He became like us so that He could bear all our iniquities and become a mercy high priest for us (Heb. 2:14-18).

Christianity does not produce a changed life but an exchanged life. Christ does not reform us, but He transforms us through His union with us. In the same way that the eternal Christ could come and inhabit the body of an infant, and still retain all His deity, He now inhabits our bodies through the new birth, in all His glory and power. Like Jesus, grow in your wisdom and understanding of who you now are in Christ.

JANUARY 23
THE MINISTRY OF JOHN THE BAPTIST
MATTHEW 3:1-12; MARK 1:1-8; LUKE 3:1-18

Matthew 3:1 "In those days came John the Baptist, preaching in the wilderness of Judaea."

These scriptures record the ministry of John the Baptist. He spent 30 years in the deserts of Judaea preparing for this ministry. Then it only lasted about six months before He baptized Jesus and men started following the Messiah. Yet in those brief six months, He turned an entire nation to God.

He did not take the normal approach and go where the people were. He was out in the wilderness and the people came to him. He had no advertisements other than the testimonies of those who had heard him. He wasn't a flashy evangelist wearing the latest styles of the day. He didn't do anything the way the religious leaders taught it was supposed to be done in their seminaries; yet it worked.

In six short months, an entire nation was stirred in anticipation of their Messiah through a man who was not normal.

One thing that keeps many of us from being used by God is our herd instinct. We are so afraid of what someone else will think. We try to be like everyone else and then we wonder why we are getting the same results as everyone else. That's not smart.

John was completely yielded to the Holy Spirit and he succeeded against all the odds. Dare to follow the Holy Spirit, even against the crowd, and you will get supernatural results too!

JANUARY 24
A GREATER HUMILITY
MATTHEW 3:13-17; MARK 1:9-11; LUKE 3:21-23

Matthew 3:14 "But John forbad him, saying, I have need to be baptized of thee, and comest thou to me?"

John the Baptist was overwhelmed that Jesus asked him to baptize Him. John had already declared himself unworthy to unloose the latchet of the Christ's shoes, and now the Christ was asking him to administer His baptism (Lk. 3:16).

Likewise, we are often overwhelmed by the idea that the Lord could use us. Who are we to proclaim the unsearchable riches of Christ? It is easy to disqualify ourselves and not fulfill God's instructions. However, Jesus told John that he had to do it to fulfill all righteousness.

As wonderful as it may seem, the Lord has chosen to use us. God's Word could not have been fulfilled without John's cooperation. The Lord works through men.

We can do nothing by ourselves, but the Lord will do nothing by Himself (Jn. 15:5; Eph. 3:20). A lack of understanding this has caused many people to miss God's blessings. They pray and desire God's best, but wait on God to move independent of them. There are things that we must do to fulfill the righteousness of God in our lives.

John was not seeking to exalt himself, but failing to baptize Jesus would not have been an act of humility; it would have been an act of stupidity. It takes great humility to recognize the call of God on your life and let Him use you.

JANUARY 25
KNOWING WHO WE ARE
MATTHEW 4:1-11; MARK 1:12-13; LUKE 4:1-13

Matthew 4:3 "And when the tempter came to him, he said, If thou be the Son of God, command that these stones be made bread."

Two of Satan's three temptations began with the words, "If you be the Son of God."

Jesus was God, but He did have a human body that had to grow in the knowledge and wisdom of God (Jn. 1:1; 1 Tim. 3:16; Lk. 2:52). It took faith for the physical mind of Jesus to believe the witness of the Spirit within Him, that He was the Messiah. Satan was attacking the most basic of His beliefs. This must have been a temptation for Jesus, or Satan would not have used it.

Satan is very subtle in his temptations. It may have looked like he was trying to get Jesus to perform a miracle, but he was actually trying to make Jesus waiver in His faith of who He was. He tried to get Jesus to draw on the supernatural power of God to confirm it to the devil and Himself.

Unlike Jesus, we sometimes fall for this trick of the devil. We may say that we are arguing for some truth of the gospel, but many times we are hoping to convince ourselves. Someone who really knows who he is in Christ and knows what he believes, doesn't have to prove anything to anyone.

Isaiah 30:15 says, *"For thus saith the Lord GOD, the Holy One of Israel; In returning and rest shall ye be saved; in quietness and in confidence shall be your strength...."* Let the Lord build your confidence in who you are in Him.

JANUARY 26
THE WEAPON OF THE WORD
MATTHEW 4:1-11; MARK 1:12-13; LUKE 4:1-13

Luke 4:4 "And Jesus answered him, saying, It is written, That man shall not live by bread alone, but by every word of God."

Jesus answered every temptation with, "It is written." The Word of God is the sword of the Spirit (Eph. 6:17). It is the only offensive spiritual weapon we have.

Since Jesus was the Word of God (Jn. 1:1), anything he would have spoken would have been the Word. He could have said, "scat" and the devil would have had to go, yet He quoted the written Word of God three times.

This gives us great assurance that the written Word of God is sufficient for us. Jesus, in the face of the greatest temptations that Satan had to offer, did not need to say anything that was not already recorded in scripture.

It is likely that when Jesus returns to this earth and destroys His enemies, He will just speak the Word that has already been given in scripture.

No wonder Satan tries to keep us from studying and knowing God's Word. Even our good works will hurt us if they keep us from really knowing the scriptures.

God has given us the mighty weapon of His Word! When we speak the Word in faith, hell shakes. Satan and his minions have already experienced what the Word can do. They know its power. We need to know it too.

JANUARY 27
SATAN'S POWER IS LIMITED
MATTHEW 4:1-11; MARK 1:12-13; LUKE 4:1-13

Luke 4:13 "And when the devil had ended all the temptation,
he departed from him for a season."

The wording of this verse implies that Satan exhausted his arsenal of temptations on Jesus and then had to leave.

We have mistakenly given Satan too much credit. He does not have a limitless number of temptations that he can pull on us. As 1 John 2:16 says, there are three areas where the devil tempts us: One, the lust of the flesh; two, the lust of the eyes, and three, the pride of life. Jesus' three temptations correspond to these.

By ascribing to Satan limitless temptations and abilities, we have built up our adversary to be bigger than he is. The truth is, *"There hath no temptation taken you but such as is common to man: but God [is] faithful, who will not suffer you to be tempted above that ye are able; but will with the temptation also make a way to escape, that ye may be able to bear [it]"* (I Cor. 10:13).

Satan would like you to think that he is tougher than he really is. One of his greatest weapons is intimidation, but he has been defeated. His teeth have been pulled. Now he can only roar as a lion seeking to devour uninformed souls who don't know their authority in Christ (1 Pet. 5:8).

Today, realize that whatever Satan is fighting you with is only temporary. Don't quit. In due season you will reap, if you faint not (Gal. 6:9).

JANUARY 28
KNOWING GOD'S PLAN
JOHN 1:19-36

John 1:23 "He said, I [am] the voice of one crying in the wilderness, Make straight the way of the Lord, as said the prophet Esaias."

John knew who he was and what he was called to do. This was one of the keys to his success.

Unlike most of us, John did not have an identity crisis growing up. He knew God's plan and purpose for his life from the beginning, and he spent his entire life preparing for it.

God has a plan for your life just as surely as he did for John the Baptist. To succeed in life, you must find God's plan for your life and then devote yourself to fulfilling that plan.

It is not enough to simply do your own thing and then ask God to bless it. Once you know you are doing God's will, you never have to ask for His blessing. God's will is already blessed.

The Lord created you with a purpose in mind. Your talents and abilities were given to you to fulfill His purpose. Although you may find limited success using these talents for your own use, you will only find your true potential when you receive direction from the Lord and use your talents for His purpose.

The good news is that God wants to reveal to you His perfect plan for your life more than you want to know it. You can rest assured that if you ask for knowledge of His plan for your life, you will receive it (Mt. 7:7). He will show you His good, acceptable and perfect will (Rom. 12:1-2).

JANUARY 29
SHARING OUR FAITH
JOHN 1:37-42

John 1:41 "He first findeth his own brother Simon, and saith unto him, We have found the Messias, which is, being interpreted, the Christ."

Andrew was the first disciple of Jesus to share his faith and bring another to Christ. Look who it was that he brought—Peter.

Peter became one of the greatest apostles of Jesus. He preached on the day of Pentecost and saw 3,000 people born again. He healed a lame man at the gate of the temple and 5,000 were born again as a result. He raised Dorcas from the dead, introduced Christianity to the Gentiles, and wrote two books of the Bible that have ministered to millions of people through the centuries.

Just think of how many millions of people Peter touched, and how Andrew was responsible for it all. The accomplishments of Peter recorded in scripture, far outnumber those of Andrew, yet without Andrew, Peter would have not known Jesus.

In the eyes of God, what Andrew did was just as important as what Peter did. As the one who introduced Peter to Jesus, Andrew had a part in all Peter's exploits. In the day when we receive our rewards from the Lord, Andrew will share every reward that Peter receives.

Very few of us will shake our world as Peter did his, but all of us are called to share our faith with others as Andrew did. Who knows, one person that you reach could be the next Peter.

JANUARY 30
SETTLING OUR DOUBTS
JOHN 1:43-51

John 1:46 "And Nathanael said unto him, Can there any good thing come out of Nazareth? Philip saith unto him, Come and see."

Nathanael suffered from a skepticism that afflicts many people today. However, it is to his credit that he came to the Lord and gave Him a chance to prove who He was.

We can only speculate what it was that Jesus saw Nathanael doing under that fig tree (v. 50), but it is clear that it was something that proved beyond a doubt that Jesus was the Christ.

Jesus didn't rebuke Nathanael for his doubts; instead, he removed them. The Lord has an answer for every doubt that we have. We need to be without guile before the Lord as Nathanael was (v. 47), and go to Him when we are plagued with doubts instead of running from, or avoiding Him.

Jesus knows our frame. He remembers that we are but dust (Ps. 103:14). It is not a sin to doubt, but it becomes sin if we harbor those doubts. We should do as Nathanael did and bring our doubts to the Lord. Let's allow Him to deal with them.

JANUARY 31
DO WHAT HE SAYS
JOHN 2:1-11

John 2:5 "His mother saith unto the servants, Whatsoever he saith unto you, do [it]."

Mary knew Jesus as no one else did at this point. The Bible supplies no details of Jesus' childhood except his trip to Jerusalem when he was 12. Although it is certain that Mary knew Jesus was no ordinary man, her request of Jesus to provide the guests with more wine reflects her belief that He could do things others could not.

Her instructions to the servants were, "*Whatsoever he saith unto you, do it.*" This shows that she not only knew Jesus could work miracles, but she knew His way of doing things did not always conform to conventional thought. Sure enough, Jesus told the servants to fill the pots with water and then take it to the governor of the feast.

This defied logic! Everyone knew the guests wanted more wine, not water. Yet these servants, at Mary's bidding, did exactly what Jesus told them and the results were wonderful. This miracle would not have taken place if the servants had not done what seemed foolish to them.

The Lord's ways are not our ways and His thoughts are not our thoughts (Isa. 55:8). To see His miraculous power in our lives, we must do whatsoever He tells us to do, regardless of how foolish it may seem. The foolishness of God is wiser than the wisdom of men, and the weakness of God is stronger than men (1 Cor. 1:25). Today, whatsoever He says unto you, do it!

FEBRUARY 1
GOD IS NOT CHEAP!
JOHN 2:1-11

John 2:6 "And there were set there six waterpots of stone, after the manner of the purifying of the Jews, containing two or three firkins apiece."

God has been represented as a God who is on a tight budget and disapproves of us asking for anything more than just the necessities. This first miracle of Jesus disproves this.

Scholars suggest that a firkin was equal to about nine U.S. gallons. This would mean that six of these water pots would hold 162 gallons of wine. That's a lot of wine!

In a similar instance, when Jesus was asked to provide food for the multitude, He again, supplied more than the need (Mt. 14:15-21; Mk. 6:33-44; Lk. 9:11-17).

These examples show the Lord's willingness to meet our needs with plenty to spare. God is not cheap!

Today, don't limit God to barely meet your needs. If you have enough, then believe for extra so that you can bless someone else. "*Let God be magnified, who has pleasure in the prosperity of His servants*" (Ps. 35:27).

FEBRUARY 2
THERE IS A RIGHTEOUS ANGER
JOHN 2:12-14

John 2:15 "And when he had made a scourge of small cords, he drove them all out of the temple, and the sheep, and the oxen; and poured out the changers' money, and overthrew the tables."

Jesus brought the message of "love your enemies" to the world and demonstrated it in such a way that some people have forgotten instances like this, when Jesus showed anger. Anger can also be a godly emotion.

Ephesians 4:26, tells us to "*be angry and sin not.*" This means there is a righteous type of anger that is not sin. This is why we are told to hate evil (Ps. 45:7; 119:104, 163; Pro. 8:13; Rom.12:9).

Ephesians 4:26, goes on to say, "*Let not the sun go down upon your wrath.*" That doesn't mean that it's alright to be angry during daylight as long as we repent by nightfall. Rather, it speaks of this righteous type of anger. We are never to let it rest. Don't ever put it to bed, but keep yourself stirred up against the things of the devil.

The key to distinguishing between a righteous anger and a carnal anger is to discern your motives and the object of your anger. Godly anger is directed at the devil with no consideration of self. If you are angry with people, that's carnal (Eph. 6:12). If your motivation is self-serving, then it's wrong.

FEBRUARY 3
HE USES THE USABLE
JOHN 2:18-25

John 2:24 "But Jesus did not commit himself unto them, because he knew all [men]."

This was the first time Jesus had ministered in Jerusalem. Multitudes believed on Him when they saw the miracles He performed (v. 23). This looked like a perfect opportunity for Jesus to take these people and use them to spread the news far and wide that He was the Christ. Instead, Jesus did just the opposite. He didn't want people proclaiming His Gospel in their own abilities.

This reveals an attitude of Jesus that is lacking among many Christians today. Jesus is more concerned with the quality of ministry than the quantity of ministry. In contrast, today's Christians often feel that the end justifies the means.

We take new converts and place them in leadership; this is directly opposed to the Bible's instructions (1 Tim. 3:6). Many times, movie stars or other famous people who have come to the Lord are made spokesmen for the Christian faith. This can harm these people and the body of Christ as a whole.

Some of you cannot understand why the Lord hasned you, but rest assured the Lord is using everyone who is usable. Instead of looking at the need and begging God to use you, take a hard look at yourself and ask the Lord to make you usable.

FEBRUARY 4
THE BORN AGAIN EXPERIENCE
JOHN 3:1-21

John 3:10 "Jesus answered and said unto him, Art thou a master of Israel,
and knowest not these things?"

The Greek word translated "master" here actually means, "an instructor, doctor, teacher." Nicodemus was an educated man in religious matters, yet he didn't have the slightest idea what Jesus was talking about.

Nicodemus' relationship with God was all academic. He knew a lot about God, but he didn't know God personally. Jesus had a union with God that was unique and Nicodemus was intrigued. God was Jesus' father. This was foreign to Nicodemus.

Jesus had not been educated by man, yet He knew God in a way that the theologians and seminary graduates of His day didn't. He shocked Nicodemus when He told him that the only way to truly know God was through an experience of being born again.

The number one thing that sets Christianity apart from religion is the born again experience. We don't just have a different doctrine than others; we have been *born* from above. We have Jesus Himself living in our hearts.

Christianity is a relationship, not a religion. We truly fellowship with God as our Father. A man with a born again experience is never at a loss when confronted by a man with an argument.

FEBRUARY 5
ETERNAL LIFE—A QUALITY OF LIFE
JOHN 3:1-21

John 3:16 "For God so loved the world that he gave his only begotten Son, that whosoever
believeth in him should not perish but have everlasting life. "

Most people focus on the part of this verse that promises us we won't perish. Although it's certainly a wonderful promise, it is not the focus of this verse. The primary purpose of Jesus' coming to this earth was not forgiveness of sins, but to give us eternal life.

Sin separated us from God, so Jesus dealt with sin. However, His payment for sin was just a step toward His ultimate purpose of reconciling man to God. If someone believes that Jesus died for his sins, but doesn't go on to enter into the close fellowship with God that Jesus made available, then he is missing eternal life.

Eternal life is not a length of life, but rather a quality of life. Eternal life is intimacy with the Father and Jesus (Jn. 17:3). Many people have been done a disservice in being told that Jesus came to forgive us of our sins—period. If that was all He did, it would have been wonderful, and much more than we deserved, but much less than what He actually accomplished.

Today, take full advantage of your salvation and go beyond the basic forgiveness of your sins into intimacy with Almighty God.

FEBRUARY 6
HUMILITY BEFORE HONOR
JOHN 3:22-36

John 3:30 "He must increase, but I [must] decrease."

John the Baptist spent 30 years in preparation for his ministry. He didn't enjoy the normal benefits of childhood or adolescence. He lived out in the deserts separated unto God instead (Lk. 1:80).

For approximately six months, he enjoyed success in his ministry like no other man ever had. He started preaching in the wilderness—not the centers of commerce. Still the multitudes flocked to him. He became the most influential man in Israel and even shot the hearts of Roman rulers. Everything was going John's way.

Then he baptized Jesus and proclaimed Him as the long-awaited Messiah (Mt. 3:13-17; Jn. 1:29). From that time on, the multitudes who once followed John began to follow Jesus in ever increasing numbers (Jn. 3:26). His own disciples left him to follow Jesus (Jn. 1:36-37). This would have destroyed most men.

Yet when he was questioned about this, John replied, "*He must increase but I must decrease.*" Surely this is one of the characteristics that made John the Baptist the greatest of all Old Testament prophets (Mt. 11:11). Jesus later revealed that "he that is greatest among you shall be your servant" (Mt. 23:11). John is one of the greatest examples of humility in the Bible. "*Before honor is humility*" (Pro. 18:12).

FEBRUARY 7
GOD'S IDEA OF GREATNESS
MATTHEW 4:12; MARK 1:14, 17-18; LUKE 3:19-20; JOHN 4:1-3

Luke 3:20 ". . . he shut up John in prison."

John spent 30 years preparing for a six-month ministry, followed by one-and- a-half years in prison, before he was beheaded. Many people would not consider his life successful, yet Jesus said John was the greatest man who was ever born (Mt. 11:11).

John's greatness didn't lie in his own success, but in the success of another. John stirred up the hearts of an entire nation in expectancy of their Messiah. The ministry of Jesus owed much of its success to the work of John. John prepared the people to meet their God (Mal. 3:1).

In our celebrity conscious society, few people want to be the backup singer or the announcer who introduces the main speaker. We have adopted a mentality that unless we are in the limelight we have failed. That's not the way the Lord looks at things.

When the Lord passes out rewards in heaven, we may be shocked to see how He evaluates greatness. Many people who did not receive recognition while on earth will shine like the stars in eternity. The Lord will judge our works on what **sort** they were and not what **size** they were (I Cor. 3:13).

FEBRUARY 8
HE LEFT JUDAEA
MATTHEW 4:12; MARK 1:14; JOHN 4:1-3

John 4:1 and 3"When therefore the Lord knew how the Pharisees had heard that Jesus made and baptized more than John. . . He left Judaea."

This is an interesting passage of scripture. On the surface, it might look like Jesus was running from a fight. Now that John the Baptist was out of the way (he had been imprisoned), it was inevitable that the Pharisees would attack Jesus.

One thing we can be sure of is that there was no fear on our Lord's part. On other occasions He demonstrated that no one could do anything to Him if He didn't allow it (Lk. 4:29-30; Jn. 7:30, 44-46; 8:20, 59; 10:39).

Therefore, we can assume that Jesus left because He knew it was God's will. On another occasion when His half brothers dared Him to go to Jerusalem and confront the Pharisees, He told them that it wasn't time for Him to go yet (Jn. 7:1-6). A lesser man would have been intimidated into showing His superiority.

Jesus was the most selfless person who ever walked the earth. He did not come to earth for Himself, but for us. If He would have defended Himself, we would have never been saved. The humility of Jesus was surely interpreted by some to be weakness, but in truth it was love. Not love for Himself, but love for a dying world for which He was the only hope.

FEBRUARY 9
GOD IS THE GREATEST GIVER
JOHN 4:10

John 4:10 "Jesus answered and said unto her, If thou knewest the gift of God, and who it is that saith to thee, Give me to drink; thou wouldest have asked of him, and he would have given thee living water."

Jesus asked this woman for a drink of water, but He wasn't interested in the water. He wanted to give this woman eternal life.

God is the greatest giver there ever was. He lives to give. When He asks something of us, we can be assured that it is only so He can multiply it and give it back to us.

God is not interested in the water we can give Him. We don't have anything to offer God that He doesn't already have. God wants us. By asking us to give of our time, money and desires, He is really asking us to give ourselves.

Many people have walked away from God sad, like the rich young ruler, because all they could think about was what they would have to give up (Mk. 10:22). All of our achievements and possessions are nothing compared to what God offers us in exchange.

Just as Jesus turned this woman's attention toward what He had to offer her, we need to focus our attention on what the Lord has given us in Christ. **He is no fool who gives up what he can not keep to receive what he cannot loose.**

FEBRUARY 10
THIRSTY?
JOHN 4:4-26

John 4:14 "But whosoever drinketh of the water that I shall give him shall never thirst; but the water that I shall give him shall be in him a well of water springing up into everlasting life."

Jesus painted a beautiful picture of salvation in this passage. The salvation Jesus brings is like an artesian spring, that doesn't have to be pumped. It bubbles up constantly.

Unfortunately, not every Christian's experience matches Jesus' description. Many people relate more to an old pump that has to be pumped and pumped. Just as a trickle of water comes, they have to rest. They lose their prime. The water stops. Then they have to start all over again.

Jesus said we would **never** thirst again. This doesn't mean that one drink will satisfy us forever, but as we continue to partake of this water of life daily, we will be constantly refreshed. The well of His life is available, but we must partake of it.

The dryness in a Christian's life comes when he substitutes other things for the living water that only Jesus can give. Any time a Christian begins to thirst again, it is not a reflection on the living water that Jesus gives, but an indication that he has been drinking from another source. *"Therefore with joy shall ye draw water out of the wells of salvation"* (Isaiah 12:3).

FEBRUARY 11
GOD LOOKS INSIDE
JOHN 4:4-26

John 4:19 "The woman saith unto him, Sir, I perceive that thou art a prophet."

This statement didn't take any great discernment on the woman's part. Jesus had just "read her mail." He told her the most intimate details of her life. Anyone could have perceived Jesus was a prophet after something like that.

This woman suddenly realized that she was dealing with more than just a man. God was speaking to her. What was her reaction? She changed the subject. She brought up a doctrinal issue concerning the proper place to worship—anything to get Jesus' attention off of her.

We all have a tendency to build walls of privacy around the intimate details of our lives. We are afraid to let anyone, especially God, look inside. God already knows our hearts and He wants all of our hearts.

Jesus brought this woman right back to the subject of her personal relationship with God. The place of worship or the forms of worship weren't important. God was looking for people who would open their hearts—even the hidden parts, for Him to inhabit.

Likewise today, Satan tries to get us occupied with everything except the one thing that counts. God wants us to worship Him in spirit and truth. Anything less than that is not enough.

FEBRUARY 12
WORSHIP HIM IN SPIRIT
JOHN 4:4-26

John 4:24 "God [is] a Spirit: and they that worship him must worship [him]
in spirit and in truth."

Man dwells primarily in the physical and emotional realm, but God is a Spirit (1 Sam. 16:7). To have true fellowship with God, we have to relate to God on a spiritual level.

In order to make this possible, God changed our spirits. At salvation, our spirits became totally new (2 Cor. 5:17). They are now righteous and truly holy (Eph. 4:24). Our spirits are now exactly the way Jesus is, because our born again spirits are the spirits of the Lord Jesus Christ (1 Jn. 4:17; 1 Cor. 6:17; Rom. 8:9; Gal. 4:6).

In our spirits we are worthy to come before God and worship Him without any fear. Our spirits are the only part of us that are worthy. That's why we **must** worship Him in spirit and in truth.

When we come before God dwelling on our failures and problems, we are not approaching Him through our spirits. Our spirits are not our problem. Our born again spirits are perfect.

There is a time for mentioning our problems and failures, but it's not the part of us that has been saved and is in fellowship with God. We must always base our relationship with the Father on who we are in our spirits through Christ Jesus.

FEBRUARY 13
SPIRITUAL FOOD
JOHN 4:27-46

John 4:32 "But he saith unto them, I have meat to eat that ye know not of."

Food is essential for life. Without it we can't grow. We get strength and vitality from food; however, food can kill us. Improper diets have killed more people than any disease has.

Our souls need nourishment too. The things we think on and the desires we have, are food for our souls. Jesus said, *"Man shall not live by bread alone, but by every word that proceedeth out of the mouth of God"* (Mat. 4:4).

Jesus valued spiritual nourishment more than He valued physical nourishment. He was thrilled to see this woman and the people of this town respond to His gift of salvation. Likewise, we should set our desires on the things of God so that spiritual matters are more important to us than physical ones.

The wrong diet for our souls is the leading cause of failure and depression in the lives of Christians. Being spiritually minded produces life and peace. Being carnally minded produces death (Rom. 8:6).

In our health conscious society, many of us wouldn't dream of abusing our bodies by having poor diets. Yet in our souls, we are killing ourselves by feeding on the wrong things. Today, treat yourself to a healthy spiritual meal.

FEBRUARY 14
GOD'S WORD HAS NO LIMITS
JOHN 4:46-54

John 4:50 "Jesus saith unto him, Go thy way; thy son liveth. And the man believed the word
that Jesus had spoken unto him, and he went his way."

Jesus didn't have to touch the child. He didn't have to send anything home with the father to bring about the cure. All He did was speak, and the son was instantly healed (v. 53).

This man traveled over 15 miles from Capernaum to Cana, to find Jesus. Therefore, the son was not within earshot so that Jesus' words could spark some cord of hope in his heart, thereby releasing God's power. Jesus' spoken word had so much power that no barriers (such as time or space) had any effect on it whatsoever.

This is hard for us to comprehend. We spend an entire lifetime learning physical limitations and adapting to them, but there are no limits to the power of God's Word. Jesus created everything in this physical universe by His words, and that creation will respond to anything He says.

The Lord gave His Word to the Jews, but they didn't believe it. Hebrews 4:2 says, "... *the word preached did not profit them, not being mixed with faith in them that heard [it]."* We have been given God's words too, in the Bible. If we will speak God's Word in faith, we will get the same results that Jesus did.

FEBRUARY 15
OUR DEBTS HAVE BEEN CANCELLED
LUKE 4:16-30

Luke 4:19 "To proclaim the acceptable year of the Lord."

This scripture was written prophetically by the prophet Isaiah about 650 years prior to this time. It was read in Jewish synagogues thousands of times, but the person this verse referred to had never voiced it. With this pronouncement, Jesus began the year of Jubilee.

The year of Jubilee was described in Leviticus, chapter 25. It was a year when everyone left their fields unworked and kept a sabbath unto the Lord. The Lord gave the people a miraculous provision the year before this jubilee started, that sustained them for three years until their crops could once again be harvested.

This jubilee was different than the other sabbatical years in that every debt was cancelled. All property was returned to its original owner and anyone who had been sold into slavery was set free. It was a year of new beginnings.

Jesus proclaimed a spiritual jubilee. We now live in a time when all our debts to God have been cancelled and all the things the devil stole from us have been returned. Even our slavery to the devil has come to an end through the redemptive work of our Lord Jesus Christ. This is a time for rejoicing. Jesus is our jubilee.

FEBRUARY 16
FAMILIARITY BREEDS CONTEMPT
LUKE 4:16-30

Luke 4:24 "And he said, Verily I say unto you,
No prophet is accepted in his own country."

A modern day equivalent of this verse is "familiarity breeds contempt." Those who know the most about us also know more of our faults than anyone else. As a general rule, our weaknesses will blind most people to our strengths.

However, in the case of Jesus, there were no faults or failures to bias these people. In this instance, the problem stemmed from the people's lack of perception. They knew Jesus in the flesh, better than most, but they failed to see who He was in the spirit.

Jesus was God in all His power and majesty, yet He was clothed in flesh—a human in every respect (1 Tim. 3:16; Heb. 1:3). These people looked on Jesus' outward appearance and failed to see God within (1 Sam. 16:7).

Likewise, we fail to see the potential in others and even in ourselves because of our preoccupation with the outward appearance and actions. Within every born again person is a new creation that is waiting to be released (2 Cor. 5:17). All it takes is someone who believes.

Today, look beyond the exterior in yourself and others, and help bring into reality what we can be in Christ.

FEBRUARY 17
THE CHOSEN ONES
MATTHEW 4:13-22; MARK 1:16-20; LUKE 5:27; JOHN 5:38

Mark 1:16 "Now as he walked by the sea of Galilee, he saw Simon and Andrew his brother
casting a net into the sea: for they were fishers."

Jesus never chose an apostle from among the religious people. Every one of his 12 disciples were men that He chose from the secular world. It wasn't because God didn't have faith in those who were religious; it was just that most of those who were part of the religious system didn't have any faith in God.

One of the most common mistakes religious people make is to put faith in themselves. They think God will use them because of their great holiness or special abilities.

Paul said, "*But God hath chosen the foolish things of the world to confound the wise; and God hath chosen the weak things of the world to confound the things which are mighty; And base things of the world, and things which are despised, hath God chosen, [yea], and things which are not, to bring to nought things that are" (1 Cor. 1:27-28).*

People who recognize their own inabilities are more dependent on God out of necessity. That is the way God wants it. The Lord is constantly searching for someone who recognizes he is nothing, so He can do something through him (2 Ch. 16:9).

Instead of thinking of your responsibility, just respond to His ability.

FEBRUARY 18
DEMONS IN CHURCH
MARK 1:21-28; LUKE 4:33-37

Mark 1:23 "And there was in their synagogue a man with an unclean spirit; and he cried out; . . . ."

Many people don't associate demon possessed people with places of worship. Yet, most of the demons that Jesus cast out were encountered in the church. Why would demon possessed people be in church?

In some cases, the people were there because they were seeking help. The church, like a hospital, offers people the cure; therefore, attracts those who are sick.

In other cases, the devil sows these types of people in the church to spread spiritual disease. A church that is teaching the true Word of God should either try to evangelize these people or make them so convicted that they will move on. Sad to say, demon possessed people can thrive in most religious settings today.

We always need to show love for the sinner as Jesus did, but we should cut the devil no slack. If a person wants to keep an evil spirit on the inside of him, he should not feel at home in church.

Let the Spirit of God live through you as He did through Jesus and you will either make people mad or glad, but there will not be indifference.

FEBRUARY 19
MINISTRY IN ACTION
MATTHEW 8:14-17; MARK 1:29-34; LUKE 4:38-41

Mark 1:31 "And he came and took her by the hand and lifted her up; and immediately the fever left her, and she ministered unto them."

How did Peter's mother-in-law minister unto Jesus and His disciples? Did she sit them down and preach to them? Certainly not. Yet sometimes people think the only way we can minister to others is to admonish them with the scriptures.

Peter's mother-in-law apparently ministered to them by serving them. The word translated "minister" is the same word that was translated "deacon" twice in the New Testament, and "serve, served or serveth" eight times.

We can minister for the Lord by doing some of the menial tasks that many consider to be unimportant. Jesus said that even a cup of cold water given in His name would not go unrewarded (Matthew 10:42).

Many people are waiting for the important jobs to come along where they can make a big impact or receive a lot of recognition, while they pass by the lesser opportunities. In the kingdom of God, we won't be given any great opportunities until we are proven faithful in the small things (Luke 16:10).

Today, ask the Lord to show you ways you can minister to others by serving them.

FEBRUARY 20
DRAWN BY HIS POWER
MARK 1:35-39; LUKE 4:42-44

Mark 1:37 "And when they had found him, they said unto him, All [men] seek for thee."

This is an amazing statement. Jesus' ministry was only a few months old and the masses of people were already seeking Him out.

This is even more astonishing when you realize that Jesus did not use any of the conventional methods of publicity. Jesus had already rejected publicity during His first ministry in Jerusalem (Jn. 2:24-25). There was no natural explanation for Jesus' success.

God is the one who promoted Jesus, and He used supernatural means to do it. It was not the slick techniques of Madison Avenue that brought the crowds—it was the awesome manifestation of God's power.

Just the day before, Jesus had cast a demon out of a man at the synagogue in Capernaum (Mk. 1:21-28). This caused the whole city to gather at Peter's house and Jesus healed every one of them (Lk. 4:40).

Jesus' display of the miraculous power of God was the spark that the Holy Spirit used to light a fire in the hearts of these people. Jesus had this power because of His intimate relationship with His father. It is no accident that He was praying while all men were seeking Him.

As you seek to touch others with the new life you've found in Christ, let God confirm His Word with the miraculous manifestations of His power through you.

FEBRUARY 21
AT THY WORD
LUKE 5:1-11

Luke 5:5 "And Simon answering said unto him, Master, we have toiled all the night, and have taken nothing: nevertheless at thy word I will let down the net."

Peter and his companions had been working hard all night. Their efforts had not produced even one fish. They had given up and were headed home, but Jesus told them to try it just one more time.

It would have been easy for Peter to reject Jesus' command. After all, Peter had been a fisherman all his life. Jesus was just a preacher. What did He know about fishing? Yet something, or rather someone, caused Peter to try just once more.

Many people are like Simon Peter and his partners. They have done all that they know to do, yet they've come up empty-handed. This breeds despair and hopelessness, which causes them to quit trying. Yet, just one word from Jesus could make the same tasks that have been unproductive on your own, bear great fruit.

The key to success or failure lies in doing things at the word of Jesus. Peter said, "At thy word I will let down the net." God's words always get results.

Today, make sure your efforts are directed by God and you will experience the results that have eluded you in the past.

FEBRUARY 22
ONLY THE HUNGRY ARE FED
MATTHEW 5:1-9

Matthew 5:6 "Blessed [are] they which do hunger and thirst after righteousness:
for they shall be filled."

In the natural world, people eat even when they aren't hungry. Many of us can prove that by turning sideways and looking at ourselves in the mirror. In the spiritual realm, only those who are hungry can get fed. One of the worst things that can happen to us is to become spiritually complacent.

Being hungry for the things of God is one of the best things that can happen to you. Most people don't feel that way. They would rather have the feeling of being full, but Jesus promised us that fullness would follow hunger: no hunger, no fullness.

Therefore, what many people hate is actually a sign of spiritual health. Longing for more of God is a healthy sign. No one hungers for God on his own. That is not the nature of man. No man hungers for God unless the Spirit of God is drawing him (Jn. 6:44).

Hungering for God doesn't cause God to move in our lives, but it is a sign that God is already at work in us. We should praise God for spiritual hunger and be encouraged. He doesn't make us hungry and then lets us starve. He makes us hungry so He can fill us with His blessings and love. We need a hunger that will never be satisfied until the marriage supper of the Lamb.

FEBRUARY 23
HE WILL SHARE HIS REWARD
MATTHEW 5:10-12

Matthew 5:12 "Rejoice, and be exceedingly glad: for great [is] your reward in heaven: for so
persecuted they the prophets which were before you."

Jesus is saying that persecution should actually cause us to rejoice. There are many positive things about persecution, but one of the best reasons to rejoice is because of the reward awaiting us in heaven.

Jesus takes the persecution of His saints seriously, as can be seen during the Damascus road experience of the Apostle Paul. The Lord asked Paul (then Saul), "*Why are you persecuting me?*" (Acts 9:4). He didn't say, "Why are you persecuting my people?" but "Why are you persecuting **me?**"

It is not actually us that people are rejecting; they are rejecting the one we represent. Therefore, Jesus promised to share His reward with us. All the glory and honor that Jesus has and will receive will, be shared with those who have suffered shame for His name's sake (Rom. 8:17). What a great reward!

Focusing on the reward instead of the persecution can actually make us rejoice when people speak against us (Acts 5:41). Paul actually longed to experience the fellowship that Jesus provided to those who suffered for His sake (Phil. 3:10). God's reward is infinitely greater than any suffering we will ever encounter.

FEBRUARY 24
SALT SHAKERS
MATTHEW 5:13-16

Matthew 5:13 "Ye are the salt of the earth: but if the salt have lost his savour, wherewith shall it be salted? it is thenceforth good for nothing, but to be cast out, and to be trodden under foot of men."

What is it that will be cast out and trodden under foot of men? Is it the salt, or is it possible that Jesus is speaking about the world? If we as believers lose our preserving influence, then there is no other way for the Lord to save the world. It will be dominated by men.

God flows through His people. It is not our own power that changes people. It's God's power in us, but God will not do it without us. It's a partnership.

Many people spend a lifetime praying for God to move, not understanding that He is going to flow through them. It is not God who is failing to intervene. It is God's people who are failing to cooperate and let Him flow through them.

All Christians have God living in them. Therefore, we are carrying around other people's miracles. If we fail to walk in the supernatural power of God, then somone may miss his miracle. We are God's salt to preserve this putrefying world. Today, get out of the shaker and let the life of God, which is in you, flow to someone who needs it.

FEBRUARY 25
THE BEST SINNER
MATTHEW 5:17-22

Matthew 5:20 "For I say unto you, That except your righteousness shall exceed [the righteousness] of the scribes and Pharisees, ye shall in no case enter into the kingdom of heaven."

What did Jesus mean? Since the Pharisees fasted twice a week, does this mean we have to fast three times a week? Since they paid tithes on everything, including spices, does this mean that anyone who fails to tithe is doomed to hell?

No! Definitely not. The Pharisees' righteousness was based on their actions. Jesus is advocating a righteousness that is based on faith in what He did for us.

Trusting in our own actions will never grant us access to God. We may be better than others, but who wants to be the best sinner in hell? We have all sinned and come short of perfection, which is what God requires (Rom. 3:23).

The only one who was ever good enough to earn right standing with God is Jesus. His righteousness is offered as a gift to anyone who will put his faith in Him as his Savior.

Jesus offers us a righteousness by faith that is so far superior to the self-righteousness that the Pharisees had, that there is no comparison. This is the righteousness that we need, and it is available to us only through faith in Christ.

FEBRUARY 26
SPIRITUAL FITNESS
MATTHEW 5:23-30

Matthew 5:29 "And if thy right eye offend thee, pluck it out, and cast [it] from thee: for it is profitable for thee that one of thy members should perish, and not [that] thy whole body should be cast into hell."

Is Jesus advocating dismembering our bodies? Quite the contrary. He is drawing on the universal drive of self preservation that is inside every person, to make a point. If you value your body so much that you would never sacrifice one of its parts, then you need to esteem your spiritual well-being much higher.

Ever since the fall of Adam and Eve, man's priorities have been misplaced. Great effort is put into preserving our physical lives while our spiritual conditions are often overlooked. They constantly get put on the back burner while we tend to more urgent matters of this life.

Yet, our physical bodies are just temporary. If we live 70 years or more, that is just a fraction of a second in the light of eternity. Our spiritual man lives forever. The state in which it exists is determined by choices made in this life.

Therefore, choose to make your spiritual condition your top priority. Spend more time on your spiritual well-being than you do on your physical well-being. You and everyone around you will be eternally grateful that you did.

FEBRUARY 27
COMMANDMENTS LEAD TO HAPPINESS
MATTHEW 5:31-32

Matthew 5:32 "But I say unto you, That whosoever shall put away his wife, save for the cause of fornication, causeth her to commit adultery: and whosoever shall marry her that is divorced committeth adultery."

God's commandments are not intended to make us miserable—they're meant for our own happiness. Satan's lie in the Garden of Eden caused Eve to question God's motives behind His command (Genesis 3:5).

Malachi 2:15 says that God hates divorce. God doesn't hate the people who divorce. He hates the act of divorce because of the damage it does to people. God loves people.

Today, people see divorce as an easy way out of marital problems. This is based on the misconception that the mate is the problem—which is rarely the case.

People who blame their mates for their problems, give in easily to divorce, thinking that a new partner will solve the situation. Yet, second marriages have more than twice the failure rate as first marriages. That's because we take ourselves and all our unresolved problems into the next marriage.

You can't control other people—not even your mate. Although, through obeying the Lord, you can control yourself and have fullness of joy. God's commands tell us what will produce true happiness in our lives.

FEBRUARY 28
MORE THAN JUST WORDS
MATTHEW 5:33-37

Matthew 5:37 "But let your communication be, Yea, yea: Nay, nay: for whatsoever is more than these cometh of evil."

A person who has to swear or make a promise to validate his statements is a person whose word is no good. The thrust of Jesus' teaching here, is that we should live in such a manner that no one would need additional proof that we are telling the truth. Our word should be our bond.

We have all heard the story of the young shepherd boy who cried wolf when there was no wolf, until finally, no one believed him when the wolf really came. Our lack of integrity in performing our word has the same effect on people today.

Very few people conduct business anymore with their word and a handshake. Even contracts are not sacred if an individual can afford a good lawyer. This is not the way God intended it to be.

God has fulfilled every word He has ever spoken. We were created in His image and He planned for us to be like Him. Even our physical bodies respond adversely when we lie. That's why lie detectors work.

Today, commit yourself to be a new man or woman of your word. You will not only experience a new respect from others, but you will find the joy of a clear heart and mind.

MARCH 1
THE BEST DEFENSE
MATTHEW 5:38-48

Matthew 5:39 "But I say unto you, That ye resist not evil: but whosoever shall smite thee on thy right cheek, turn to him the other also."

Which would you rather have—God defending you, or you defending yourself? That's the choice that Jesus offers here. "Turning the other cheek" is not a prescription for abuse, but rather the way to get the Lord involved in your defense.

Many people feel that these instructions of Jesus guarantee that others will take advantage of them. That would be true if there was no God, but when we follow these commands of Jesus, the Lord is on our side. He said in Romans 12:19, "*Dearly beloved, avenge not yourselves, but [rather] give place unto wrath: for it is written, Vengeance [is] mine; I will repay, saith the Lord.*"

When we fight back, we are drawing on our own strength, but when we turn the other cheek, we are invoking God as our defense. Once we understand this, it becomes obvious that these instructions are for our own good.

James 1:20 says that the wrath of man does not accomplish the righteousness of God. Regardless of how appropriate our anger may seem, and how we think our wrath could make a person or situation change, we will never achieve God's best that way.

When we defend ourselves, we stop God from defending us. It has to be one way or the other. It cannot be both ways. When we turn the other cheek to our enemies, we are loosing the power of God on our behalf. Let God defend you today.

MARCH 2
WHAT'S YOUR MOTIVATION
MATTHEW 6:1-4

Matthew 6:1 "Take heed that ye do not your alms before men, to be seen of them: otherwise ye have no reward of your Father which is in heaven."

The motive behind your gift is more important than the gift itself. Paul said if he gave all of his goods to feed the poor, or if he made the ultimate sacrifice of giving his own life for someone else, but it wasn't motivated by love, then his gift would profit him nothing (1 Cor. 13:3).

Many Christians give faithfully, but never see the hundredfold return that the Lord promised because their motives are wrong. (Mk. 10:29-30). Paul said that God loves a cheerful giver—not one who gives grudgingly or out of debt (2 Cor. 9:7).

Jesus gave us the key to purifying our motives in this same teaching. He said, *"But when thou doest alms, let not thy left hand know what thy right hand doeth"* (Mt. 6:3). Giving in a manner in which you will not receive recognition for your gifts will guarantee that your motives are right and grant you the true joy that comes through selfless giving (Acts 20:24).

Ask the Lord to show you an opportunity today to give a kind word or a helping hand to someone who will not be able to repay you, and where others will never know about it. This could be a motorist in a traffic jam, a co-worker, a spouse, a child who won't even notice your kind deed, or any number of other people. Opportunities are all around us.

MARCH 3
QUALITY PRAYER
MATTHEW 6:5-8

Matthew 6:7 "But when ye pray, use not vain repetitions, as the heathen [do]: for they think that they shall be heard for their much speaking."

Some of the most effective prayers are the shortest prayers. Jesus said, "Peace, be still," and the wind and the waves ceased (Mk. 4:39). He said, "Lazarus, come forth," and Lazarus came back from the dead (Jn. 11:43-44).

Today, there is a new emphasis on the quantity of prayer instead of the quality of prayer. Jesus never advocated long prayers, and there are only a few instances where Jesus prayed long prayers. This is not to say that communion with God is not important. It certainly is, but formal prayer is only one part of our communion with the Lord.

Psalm 5:1-2 uses the words "prayer" and "meditation" interchangeably. Therefore, communing with God through keeping your mind stayed on the things of the Lord is also prayer. There are also times in prayer when we need to be still and know that God is God (Ps. 46:10).

Many times we ask the Lord to speak to us, but He can't get a word in edgewise. We're doing all the talking.

MARCH 4
A LOVING FATHER
MATTHEW 6:9-13

Matthew 6:9 "After this manner therefore pray ye: Our Father which art in heaven, Hallowed be thy name."

Although God was referred to as, "Our Father" 13 times in the Old Testament, Jesus' frequent use of this title brought a whole new understanding of our relationship with God. Jesus referred to God as His father over 150 times, and He spoke of God as being our father 30 times. This infuriated the religious Jews of Jesus' day who considered it blasphemy to call God their father, because they understood that to mean they were equal with God (Jn. 5:17-18).

This title has become so common in the church today that many times, we don't perceive its real significance. The revelation that we are instructed to call God "our Father" reveals the kind, gentle, loving nature of our God (1 Jn. 4:8). Paul amplifies this by using the term *"Abba Father" (Rom. 8:15)*, which is an affectionate term that a young child would use for his father, and it corresponds to our English word, "daddy."

We are instructed here to recognize our relationship with God and praise Him for it. It's a relationship that goes beyond any human relationship we could ever have on earth. It's a relationship of belonging to a father who loves us because we are His. Run to Him, drop all pretense and formality, and call Him "Daddy."

MARCH 5
SALVATION BEGINS NOW
MATTHEW 6:9-13

Matthew 6:10 "Thy kingdom come. Thy will be done in earth, as it is in heaven."

We do not have to live a beggarly existence here on earth and have to wait until we get to heaven to begin experiencing the benefits of our salvation. Jesus told us to pray, "Thy will be done in earth, as it is in heaven." In heaven, He will "wipe away all tears from our eyes" (Rev. 21:4); therefore, on earth, we can pray and believe to receive "joy unspeakable and full of glory" (1 Pet. 1:8). Healing, prosperity, and all the other benefits of heaven are ours on earth, to the degree that we can believe and receive them.

It is God's will to deliver us from this present evil world. The Lord didn't save us from our sins so we could be "saved and stuck" until we go to heaven. He made provision for our success in this life as well. Our salvation is effectual in this life too, not just the one to come. Some people have relegated all the benefits of salvation to when they all get to heaven. This is not true. Through the atonement of Jesus, we have been delivered from sickness, poverty, demonic control, and sin, in this present life. To the degree we believe this, we will begin to experience the physical benefits of our salvation in the "rough now and now," not just in the "sweet by and by."

Our salvation is not just pie in the sky, but it is victory in this present life. Today, believe God and start receiving every benefit of your salvation in this life, and help others to receive what has been purchased for them. We don't have to wait until we get to heaven.

MARCH 6
VICTORY: A PROVISION
MATTHEW 6:9-13

Matthew 6:13 "And lead us not into temptation, but deliver us from evil: For thine is the kingdom, and the power, and the glory for ever. Amen."

A temptation can be a difficult situation or a pressure. Contrary to popular belief, God is not the source of our temptations (Jas. 1:13). When we are under pressure, it is important to realize that God is not trying to entrap us. Satan is called the tempter (Mt. 4:3; 1 Th. 3:5). Then why did Jesus instruct us to pray that the Father would not lead us into temptation? This was simply a request for guidance so that we could be delivered from evil.

Jesus himself was tempted by Satan (Mt. 4, Lk. 4). He trusted God fully for provision, protection, and purpose. The Father would no more lead us into temptation than He would withhold our daily bread. Although, as stated in James 4:2, *"Ye have not because ye ask not."* The statements, *"give us our daily bread"* and *"lead us not into temptation"* are simply requests for what has already been provided for us. This part of prayer serves as a reminder to us of God's promised protection (Ps. 91) and gives us an opportunity to release our faith and appropriate what has already been provided.

"No temptation has seized you except what is common to man. And God is faithful; he will not let you be tempted beyond what you can bear. But when you are tempted, he will also provide a way out so that you can stand up under it" (1 Cor. 10:13 NIV). The victory demonstrated by Jesus is available to us. *"But thanks be to God, which giveth us the victory through our Lord Jesus Christ."* (1 Cor. 15:57). He has given it to you. Believe and receive it.

MARCH 7
THE BENEFITS OF FASTING
MATTHEW 6:14-18

Matthew 6:16 "Moreover when ye fast, be not, as the hypocrites, of a sad countenance: for they disfigure their faces, that they may appear unto men to fast. Verily I say unto you, They have their reward."

It was a Jewish custom to anoint yourself with olive oil and in Jesus' day it was apparently customary to also anoint the heads of your guests. (Lk. 7:46). At times, ointment or perfumes were used in this personal anointing. A lack of having your head anointed was associated with mourning or sorrow. Jesus says that there should be no external sign of fasting or sorrow, but it should be done secretly to the Lord to receive a full reward. Paul stated in 1 Corinthians 7:5, that abstinence from the physical relationship in marriage for the purpose of fasting should not be done without the consent of your spouse. A fast does not always have to be totally secretive to be productive. Rather, Jesus is once again dealing with the motives behind our actions. The fast must be directed toward God and not men.

Fasting accomplishes many things. One of the greatest benefits of fasting is that through denying the lust of the flesh, the spirit man gains ascendancy. Fasting was always used as a means of seeking God to the exclusion of all else. Fasting does not cast out demons, but rather it casts out unbelief. Therefore, fasting is beneficial to every aspect of the Christian life—not only in casting out devils.

The real virtue of a fast is humbling yourself through self-denial, and it can be accomplished through ways other than total abstinence from food. Partial fasts can be beneficial, as well as fasts of our time or pleasures. However, because appetite for food is one of man's strongest drives, fasting from food seems to get the job done the quickest. Fasting should be a much more important part of our seeking God. Seek to live a lifestyle of fasting, whether it is denying yourself through food, or denying your own wishes. Exalt Jesus today. Put Him first in everything you do.

MARCH 8
KNOWING GOD IS OUR GREATEST TREASURE
MATTHEW 6:19-21

Matthew 6:21 "For where your treasure is, there will your heart be also."

If isolated from the rest of God's Word, there are some scriptures that could be interpreted that having money or wealth is wrong; however, there are other scriptures that speak of riches as a blessing. The harmony between these two apparently opposite positions is that money is neither good nor bad. It is the love of money that is the root of all evil, and many have committed the sin of loving money who don't even have a dime (1Tim. 6:10). The love of things (covetousness) is idolatry, and this is what Jesus is addressing.

Because it is so easy to lust after money and the things it can provide, the Lord established a system whereby prosperity is a by-product of putting God first. As Matthew 6:33 states, *"But seek ye first the kingdom of God and his righteousness and all these things shall be added unto you."* We should no more reject the blessing of prosperity than we should covet it—that is idolatry.

The reason for not laying up treasures on this earth is so that we will not have our hearts drawn away from the things of God. A key to success in the kingdom of God is singleness of purpose. We don't have the capacity to do our best in two areas at the same time. If we will simply put God and His kingdom first in every area of our lives, He will add to us all the wealth that we need. What is more valuable or important than knowing Him?

MARCH 9
SINGLENESS OF VISION
MATTHEW 6:22-24

Matthew 6:24 "No man can serve two masters: for either he will hate the one, and love the other; or else he will hold to the one, and despise the other. Ye cannot serve God and mammon."

Jesus is speaking of spiritual vision. If we keep our attention (eyes) solely upon Jesus and the Word, then all that we will be filled with is the light of His Word (Jn. 1:1-14; Ps.119:105). The key to victory is this singleness of purpose (Phil. 3:13).

The strength of a laser is that all the light is concentrated on one single point. Likewise, the strength of a Christian is in how single his vision is upon Jesus, "the author and finisher of our faith" (Heb. 12:1-3).

You may have God and riches, but you can only serve one of them. In Matthew 6:24, the Lord amplifies this by saying that you cannot serve two masters. Why is this so? Because you do not have the capability of faithfully serving both of them. You will cleave to one more than the other. You cannot serve both with all of your heart. You just don't have the capacity to do your best in two areas at the same time. God wants singleness of vision, and singleness of purpose. He wants you to serve Him with all of your heart.

You may be wondering how you can still make a living without always thinking about money. Where will it come from? How will you get more of it? In verse 33, Jesus goes on to say that He will supply all of your need when you seek first the Kingdom of God. All of these other things (food and clothing etc.) will be added unto you. If you will simply put God and His Kingdom first in every area of your life, He will add to you all the wealth that you need.

It's when we covet after money that we "pierce ourselves through with many sorrows" (1 Tim. 6:10). Put God to the test today. Put Him first in every area of your life and see if He won't provide all the other things you need.

MARCH 10
TAKING THOUGHTS—OR NOT
MATTHEW 6:25-34

Matthew 6:31 *"Therefore take no thought, saying, What shall we eat? or, What shall we drink? or, Wherewithal shall we be clothed?"*

The Greek word used here for "thought" is "merimnao" and denotes "to be anxious or careful." In this passage, as well as the parallel passage in Luke 12:22-32, Jesus commands us not to worry or be anxious about our material needs being met. It would be impossible to have no thought whatsoever about our physical needs. Even Jesus thought about His need for money to pay taxes (Mt. 17:24-27). We are simply not to be preoccupied with thinking about riches or spending our time worrying about necessities. These things will be added unto us as we seek first the Kingdom of God.

The way we take or receive an anxious thought is by speaking it. Doubtful thoughts will come, but we do not sin until we entertain them. According to this verse, speaking forth these thoughts is one way of entertaining them; therefore, don't speak forth these negative thoughts.

It is imperative that we watch the words we say. Begin to speak words in faith that line up with God's Word, then positive results will follow. If we speak words of doubt, we will eventually believe them and have the negative things that these words produce. There are no such things as "idle" words that will not work for or against us. Death or life is in the power of every word we speak (Prov. 18:21). Our words can be our most powerful weapon against the devil, or they can become a snare of the devil (Prov. 6:2).

Today watch your words. Speak only things that will express your faith, trust, and confidence in the Lord and not your fear about the situations you face.

MARCH 11
RIGHTEOUS JUDGMENT
MATTHEW 7:1-5

Matthew 7:1 *"Judge not, that ye be not judged."*

There are many examples of people judging others in the scriptures. Paul prayed that our love would abound more and more in all judgment (Phil. 1:9). In light of the scriptures where Jesus and the disciples spoke of judging, it is evident that there must be a right and a wrong type of judging.

In Luke 12:56-57, Jesus uses the words "discern" and "judge" interchangeably. The dictionary defines "judge" as many things from "condemn to appraise, to form an opinion about; to think or consider." There is certainly nothing wrong with discerning or appraising a situation or person. Quite the contrary, we need to try the spirits (1 Jn. 4:1). Judging when done as discernment is good.

It is the condemning type of judgment that is wrong. We can defer passing sentence on people to God, and know that He will make a perfect judgment (Rom. 2:2, Rev. 20:13). God is ultimately the only qualified judge.

Jesus is not forbidding judgment, but He is warning us to be careful with our judgment because we will be judged accordingly. There are certain cases where we have to pass a condemning sentence as Paul did or as a judge would do today. Pastors and elders are charged with rebuking and even disciplining church members, but it is not something to be done lightly. Judging is not aimed at the person, but at the actions of that person. This warning constrains us to be certain that we have heard from God. We must not simply vent our own frustrations.

Every Christian has a need for wisdom in making judgments about how to live from day to day. How wonderful to know that God through His Word has already equipped us to judge.

MARCH 12
GOD ANSWERS EVERY PRAYER
MATTHEW 7: 6-8

Matthew 7:7 "Ask, and it shall be given you; seek, and ye shall find; knock, and it shall be opened unto you:"

Prayer that meets the requirements outlined in God's Word is always answered. Many times we don't perceive the answer because it always comes in the spiritual realm before it is manifested in the physical realm. If we waver from our confident faith, then we abort the manifestation of that answer (Jas. 1:6-7; Heb. 10:35), but God did answer. Everyone who asks receives.

In the book of Daniel chapter nine, Daniel prayed a prayer and waited a relatively short period of time to see his answer. In less than three minutes, the angel Gabriel appeared and answered all of his questions. This same man prayed another prayer in chapter 10, but this time it took three weeks before he had an angelic messenger come and answer his questions. What was the difference? Most people believe that God answered one prayer in three minutes and the next prayer in three weeks. But Daniel 10:12, says *"from the first day that thou didst set thine heart to understand. . .thy words were heard, and I am come for thy words."* Satan had hindered the second prayer from reaching Daniel. God was not the variable. God answers every prayer.

This is confirmed in Matthew 7:8, which says that everyone who asks receives; he that seeks will find, to him that knocks it is opened. God answers, but Satan can hinder our prayers in the spiritual realm before they ever physically manifest. If we understand that God gives the answer and that Satan is the one hindering, the truths of these scriptures will encourage us. God does answer prayer.

God is always answering your prayers. If you haven't seen them manifest, don't doubt God, but recognize that you're fighting an enemy, and must persevere. Stand on your faith. Pray without ceasing until you see the answer.

MARCH 13
GOD TAKES PLEASURE IN MEETING OUR NEEDS
MATTHEW 7: 9-11

Matthew 7:11 "If ye then, being evil, know how to give good gifts unto your children, how much more shall your Father which is in heaven give good things to them that ask him?"

What kind of parents would ever deny their children the necessities of life? If you have children, would you fail to feed them? Or provide for them? If they ask you for food, would you give them poison instead? Of course not. This is the point Jesus is making.

"God is love" (1 Jn. 4:8). His love for us is infinitely greater than any loving relationship on earth. We can apply this truth about God's love for us to any command or example we find in God's Word where His standards for relationship are revealed. Be assured that He will much more than meet those standards Himself.

This gives us confidence that in the same way we respond in love to our children and to those who are in need, our God, who is love, will also respond to us. God is a faithful God, and He will always give us the things that we need.

Today, let the Lord be magnified in your life as Psalm 35:27 says, *"Let the LORD be magnified, which hath pleasure in the prosperity of his servant."* It pleases God to minister to you. Let God have pleasure today by meeting your needs. You have not, because you ask not (James 4:2). God wants you to ask so that you can receive (John 16:24). Believe God. He gets pleasure when you ask Him.

MARCH 14
A LIFESTYLE CHECK
MATTHEW 7:12-20

Matthew 7:20 "Wherefore by their fruits ye shall know them."

The way that you can tell whether a person is genuine is by the fruit he produces. This fruit is his lifestyle. Jesus made the point that you don't get bad fruit from a good tree, and you don't get good fruit from a bad tree. Many people say one thing, but their actions speak so loudly to the contrary, that you really can't hear what they are saying. If you are in doubt about whether a person is genuine, or whether you should receive from him and follow his teaching, look at the fruit he is producing.

In evaluating ministers and ministries, more attention should be given to the fruit they are producing. Failure to do this could lead someone to reject and even discredit a minister who simply makes a mistake or is wrong in one area. Every minister has shortcomings, just as every other member of the body of Christ does, but that doesn't mean his ministry is bad. Look at the fruit. Fruit is the true test of ministers and ministries. If people are being saved, if lives are being changed, there is good fruit. Even though the minister may say something bad and make mistakes, the fruit is good. Therefore, you can say that the tree is good. When a person says all of the right things and seems sincere, but the lives of the people around him are shattered, torn, and in confusion and distress, then the fruit is bad. You can judge the effectiveness of a person by the fruit he is producing in his life. In ministry you can judge the effectiveness of a minister by the fruit his ministry is producing.

Today, make sure that the fruit produced from your life is good fruit. Make sure that you are making a positive impact on people's lives; that you are turning people to the Lord and not leaving them hurt and confused. People are looking at you to see what type of fruit you are bearing.

MARCH 15
HEALING IS GOD'S WILL
MATTHEW 8:1-4

Matthew 8:2 "And, behold, there came a leper and worshipped him, saying, Lord, if thou wilt, thou canst make me clean."

Leprosy was a hated disease and its symptoms are described in detail in Leviticus 13:1-46. This leper believed Jesus could heal him, but doubted His willingness to heal him. Jesus showed him His willingness to heal, and since He is no respecter of persons, He established a precedent for us (Rom. 2:11). This leper did not know God's will concerning healing, but this is not the case with us. The Word of God is the will of God, and it reveals that it is always God's will to heal.

Isaiah 53:5, makes it clear that when Isaiah said "with his stripes we are healed," he was speaking of the physical healing of our bodies. Jesus provided for physical healing as well as forgiveness of sins. The word "save" (Gk.-"sozo") is translated "made whole" in reference to physical healing in Matthew 9:22, Mark 5:34, and Luke 8:48. James 5:15 says, "the prayer of faith shall save (Gk.-"sozo") the sick." Many scriptures mention the healing of our bodies in conjunction with the forgiveness of our sins. Healing is a part of our salvation, just as much as the forgiveness of our sins.

Nowhere do we find Jesus refusing to heal anyone. In light of Jesus' statement that He could do nothing of Himself, but only what He saw the Father do (Jn. 5:19 and 8:28-29), His actions are proof enough that it is always God's will to heal. There are certain things Jesus suffered for us that we should not suffer. Jesus died for our sins so that we would not have to pay for them (Rom. 6:23). Jesus took our sicknesses and diseases so that we could walk in health (Mt. 8:17; 1 Pet. 2:24). Jesus became poor so that we, through His poverty, might be rich (2 Cor. 8:9). If God is for us, then no one can successfully be against us.

The Lord has made every provision for you to walk in all He has provided for you today. Don't put it off a minute longer.

MARCH 16
TOUCHED BY LOVE
MATTHEW 8:1-4; MARK 1:40-45; LUKE 5:12-15

Mark 1:41 "And Jesus, moved with compassion, put forth his hand, and touched him . . .and he was cleansed."

Only Mark records this important statement that Jesus was "moved with compassion" in the healing of this leper. There are three other instances in the gospels when Jesus was moved with compassion, that resulted in healing (Mt. 14:14; 20:34; Lk. 7:13;) and one that resulted in deliverance (Mk.5:19). Many times, the difference between seeing a person healed or not healed is this all-important ingredient: love.

All three of the Gospel accounts record Jesus touching this leper. This not only illustrates the doctrine of "laying on of hands," but was probably included because according to Numbers 19:22, this action would have made Jesus unclean. This illustrates the New Testament ministry of the Spirit versus the Old Testament ministry of the letter of the law (2 Cor. 3:6). Jesus did not have to avoid the ceremonial uncleanness that would come from physical contact with a leper because He came to bear our sins in His own body. As can be seen from Mark's account, two things happened: First, the leprosy departed and second, the man was cleansed. Jesus not only removed the disease, but restored the damaged parts of the leper's body. This leper was healed as soon as Jesus spoke.

The Word of God is the will of God, and it reveals that it is always God's will to heal. Jesus often healed people by touching them, and others received their healing as they touched Jesus. You can transmit the power or the anointing of God through the laying on of hands. Let Him use you today to touch others.

MARCH 17
FAITH THAT IS SEEN
MATTHEW 9:1-8, MARK 2:1-12; LUKE 5:17-26

Mark 2:5 "When Jesus saw their faith, he said unto the sick of the palsy, Son, thy sins be forgiven thee."

Faith can be seen. Just as Jesus explained to Nicodemus in John 3:8; faith is like the wind. Faith itself is invisible, but saving faith is always accompanied by corresponding actions that can be seen (Jas. 2:17-26).

It was not only the faith of the paralytic that Jesus saw, but also that of his four friends (Mk. 2:3). This demonstrates the effect our intercession in faith can have upon others. Jesus saw their faith. Although our faith released on behalf of others is powerful, it is not a substitute for their faith. It is simply a help. The person who is to receive the miracle must have some degree of faith also. Even Jesus could not produce healing in those who would not believe (Mk. 6:5-6). In this instance, it is evident that the paralytic also had faith because he was not resistant to the four who brought him, and he got up and obeyed Jesus' command (v. 7) without having to be helped.

Why did Jesus minister forgiveness of sins to this man instead of meeting the obvious need he had of healing? God is more concerned with the spiritual health of a man than his physical health. Or, Jesus, through a word of knowledge, may have perceived that the real heart-cry of this man was to be reconciled to God. In some instances, sickness was a direct result of sin (Jn. 9:2-3)Therefore, Jesus dealt with the root of the paralysis. It's not certain whether this man's paralysis was a direct result of sin, but sin in our lives (that has not been forgiven) will allow Satan to keep us in bondage. Through Jesus' act of forgiving this man's sins, the paralytic was free to receive all the blessings of God, which certainly included healing.

The point Jesus is making is that both forgiveness of sins and the healing of the paralytic are humanly impossible. If Jesus could do one of these things, He could do the other. He then healed the paralytic showing that He did, indeed, have the authority to forgive sins. In Jesus' day, the people were more inclined to accept His willingness to heal than they were to accept His forgiveness of sins without the keeping of the law. Today, the church world basically accepts forgiveness of sins, but doubts God's willingness to heal. They were never meant to be separated. Believe and receive all that God has for you today.

MARCH 18
LET CHRIST LIVE THROUGH YOU
MATTHEW 9:9-10; MARK 2:14-15; LUKE 5:27-29

Matthew 9:9 "And as Jesus passed forth from thence, he saw a man, named Matthew, sitting at the receipt of custom: and he saith unto him, Follow me. And he arose, and followed him."

To "follow" means to come or go after; move behind in the same direction; to come or go with; to accept the guidance or leadership of; to adhere to the cause or principles of; to be governed by; obey; comply with (Jn. 10:27-29; Rom. 10:9-10, 13).

When a person first comes to Jesus, it is impossible to know everything that following Jesus entails. No one, however, should be fearful of making a total commitment to Him because of some imagined problem that may never come to pass. There should be a willingness to forsake everything to follow Jesus. Once we make that decision, then Christ begins to live through us and we find a strength that is not our own, and is equal to whatever test we may encounter (Gal. 2:20).

It is Christ living through us that is the secret of victorious Christian living. It is not us living for Jesus, but Jesus living through us. Failure to understand this simple truth is at the root of all legalism and the performance mentality. The law focuses on the outer man and tells it what it must do. Grace focuses on the inner man and tells it what is already done through Christ. Those who are focused on what they must do are under law. Those who are focused on what Christ has done for them are walking under grace.

Just as the life of a root is found in the soil, or a branch in the vine, or a fish in the sea; the believer's true life is found in union with Christ. The Christian life is not just hard to live; it's impossible in our human strength. The only way to walk in victory is to let Christ live through you.

MARCH 19
SOMETHING NEW
MATTHEW 9:11-17; MARK 2:16-22; LUKE 5:30-39

Luke 5:36-37 "And he spake a parable unto them; No man putteth a piece of a new garment upon an old; if otherwise, then both the new maketh a rent, and the piece that was taken out of the new agreeth not with the old. And no man putteth new wine into old bottles; else the new wine will burst the bottles, and be spilled, and the bottles shall perish."

These two parables are in response to the scribes' and Pharisees' criticism (v. 30) and the question from John's disciples about why Jesus didn't act according to their religious traditions and expectations (Mt. 9:14; Mk. 2:18). The gist of these parables was to show that Jesus came to do a new thing that would not mix with the old covenant ways that were familiar to the people (Isa. 43:18-19; Jer. 31:31-34; Heb. 8:7-13).

A new cloth sown on an old garment in Jesus' day would shrink the first time it was washed. Then it would tear away from the old garment that was already shrunk, making the hole worse. This illustrates that Jesus did not come to patch up the old Mosaic covenant, but to replace it (Heb. 7:18-19).

Also, new wine (not yet fermented) had to be put into new or reconditioned wineskins to allow for the expansion of gases within the skin as the result of the fermentation process. Otherwise, an old wineskin that had already been stretched by use would simply burst and all the wine would run out. The Old Testament laws could never stretch enough to accommodate the New Testament truths of mercy and grace (Heb. 10:1-10). Jesus set us free from the judgment of the Old Testament laws (Rom. 6:14; 7:1-4; 8:2; 10:3-4; Gal. 3:12- 14,23-24; 5:4; Phil. 3:9).

These religious scribes and Pharisees (Lk. 5:30) were making the terrible mistake of trusting in their own efforts to produce their right standing (righteousness) with God. Jesus did not come to accept our sacrificial acts, but to make Himself a sacrifice for our sins. He did all this to give us new life in Him. Thank Him for His grace today.

MARCH 20
NATURALLY HOLY
JOHN 5:1-15

John 5:14 "Afterward Jesus findeth him in the temple, and said unto him, Behold, thou art made whole: sin no more, lest a worse thing come unto thee."

In saying this, Jesus shows that sin causes the tragedies that come into our lives. The reason for holiness in the life of the believer is that when we give in to sin, we yield ourselves to Satan, the author of that sin. Yielding to sin is yielding to a person—Satan. God doesn't impute the sin to us, but the devil does. Our actions either release the power of Satan or the power of God in us.

Although God is not imputing our sins unto us, we cannot afford the luxury of sin because it allows Satan to have access to us. When a Christian sins, he gives the devil an opportunity to produce death in his life. The way to stop this is to confess the sin, and God who is faithful and just, will take the forgiveness that is already present in our born again spirits and release it in our flesh. This removes Satan and his strongholds.

The sins of a Christian don't make him a sinner any more than the righteous acts of a sinner make him righteous. Sin is a deadly thing that even Christians should avoid at all costs, but it does not determine our standing with the Lord. A person who is born again is not "in" the flesh even though he may walk "after" the flesh.

What is the motive for living a separated life? We live separated lives because our natures have been changed. We were darkness, now we are light (Eph 5:8). Many people argue for holiness in order to obtain relationship with God. We need to live holy lives because of the relationship that we already have. It's the nature of a Christian to walk in the light and not in the darkness. If Christians were rightly informed of who they are and what they have in Christ, holiness would just naturally flow out of them. It's their nature. It's our nature.

MARCH 21
REST IN HIS LOVE
JOHN 5:16-27

John 5:16 "And therefore did the Jews persecute Jesus, and sought to slay him because he had done these things on the sabbath day."

The Sabbath was first mentioned in scripture in Exodus, chapter 16, when the Lord started miraculously providing the children of Israel with manna in the wilderness. The Israelites were commanded to gather twice as much manna on the sixth day because God would not provide any on the seventh day. Shortly after this, the Lord commanded the observance of the Sabbath day in the ten commandments, written on two tablets of stone, and communicated to Moses on Mt. Sinai (Ex. 20:8-11). In this command, God connected the Sabbath day with the rest that He took on the seventh day of creation.

As revealed in Colossians 2:16-17, the Sabbath was symbolic. According to Exodus 23:12, one of the purposes of the Sabbath was to give man and his animals one day of physical rest each week. Today's medical science has proven that our bodies need at least one day of rest each week to function at their peak. Deuteronomy 5:15, also clearly states that the Sabbath was to serve as a reminder to the Jews that they had been slaves in Egypt and were delivered from bondage—not by their own efforts, but by the supernatural power of God. However, in the New Testament, there is an even clearer purpose of the Sabbath stated. In Colossians 2:16-17, Paul reveals that the Sabbath was only a shadow of things to come and is now fulfilled in Christ. Hebrews 4:1-11, talks about a Sabbath rest that is available to, but not necessarily functional in all New Testament believers. This New Testament Sabbath rest is simply a relationship with God in which we have ceased from doing things by our own efforts and are letting God work through us (Gal. 2:20; Heb. 4:10).

The Sabbath is not a day, but rather a relationship with God through Jesus. Rest in His love and let Him use you today.

MARCH 22
JESUS SHARED HIS FATHER'S GLORY
JOHN 5:16-27

John 5:18 "Therefore the Jews sought the more to kill him, because he not only had broken the sabbath, but said also that God was his Father, making himself equal with God."

When the Jewish authorities heard Jesus call God his "own Father," they immediately understood that Jesus claimed for Himself deity in the highest possible sense of the term. That claim was either blasphemy, to be punished by death, or else Jesus was who He claimed to be.

Jesus never associated Himself with His disciples by using the plural pronoun "our" Father. Rather, He always used the singular "my" Father, since His relationship was unique and eternal, whereas theirs was by grace and regeneration.

We should ponder carefully our Lord's conception of who He was. He said, "I am from above" (Jn. 8:23); "Before Abraham was, I AM" (Jn. 8:58); "I and my Father are one" (Jn. 10:30); "He that hath seen me hath seen the Father" (Jn. 14:9); "I am not of the world" (Jn. 17:16). He also declared His eternal preexistence and that He shared the Father's glory (Jn. 6:62; 17:5).

We can't just honor Jesus, but we have to honor Him "even as" (in like manner or the same way) we honor the Father. This is what separates true Christianity from the religions of the world. Many religions (Islam, Unification Church, Jehovah's Witnesses) honor Jesus as a great man, but they are violently opposed to making Jesus equal with Almighty God (1 Jn. 2:23). The names and titles given to Jesus in John's Gospel clearly present Jesus as being equal to God. He is all you need Him to be.

MARCH 23
PLEASE GOD, NOT MAN
JOHN 5:28-47

John 5:43-44 "I am come in my Father's name, and ye receive me not: if another shall come in his own name, him ye will receive. How can ye believe, which receive honour one of another, and seek not the honour that cometh from God only?"

This is in reference to Jesus coming in the power and authority of His Father to point men to Father God. Jesus existed before His advent on this earth in the form of God, and He was equal to God. Yet, He humbled Himself and became a servant while on earth (Phil. 2:6-8).

He did not come to promote Himself, but to give His life to provide the way to the Father (Jn. 14:6). In the same way, the Holy Spirit does not exalt Himself, but points all men unto Jesus. Jesus came, meek and lowly, totally submitted unto and seeking only to please the Father.

This is radically different from the way so called great men present themselves. The Roman caesar of Jesus' day proclaimed that he was God and demanded worship. Lesser leaders ruled by exalting themselves over the people they governed. Jesus showed us that, ". . . whosoever will be great among you, let him be your minister; And whosoever will be chief among you, let him be your servant: Even as the Son of man came not to be ministered unto, but to minister, and to give his life a ransom for many" (Mt. 20:26-28).

If we are concerned about what people think in an attempt to gain their approval (or honor), we will never take a stand in faith for anything that might be criticized. This one thing has probably stopped as many people from receiving from God as anything else. You cannot be a man-pleaser and please God at the same time. Commit your all to Him—every thought, word, and deed.

MARCH 24
ABOUT THOSE SCRIBES
MATTHEW 12:1-14; MARK 2:23-3:6; LUKE 6:1-11

Luke 6:7 "And the scribes and the Pharisees watched him, whether he would heal on the sabbath day, that they might find an accusation against him."

The scribes were copyists of the holy scriptures. They preserved the oral law in written form and faithfully handed down the Hebrew scriptures. In New Testament times, they were students, interpreters, and teachers of the Old Testament. Their functions regarding the law were to teach it, develop it, and use it in any connection with the Sanhedrin and various local courts. They were ambitious for honor, which they demanded, especially from their pupils, as well as from the general public. This homage was readily granted them (Mt. 23:5-11).

Ezra was a scribe during the Babylonian captivity of the Jews, and he was a godly man. The office of a scribe was a worthy one, but the scribes of Jesus' day were often rebuked by Him for having gone beyond the job of copying the scriptures. They had a large volume of interpretations based on traditions, that they added to the scriptures and thus made "the word of God of none effect" (Mk. 7:13).

The scribes became an independent company of interpreters of the law and leaders of the people. Even they themselves sought to evade some of their own precepts (Mt. 23:2-4). They clashed with Christ because He taught with authority and condemned the external formalism that they fostered (Mt. 7:28-29). They persecuted Peter and John (Acts 4:3-7) and had a part in Stephen's martyrdom (Acts 6:12). Although the majority opposed Christ, some did believe (Jn. 12:42).

Later on we'll read how Jesus exposed the hypocrisy of the scribes by dealing with issues of the heart. They appeared to be holy outwardly, but their hearts were far from God. It is important for us to keep our hearts tender, receptive to His Word, and give ourselves to Him in worship. Think about the good things He has done for you today and be thankful.

MARCH 25
HIS MERCY ENDURES FOREVER
MATTHEW 12:15-21; MARK 3:7-19; LUKE 6:12-16

Matthew 12:20 "A bruised reed shall he not break, and a smoking flax shall he not quench, till he send forth judgement unto victory."

One of the ways that God's goodness is revealed is in mercy. We may describe mercy as the readiness of God to relieve the misery of fallen creatures. Many times mercy is called compassion or lovingkindness. It is expressed toward the sinner because of the misery that sin has brought upon him.

The "reed" referred to in this passage is probably speaking of the reeds that grew in the marshy areas in the land of Palestine. They were very fragile and could be easily bruised or broken. The term "smoking flax" refers to a linen wick that was made from flax and burned brightly when floating on oil in an open lamp. However, when the oil was depleted, the flax would just smoke until the oil was replenished.

The meaning of these illustrations is that Jesus ministered in mercy to those who were bruised or broken (Lk. 4:18), or who had lost their oil (spirit). He has come to fill them anew (Mt. 5:3; Acts 1:5; 2:4). The Jews were used to the judgment of the law, but Jesus came to minister grace and truth (Jn. 1:17), even to the Gentiles (Mt. 12:18-21).

God's mercy to the believer is revealed by His act of taking away the misery of sin's consequences through the New Covenant of our Savior, the Lord Jesus Christ. Salvation is given to us because of God's mercy. It's not something we've merited or earned. As the Apostle Paul states, *"Not by works of righteousness which we have done, but according to HIS MERCY He saved us"* (Ti. 3:5). God is for you, not against you. Cast all of your care upon Him, because His mercy endureth forever!

MARCH 26
MORE THAN JUST SOWING AND REAPING
LUKE 6:17-49

Luke 6:38 "Give, and it shall be given unto you; good measure, pressed down, and shaken together, and running over, shall men give into your bosom. For with the same measure that ye mete withal it shall be measured to you again."

This verse reveals one of God's cardinal laws that will work in the spiritual realm, as well as in the physical world. Just as we "give" seed into the ground to receive multiple seeds in return, so it is with everything we give. Whether it's money, possessions, an emotion such as love or hate, prayers, or our time, we will reap a harvest of whatever we give. We reap exactly what we sow and proportional to the same measure that we give (Gal. 6:7-8).

"He which soweth sparingly shall reap also sparingly; and he which soweth bountifully shall reap also bountifully" (2 Cor. 9:6). This law works on positive or negative things that we sow.

Although this is an unchangeable law of God, it can be overcome by a greater law in much the same way that we can escape the law of gravity by using the greater laws of thrust and lift. The negative things we have given don't have to come back to us if we apply the greater law of forgiveness (1 Jn. 1:9). Likewise, the good things we have sown can be voided if we don't continue in well doing (Gal. 6:9).

God is our source, but God uses people. If we pray for finances, God is not going to make counterfeit currency and put it into our wallets. He will use people to get the money to us. So, it is not always as simple as praying for money and receiving it the next minute. We need to believe the Lord hears and answers our prayers, and then pray for the people He's going to use to deliver the answer. This could mean any number of people such as your employer or the people who buy your goods. Ultimately God is your source—trust Him.

MARCH 27
GOD'S KIND OF FAITH
MATTHEW 8:5-13, LUKE 7:1-10

Matthew 8:9-10 "For I am a man under authority, having soldiers under me: and I say to this man, Go, and he goeth; and to another, Come, and he cometh; and to my servant, Do this, and he doeth it. When Jesus heard it he marvelled, and said to them that followed, Verily I say unto you, I have not found so great faith, no, not in Israel."

There were only two things in all of scripture that caused Jesus to marvel: the centurion's faith and the Jews' unbelief (Mk. 6:6). A faith that made Jesus (the author and finisher of our faith) marvel is worth examining. This centurion believed that the spoken word of Jesus was sufficient to produce his miracle. He didn't need Jesus to come to his house. He had faith in Jesus' word. Therefore, we can see that the person who simply believes the written Word of God is operating in a much higher form of faith than those who require additional proof. Compare this centurion's faith with the "little" faith of Thomas in John 20:24-29.

Thomas refused to believe what He couldn't see or feel. Our five senses were given to us by God and are necessary to help us function in this life, but if we do not renew our minds to acknowledge the limits of the five senses, they will keep us from believing. Faith can perceive things that the senses cannot (Heb. 11:1).

The type of faith that Thomas operated in was a human or natural faith that was based on what he could see. Jesus said there was a greater blessing to be obtained. That greater blessing comes from using a supernatural, God-kind of faith that is based only on God's Word.

Jesus and God's Word are one (Jn 1:1,14). Believing God's Word is not just putting your trust in some printed words on the pages of a book we call the Bible. There is much more involved. It is a relationship with a person, the person behind the words. Get to know Him through His Word.

MARCH 28
WHOSE FAITH WAS IT?
LUKE 7:11-17

Luke 7:13-14 "And when the Lord saw her, he had compassion on her, and said unto her, Weep not, And he came and touched the bier: and they that bear him stood still. And he said, Young man, I say unto thee, Arise."

This example of the widow's son being raised from the dead is often used to demonstrate that Jesus produced many miracles without any faith from those receiving the miracle, but by His faith alone. However, the prayer in Mark 6:5-6 shows that Jesus could not (nor would not) do many mighty works in His hometown because of the people's unbelief. Many scriptures reveal that faith must be present to receive from God (Mk. 11:23-24; Jas. 1:5-7).

So, whose faith was present in this instance? First, the mother of the boy responded to Jesus in faith. For this woman to allow Jesus to interrupt the funeral procession and tell her to stop weeping has to be viewed as a positive response. These people were no different from mourners at funerals today. If she had rebelled at Jesus' intrusion, the crowd would have sided with her because of pity, but none of these reactions are recorded. Jesus was in command.

Second, it cannot be proven that a dead person has no choice in what happens. We may take it for granted, but the scriptures don't state that. A person doesn't cease to exist at death; he simply leaves his body. The person is still very much alive. Many people who have been raised from the dead have mentioned that they had a choice in whether or not to enter their bodies again. Although this principle cannot be verified by scripture, it cannot be ruled out by scripture either.

In any case, to be consistent with the rest of scripture, some degree of faith had to be present in either the person receiving the miracle, or an intercessor (in this case, the mother). Reach out in faith to receive your miracle today.

MARCH 29
OUR INHERITANCE WITH CHRIST
MATTHEW 11:2-19, LUKE 7:18-35

Matthew 11:11 "Verily I say unto you, Among them that are born of women there hath not risen a greater than John the Baptist: notwithstanding, he that is least in the kingdom of heaven is greater than he."

Much of the Old Testament deals with future events and the coming Messiah and His Kingdom. Not only was John the Baptist the voice of God to his generation, he was also the fulfillment of Old Testament prophecy. He did not merely prophesy about the coming Messiah and the New Covenant, as the Old Testament prophets did, but he actually prepared the way for the hearts of the people to receive Jesus, by bearing witness to the Light.

Although John the Baptist was the greatest of the Old Testament prophets, he was not a born again "new creature in Christ." When Jesus was raised from the dead, He enabled us to be "born of the Spirit" and become children of God, heirs of God, and joint-heirs with Christ. We were enabled to become "partakers of the divine nature" and full-fledged sons of God. John operated under the Old Covenant when none of these promises were yet in effect. Jesus established a new order: "the Kingdom of God," in which these promises became effective. God saw John and all of the Old Testament prophets through the law.

The new birth is essential for entering into the Kingdom of God. Our spiritual man became dead unto (separated from) God through sin. Just as we didn't accomplish our physical birth, we cannot produce our spiritual rebirth. We are totally incapable of saving ourselves; therefore, we need a Savior. We simply believe on the Lord Jesus Christ and we are saved. Salvation is not a reformation, but rather a regeneration—a new birth, a new creation that can only be accomplished by a creative miracle of the Holy Spirit. Because of the new birth, God sees us through Jesus. Celebrate life!

MARCH 30
BEING YOKED TO JESUS
MATTHEW 11:20-30

Matthew 11:28-30 "Come unto me, all ye that labour and are heavy laden, and I will give you rest. Take my yoke upon you, and learn of me; for I am meek and lowly in heart: and ye shall find rest unto your souls. For my yoke is easy, and my burden is light."

Yokes were made of wood with two hollowed out sections on the bottom portion that rested on the necks of oxen, which were used to plow or to draw a cart. Figuratively, a yoke symbolized servitude or submission. Jesus is admonishing us to submit ourselves to Him, for true rest comes from serving Him—not ourselves.

A new ox was often trained for plowing or drawing a cart by yoking him with an experienced ox. The yoke kept the young ox from doing his own thing and he soon learned obedience to his master. In like manner, we are to commit ourselves to being yoked to Jesus. "It is not in man that walketh to direct his steps" (Jer. 10:23). Therefore, we have to "bear the yoke in our youth" (Lam. 3:27), if we want to become mature Christians, but the comparison ends here. Unlike the sometimes harsh treatment oxen are given to bring them into subjection, Jesus is "meek and lowly in heart," and wins us by love. Jesus pulls more than His share of the load; therefore, our burden is light.

The most loving father in the world cannot compare with the love our heavenly Father has for us. Yet, many times we find it easier to believe in the willingness of a father, mother, or mate to help us, than in the willingness of God to use His power on our behalf. Relatively few people really doubt God's ability, but doubt His willingness to use His ability on their behalf, which causes them to do without. Jesus assures us that God's love, and His willingness to demonstrate that love, is far greater than we can ever experience in any human relationship. Not only does He want our love, but He wants you to let Him love you today.

MARCH 31
THE UNPARDONABLE SIN
LUKE 12:10; MATTHEW 12:24-31; MARK 3:22-30

Matthew 12:31 "Wherefore I say unto you, All manner of sin and blasphemy shalt be forgiven unto men: but blasphemy against the Holy Ghost shall not be forgiven unto men."

The word "blaspheme" means "to speak evil of; defame; or revile." In context, Jesus is saying that blasphemy against the Holy Ghost is attributing the working of the Holy Spirit to the devil. Many people in the Bible did this, including Saul, who became the Apostle Paul. However, we see in 1 Timothy 1:13, that Paul said he received mercy concerning his blasphemy because he had done it "ignorantly in unbelief." Therefore, the blasphemy against the Holy Ghost that Jesus is warning against must be willfully reviling the Holy Ghost with knowledge of what is being done.

This parallels Hebrews 6:4-6, where qualifications are placed on those who can fall away from grace. This passage indicates that only a mature Christian can commit such a thing. Likewise, with blasphemy against the Holy Ghost, rash statements spoken against the Holy Spirit in ignorance or unbelief by those who don't really know what they are doing, can be forgiven.

From our human perspective, no clear line can be drawn as to when someone becomes accountable for blasphemies and has committed this unpardonable sin. We can be assured that God knows the hearts of all men and that He will judge righteously concerning this. God's Word does show us that when anyone becomes a "reprobate," they lose all conviction from God (Rom. 1:28); therefore, anyone who is convicted and repentant over having possibly blasphemed the Holy Ghost has not yet reached the place where it is unpardonable or he wouldn't care. Keep your heart tender and sensitive to Him. Listen to His voice speak to you through His Word today.

APRIL 1
SINGLENESS OF HEART
MATTHEW 12:32-45

Matthew 12:35 "A good man out of the good treasure of the heart bringeth forth good things: and an evil man out of the evil treasure bringeth forth evil things."

Our spirits are definitely a part of our hearts, but as seen in 1 Peter 3:4, they are only a part. Sin, iniquity, and unbelief come from the heart, not from the born-again spirit. Hebrews 4:12 suggests that spirit and soul are both part of the heart; hence, the scriptures admonish us to believe with all our hearts (Acts 8:37), have singleness of heart (Col. 3:22), and tell us our hearts can have two minds or ways of thinking (Jas. 4:8).

Even Christians still struggle with things like pride and foolishness which Jesus said come out of the heart. It's certain that our born again spirits are not the source of these sins. The heart encompasses more than just the spirit.

The English word "soul" comes from the Greek word "psuche," translated "heart, life, mind, and soul." The mind is the principle and leading part of the soul, followed by the will and emotions. The soul could also be described as the hidden part of all existing beings or what most people would call the personality. The soul is the center of feelings and emotions, appetites and desires, and sensory perception and consciousness

The soul may also speak of the totality of a person—his total being or self; the hidden or inward man. The soul and the body do not get born again. It is the spirit of man that becomes totally new at salvation. Although every believer receives the same miraculous spiritual rebirth, the visible results of that inward change will vary from person to person according to how much he renews his mind. The term "heart" can include all of the inner man—spirit, soul, or any portion thereof. The peace of God will keep your heart at rest in Christ Jesus. Let Himdo it.

APRIL 2
JUST WORDS
MATTHEW 12:34-37

Matthew 12:37 "For by thy words thou shalt be justified, and by thy words thou shalt be condemned."

God created the heavens, the earth and everything that is in the earth by His words (Heb. 11:3). The whole creation was made by, and responds to words. Our words, when spoken in faith, release either life or death (Prov. 18:21), and affect people, things, and circumstances. We can release the power that is in faith by our words.

Every word counts. There is no such thing as an idle word that will not work for us or against us. Our words can be our most powerful weapon against the devil, or they can become a snare of the devil (Prov. 6:2). Faith-filled words can move mountains.

The faith that made Jesus marvel was a faith in the authority of the spoken word (Mt. 8:8-10). We are to believe in the power of our words. If we begin to speak words in faith that line up with God's Word, then positive results will follow. If we continue to speak words of doubt, we will eventually believe them and have the negative things that these words produce. Death or life is in the power of every word we speak.

Faith is released by speaking words. Jesus encouraged us to speak to mountains or to whatever our problem is. Most people speak to God about their problems, but few follow Jesus' instructions and speak directly to the "mountain." God has put certain things under our authority and we must exercise it. When a problem stands in our way, we must speak to the problem and command it to get out of our way in the name of Jesus. Speak God's Word today. His Words will produce life.

APRIL 3
TO WHOM MUCH IS GIVEN
MATTHEW 12:43-45

Matthew 12:43 "When the unclean spirit is gone out of a man, he walketh through dry places, seeking rest, and findeth none."

Most often, verses 43-45 are used to teach about demon possession and deliverance from evil spirits. Jesus made it clear that getting rid of an unclean spirit is only a part of deliverance. You must also fill the place that was previously occupied by the demonic spirit with the presence and power of God as protection. If a person is cleansed from an evil spirit but left "empty," the spirit will return with even more spirits and the individual will be in worse condition. Simply being void of the devil, but not full of God, is a dangerous and short-lived condition. True deliverance is not only getting freed, but staying free.

In context, these verses refer to Jesus' rebuke of the scribes and Pharisees and His statement about the men of Nineveh and the queen of the south condemning them at the judgment. One of the laws of God concerning accountability is being dealt with here. As stated in Luke 12:48, "...For unto whomsoever much is given, of him shall be much required...." The people of Jesus' day who rejected His message will be held more accountable at the judgment than the men of Nineveh or the Queen of Sheba, because Jesus' witness and person was so much greater than either Jonah or Solomon. Just as a man who receives miraculous deliverance from an evil spirit becomes more accountable and will end up in even worse condition if he doesn't walk in that accountability, so the people of Jesus' generation were accountable for more than any other generation had ever been. A person would be better off to keep just one evil spirit than to be set free, not fill himself with God, and end up with eight demonic spirits, seven of which are more wicked than the first. The scribes and Pharisees would have been better off to have never had Jesus bring the kingdom of God unto them, than to reject such an offer. He has given you much, what will you do with it?

APRIL 4
JESUS: TEACHER AND SAVIOR
MARK 4:1-12

Mark 4:2 "And he taught them many things by parables, and said unto them in his doctrine,"

The Greek word used here for "doctrine" means "teaching" and occurs a total of 30 times in the New Testament. The four gospels refer to Jesus teaching 43 times and preaching 19 times, and six verses refer to Him preaching and teaching in the same verse. This would indicate that Jesus spent twice as much time teaching as He did preaching. Jesus' teaching is the basic building block of making disciples and a stumbling block to the religious people.

Why is it that a person who is seeking so hard to please God can be rejected, while a person who has not sought God at all can come into a righteous relationship with Him? This is an important question and the answer is one of the most profound doctrines in scripture. The answer is faith and its object. The Jews were zealous for the things of God, but their faith was in themselves. They were trusting that they could earn God's favor by their acts of righteousness. On the other hand, the Gentiles had no holiness to trust in. So, when they heard the Gospel message, that Jesus paid our debt for us, they readily accepted His "gift" of salvation, while the religious Jews could not abandon their trust in themselves for salvation.

The same problem exists today. Millions of church people are trying to live holy lives, but they do not have a true faith in Jesus as their Savior. If they were to stand before God and He was to ask them what they had done to deserve salvation, they would immediately start recounting all their acts of holiness such as church attendance, giving receipts, etc. Regardless of how good our actions are compared to others, they always come short of the perfect standard of God. The only response to this kind of question that would grant us entrance into heaven is to say, "My only claim to salvation is faith in Jesus as my Savior." Let Him be the object of your faith today. He is all you need.

APRIL 5
GOD'S TRUTHS BELONG TO HIS CHILDREN
MATTHEW 13:1-13

Matthew 13:11 "He answered and said unto them, Because it is given unto you to know the mysteries of the kingdom of heaven, but to them it is not given."

The Greek word translated "mystery" here, means "something that could not be known by men except by divine revelation, but that, though once hidden, has now been revealed in Christ and is to be proclaimed so that all who have ears may hear it."

God's truths are hidden *for* His children, not from them. God has given an open invitation to everyone to receive the spiritual rebirth that entitles them to the revelation of these mysteries of the kingdom. As stated in 1 Corinthians 2:14, a natural man cannot receive the things of the Spirit of God because they are spiritually discerned. Therefore, whoever rejects Jesus rejects the source of all wisdom and knowledge (Col. 2:3), thereby reserving the deep things of God for those who receive Jesus and draw on His wisdom through the Holy Spirit. This also safeguards the laws of God, upon which all the universe is founded, from being appropriated and misused by Satan's kingdom.

In context, Jesus is speaking about those who have revelation knowledge of the mysteries of God. They will receive even more revelation and will walk in the abundant life that Jesus provided (Jn. 10:10; 2 Pet. 1:3). Those who do not receive God's revelation will lose whatever truth they do have and will go further into deception. God reveals His truths to us in stages, not all at once (Isa. 28:9-10). Therefore, as we walk in the revelation of what the Lord has already shown us, He will reveal more of His truths to us. The truths of God are mysterious only to those who do not soften their hearts by seeking God with their whole hearts. As Jeremiah 29:13 says, *"And ye shall seek me, and find me, when ye shall search for me with all your heart."*

APRIL 6
NATURALLY HOLY
MATTHEW 13:14-23

Matthew 13:15 "For this people's heart is waxed gross, and their ears are dull of hearing, and their eyes they have closed; lest at any time they should see with their eyes and hear with their ears, and should understand with their heart, and should be converted, and I should heal them."

The word "waxed" means "to become gradually more intense or to increase," and shows that this condition of the heart is not something we are born with or that strikes us suddenly. It has to be nurtured over a prolonged period of time. This is why we should not violate our consciences, even in small things.

Guarding your conscience will keep you sensitive to God and will stop your heart from becoming hardened. If you will stay faithful to God, even in the small things, then you will also be faithful in the more important things.

Keeping the commandments doesn't affect God's willingness to love us, but it affects our *awareness* of how much He loves us. If we live in sin, our consciences become defiled and they condemn us. It's not God condemning us, but our consciences. God still loves us. John was speaking of this same thing in 1 John 3:20, when he said, *"For if our heart condemn us, God is greater than our heart, and knoweth all things."* However, as far as this earthly life goes, our awareness of God's love is everything. Therefore, we must keep Satan from blinding us to the love of God.

The most effective way of doing this is to give no place to the devil through sin. John went on to say in 1 John 3:21, *"Beloved, if our heart condemn us not, then have we confidence toward God."* Holiness is essential in keeping our hearts assured of the love of God (1 Jn. 3:19). It's the nature of a Christian to walk in the light and not in the darkness. When you are rightly informed of who you are and what you have in Christ, holiness just naturally flows out of you. That's your nature.

APRIL 7
THE POWER OF GOD'S WORD
LUKE 8:11-15

Luke 8:11 "Now the parable is this: The seed is the word of God."

It is through reading the Word and the enlightenment of the Holy Spirit, that Christ in His fullness is known. What a privilege it is today to have God's Word in our own language. Six hundred years ago there was no English translation of the whole Bible. Thanks to the efforts of John Wycliffe (1384) and William Tyndale (1523), today we are able to read and understand the writings of the apostles for ourselves. Men gave their lives to bring us God's Word. We should take advantage of this wonderful privilege.

The piece of armor known as the *"sword of the Spirit,"* is the only piece that has the ability to cut, wound, and hurt our enemy, the devil. It's not the Bible lying on your coffee table that makes the enemy flee, but it is the Word of God hidden in your heart, activated by the power of the Holy Spirit, and spoken in an appropriate situation. It's similar to what was spoken by Jesus in John 6:63; *". . . the words that I speak unto you,* they *are spirit and* they *are life."* The Word by itself doesn't make us free. It is the Word we know and speak that will deliver us (Jn. 8:32).

Why is the Word so effective? It's because it is the WORD of God. It has authority, because it is indeed the WORD of God. God's Word supersedes all authority of the church, of reason, of intellect, and even of Satan. It is the Holy Spirit that wields this Word as it is spoken in faith. Speaking God's Word in faith brings the Holy Spirit into action. In Luke, chapter four, when Jesus was tempted of the devil for 40 days, it was the Word of God that Jesus used to defeat the enemy in the time of His temptation. Jesus constantly met His temptation by quoting from God's Word as He repeatedly stated the phrase, *"It is written."* Likewise, the Christian soldier must avail himself of God's Word by placing it in his heart, so that the Holy Spirit may bring it forth at the appropriate time to accomplish a complete and total victory. It's yours!

APRIL 8
GOD'S WORD: USE AS DIRECTED
LUKE 8:4-11

Luke 8:11 "Now the parable is this: The seed is the word of God."

This parable illustrates the importance of the Word of God. God's Word contains total power, but it has to be planted in our hearts and allowed to germinate before it releases that power.

The seed is God's Word, and the types of ground are the four major conditions of people's hearts. The Word was the same in each situation, but there were different results in each case because of the condition of men's hearts—not because of the Word. The Word doesn't work for everyone because not everyone will allow the Word to work. The variable in this parable is the condition of the heart. God's Word is always the same. It has the same potential in every heart.

Good ground doesn't just happen; it must be cultivated. This is the reason why only one out of four people in Jesus' parable brought forth fruit. It takes a lot of time, effort, and diligence to be a fruitful Christian. The Christian life is not like a 100-yard dash, but rather a 26.2 mile marathon. It's quicker and easier to raise weeds than it is to raise tomatoes or corn.

In this whole parable, it was the Word that produced the fruit. The ground simply gave it a place to grow. If we will simply put God's Word in our hearts, protect it, and give it priority in our lives, the Word will produce fruit of itself. Satan has deceived many people into thinking that they don't have the talents or abilities to be fruitful Christians, but they are not the ones who bring forth fruit; it's God's Word. When we protect the Word sown in our hearts, it will do the rest.

APRIL 9
UNDERSTANDING GOD'S WORD
LUKE 8:4-13

Luke 8:12 "Those by the wayside are they that hear; then cometh the devil, and taketh away the word out of their hearts, lest they should believe and be saved."

The first type of person Jesus describes is someone who doesn't understand God's Word (Mt. 13:19). Before God's Word can penetrate your heart, you have to understand (not comprehend) what it's saying. If the Word isn't understood, then it will be like seed scattered on top of hard-packed ground (the wayside). The birds will eat the seed and there will be no fruit.

Mark 4:15 and Luke 8:12, make it clear that these birds represent Satan, and Mark says that the devil comes immediately to steal the Word. Satan did not have direct access to the Word in any of the other heart-types that Jesus described. Satan cannot steal the Word from us if we hide it in our hearts (Ps. 119:11). This first type of person simply heard the Word, but didn't receive it. He never applied it to his life, so he lost it.

Notice that Luke links belief and salvation with the Word being sown in our hearts in the same way as described in Romans 10:14-17. If there is no Word, there cannot be any belief or salvation (I Pet. 1:23). We must preach the Word—not just morality or social issues.

Luke's use of the word "saved" could include, but is not necessarily limited to, forgiveness of sins. Salvation includes much more than forgiveness of sins. This verse could describe a person who didn't receive the Word; therefore, was eternally damned. It could also be describing a Christian who simply doesn't receive the Word in a certain area of his life and therefore doesn't experience the victory that Jesus provided for him. Are you experiencing His victory in your life?

APRIL 10
NO DISTRACTIONS PLEASE
MARK 4:13-20

Mark 4:16 "And these are they likewise which are sown on stony ground; who, when they have heard the word, immediately receive it with gladness;"

The second type of person Jesus describes is one who does receive the Word, even with great joy, but his commitment to the Word is shallow. Just as a plant must establish a strong root system to sustain its growth, we must become rooted and grounded in God's Word. Too much attention on visible growth will cause us to become impatient and not take the time to become firmly established in the truths of God's Word. This will always result in fruitlessness.

A seed planted in shallow earth will germinate and grow faster than a seed planted in deep soil. The seed in deep soil will put all of its energy towards the roots first, while the seed in shallow soil has no choice but to put its effort into the growth of the plant above the ground. The plant in shallow soil will look like it is far ahead of the other seed for a while, but that will not last. It soon withers and dies, while the seed with roots grows and brings forth fruit.

Notice that afflictions, persecutions, and tribulations are instruments of the devil and are used to stop God's Word from bearing fruit in our lives. They are not good things that God brings our way to improve us. They are instruments of Satan. These things are designed to take our attention off of God's Word, thereby stopping the Word from taking root in us. It's like the runner who spends all of his time in the grandstands arguing with the hecklers over the way he's running the race. He may win an argument, but he will lose the race. We must not let anything distract us from meditating on God's Word day and night; for only then will we make our way prosperous and have good success (Josh. 1:8). By consistently putting God's Word first in every area of your life, you will let that Word become so rooted in you that nothing can remove it.

APRIL 11
WORLDLY CARES ARE THORNS
LUKE 8:5-14

Luke 8:14 "And that which fell among thorns are they, which, when they have heard, go forth, and are choked with cares and riches and pleasures of this life, and bring no fruit to perfection."

This third type of ground is characteristic of a large part of the body of Christ today. These are people who have received God's Word, committed themselves to it to the degree that they are able to remain faithful in persecution, but because of being occupied with the affairs of this life, the Word sown in their hearts is choked and no fruit is produced. Just as weeds in a garden will steal all of the nutrients and starve the plants, so the pleasures of this life, if we allow them to dominate our thinking, will stop the fruit that the Word would have produced.

Throughout history, the church has always grown in size and strength during persecution. This is because during persecution we get our priorities straight. We realize that our lives are in Jesus (Jn. 14:6), not in things (Lk. 12:15), and we focus all of our attention on the Lord. However, prosperity has been far more damaging to the body of Christ for the exact reason stated here in this verse. God wants to bless His children with things (Ps. 35:27; Mt. 6:33), but a preoccupation with these things will choke God's Word and make it unfruitful. If we would follow God's formula for prosperity found in Matthew 6:19-34, the Word would bring forth fruit and we would enjoy the physical blessings of this life too.

Notice that Jesus said that no fruit was brought to perfection. This type of person will exhibit some fruit, but it will always be small and short of what it should be. Do you feel frustrated because you are just getting by and are not really experiencing the abundant life that Jesus came to give? (Jn. 10:10) Examine your lifestyle and see if the cares of this life, deceitfulness of riches, or the pleasures of this life, could be choking God's Word.

APRIL 12
HIS LOVE IS OUR LIGHT
MARK 4:21-25

Mark 4:21 "And he said unto them, Is a candle brought to be put under a bushel, or under a bed? and not to be set on a candlestick?"

Just as a candle or lamp is not to be hid, but to be displayed so that everyone can benefit from its light, so a Christian must let his light shine before men that they might see his good works and glorify his Father who is in heaven. God has ordained us to go and bring forth fruit (Jn. 15:16). The great commission of the Church is to reach the world.

The early Christians experienced the love of Christ in an intimate and life-transforming way. This motivated them to reach their known world with the Gospel of Christ more than any other generation of Christians has since. They didn't have the benefits of our modern technology, but they did have the benefit of being full of the love of Christ. Experiencing the love of Christ causes us to be filled with the fullness of God (Eph. 3:19), and makes us a witness that the world cannot resist (Jn. 13:35).

Today, much of the emphasis of the church is placed on techniques of evangelism or spiritual warfare. We motivate people to witness through feelings of guilt, or punishment if they don't. Much of our evangelism has become as dead and nonproductive as the efforts of the cults whose people knock on doors and argue others into their way of thinking. The church today needs a revival of its personal relationship with the Lord. When we can truly say with Paul, that the love of Christ constrains us, then we will impact our world for the Lord. We can't give away what we don't possess. We need to personally know the love of Christ in an experiential way before we try to share it with others. Let Him love you, and let His love flow through you to others. The world is hungry for love, real love.

APRIL 13
TARES AMONG THE WHEAT
MATTHEW 13:24-30

Matthew 13:25 "But while men slept, his enemy came and sowed tares among the wheat, and went his way."

Satan has secretly infiltrated the church with some of his followers for the purpose of hindering the influence of the church. This has been a more effective strategy than direct opposition.

These tares that are spoken of refer to the Old World variety of darnel, which is poisonous. Virtually all grains are almost indistinguishable from tares when they send up the first blade from the ground. By the time the tares become distinguishable, they are so well rooted, that if growing in close proximity to a productive grain, uprooting the tares would also mean uprooting the productive grain. Therefore, verse 30 admonishes us to let both grow together until the harvest. The grains of the tares are long and black in contrast to the wheat, and are easily recognizable at harvest time. Many will profess Christianity, but "by their fruits ye shall know them."

There will be those who are deceived and unaware that they are not born again, who will remain among the church. Jesus warns us against trying to root them out especially since it is not always possible to discern other people's hearts. In an effort to destroy these tares, we might offend one of Christ's "little ones" and cause his or her profession of faith to waver.

It is important though, for our own personal benefit, that we be aware that the children of the wicked one are placed among the true believers. Our best defense is to preach the Word of God without watering it down. False brethren will not endure sound doctrine. They will leave when the Word, which is sharper than any twoedged sword, begins to expose the thoughts and intents of their hearts. Stick to the Word!

APRIL 14
KING OF HEARTS
MARK 4:30-34

Mark 4:30 "And he said, Whereunto shall we liken the kingdom of God? or with what comparison shall we compare it?"

The word "kingdom" means "the realm over which a king rules." When applied to God, it could refer to all creation, since "his kingdom ruleth over all" (Ps. 103:19), but the kingdom more often applies to His rule in and through those who are submitted to Him. "The kingdom of God," more specifically refers to Christ living and ruling in our hearts. So praying, "thy kingdom come" is praying for the expansion and influence of God's rule in the hearts of men everywhere and ultimately, the establishment of His physical kingdom here on earth at His second coming (Rev. 11:15; 20:4).

Throughout Jesus' earthly ministry, the Jews kept looking for Jesus to establish a physical kingdom here on earth and deliver them from the oppression of the Romans. Although during the Millenium, the kingdom of God will physically rule over the nations of the earth, Jesus' kingdom is spiritually established by His Word and not by carnal weapons (2 Cor. 10:3-5). Jesus said, "The kingdom of God cometh not with observation . . . behold, the kingdom of God is within you" (Lk. 17:20-21). Paul says we are already in the kingdom of God (Col. 1:13). Therefore, the kingdom of God is Christ's invisible church—His body. The kingdom began during His earthly ministry and is still ruling the hearts of men today.

The new birth ushers us into the kingdom of God which is infinitely greater in wonder and benefits than our finite minds can comprehend. To the degree that we do begin to understand how God's kingdom works and apply it to our lives, we can experience heaven here on earth. Pray for a release into the physical realm what is already present in your spiritual being.

APRIL 15
HIS CHOSEN TREASURES
MATTHEW 13:44-50

Matthew 13:44 "Again, the kingdom of heaven is like unto treasure hid in a field; the which when a man hath found, he hideth, and for joy thereof goeth and selleth all that he hath, and buyeth that field."

The interpretation of this parable is this: The field is the world, the man buying the treasure is God, and the treasure is the true believers in Christ. The price that was paid was the life of Jesus on the cross. Jesus saw, through His foreknowledge, a remnant of people who would receive Him as Lord, and "for the joy that was set before him," He endured the cross (Heb. 12:2), and purchased us unto Himself with His own blood (Acts 20:28). He purchased the whole world, but not everyone will receive what He did. Therefore, the church is hidden (scattered among the world) today.

Father God had the plan of salvation worked out before He even created the world. Most of us would not have created the world and mankind if we had known the heartache and terrible sacrifice this act would cost. But God is not man. In His judgment (which is the correct judgment) the prize was worth the cost.

God knows in advance those who will accept His offer of salvation. The Scriptures teach that we (believers) were chosen in Christ before the foundation of the world (Eph. 1:4). That's how infinite God's ability is. We were chosen in Christ before the world began. We are holy and without blame because God sees us through Christ. It was predetermined that we would be God's children. We have been accepted by God. The Father would no more reject us than He would reject Jesus, because we are accepted by the Father through Christ. We are redeemed and forgiven. We are truly blessed!

APRIL 16
JOINT HEIRS WITH CHRIST
MATTHEW 12:46-50

Matthew 12:50 "For whosoever shall do the will of my Father which is in heaven, the same is my brother, and sister, and mother."

We are not just heirs, we are joint-heirs with Christ. It would be wonderful to inherit any amount of God's glory and power, but the idea that we share equally with the one who has inherited everything God is and has is beyond comprehension. This is an awesome blessing, but it also places a tremendous responsibility on us.

In the same way in which a check made out to two people cannot be cashed without the endorsement of both parties, so our joint-heirship with Jesus cannot be taken advantage of without our cooperation. Unaware of this, many Christians are just trusting that the Lord will produce the benefits of salvation for them. They are acutely aware that they can do nothing without Him, but don't realize that He will do nothing without them (Eph. 3:20).

The idea that God will do exceedingly abundantly above all that we ask or think, PERIOD, is not true. He has power, but it is the use of His ability combined with the power that works in us. "No power working in us" means no power of God will come through us. The exceeding greatness of His power that is toward those who believe, is power that is not external, but is internal, within the believer. It works according to the faith that we exercise in the indwelling Savior. It was this principle that Paul was stating when he declared, *"I can do all things through Christ which strengtheneth me."*

The way we place our endorsement on the check is to believe what God promised in His Word, and act on it as if it were true. IT IS! Jesus has already signed His name to every promise in the Word. We aren't waiting for Him. He is waiting for us.

APRIL 17
PEACE IN THE MIDST OF THE STORM
MATTHEW 12:46-50; 8:23-27; MARK 3:31-35; 4:35-41; LUKE 8:19-26

Mark 4:37-38 "And there arose a great storm of wind, and the waves beat into the ship so that it was now full. And he was in the hinder part of the ship, asleep on a pillow: and they awake him, and say unto him, Master carest thou not that we perish?"

Considering that the boat was filled with water, it is amazing that the disciples had to awaken Jesus. This was not a large ship with cabins below deck, but rather a small, open boat and Jesus was, no doubt, soaked to the bone. This reflects Jesus' humanity and how tired He must have been. It also shows that Jesus must have been in a very deep sleep. Medical science has discovered that the deeper we sleep, the more rest our bodies get. This is a clue as to how Jesus could maintain the grueling pace He kept, along with an occasional all-night prayer time. He was receiving the maximum benefit from His sleep.

Jesus did not say, "Let us go out into the midst of the sea and drown in a storm." He was going to the other side. This shows that the disciples still didn't understand Jesus' authority. They were committed to Him as their Messiah, but they hadn't yet realized that Jesus was Lord even over the physical elements. Many Christians still do this today. They receive the spiritual benefits of salvation, but have not reaped the physical benefits of health and prosperity, which are also part of our salvation.

Whatever we focus upon, the storm, or the Lord in the midst of our storm, will determine how we manage the storms we face in life. He is not asleep concerning the things you face in this life; He's right there in your "ship," resting, because He knows you'll both get to the "other side." His peace is yours. Believe His Word. Rest in His love.

APRIL 18
SERVANT POWER
MARK 4:35-41

Mark 4:41 "And they feared exceedingly, and said one to another, What manner of man is this, that even the wind and the sea obey him?"

When God created this physical world and all of its inhabitants, He gave mankind authority to rule and subdue His creation. Although God still owned the universe and all that was in it, He gave control of the earth to man. When man sinned, he began to use this power against God's wishes. God did not ordain all the terrible things that have happened throughout history, yet He did not take back man's right to dominate the earth. Instead, He became a man and took back that authority to by conquest. After Jesus' resurrection, He said in Matthew 28:18, *". . . All power is given unto me in heaven and in earth."* Then He gave the great commission to His disciples, thereby conferring that authority upon them too. Jesus becoming flesh was absolutely essential for gaining all power (or authority) in heaven and in earth. Jesus was a "God-man." As stated in 1 Timothy 3:16, He was God manifested in the flesh, which is a great mystery.

Jesus came in the power and authority of His Father to point men to the Father God. Jesus existed before His advent on this earth in the form of God and was equal with God; yet, He humbled Himself and became a servant while here on earth. He did not come to promote Himself, but to give Himself as the way unto the Father.

This is radically different from the way so called "great men" present themselves. The Roman Caesar of Jesus' day proclaimed that he was God and demanded worship. Lesser leaders ruled by exalting themselves over the people they governed. Jesus showed us that, *"Whosoever will be great among you, let him be your minister; and whosoever will be chief among you, let him be your servant: even as the Son of man came not to be ministered unto, but to minister, and to give his life a ransom for many"* (Mt. 20:26-28).

APRIL 19
WORSHIP IS WARFARE
MATTHEW 8:28-34; MARK 5:1-17; LUKE 8:27-39

Mark 5:6 "But when he saw Jesus afar off, he ran and worshipped him."

The word "worshipped" is taken from the Greek word "proskuneo" which means "to pros-trate oneself in homage to; do reverence to; adore." That this tormented man ran to Jesus, and not away from Him, indicates that even demon-possessed people have a free will and Satan cannot control an individual without his consent.

Many battles have been fought over whether a Christian can be demon possessed. The Greek word for "possessed" literally means "to be demonized." The Bible makes no clear distinction between degrees of demon activity (such as oppressed, depressed, possessed, etc.), but simply refers to people as being "demonized." All Christians are fighting against spiritual powers. If we don't put on the whole armor of God, Satan can certainly affect us or even control us.

The best way to administer deliverance is through God's Word. As a person receives the Word, it will set him free and also help guard against this situation when the demon tries to come back in with seven other spirits. In severe cases of being demonized, the individual clearly needs the help of a believer, and that's the reason why Jesus equipped all believers with authority over evil spirits.

Anointed praise and worship will also drive off evil spirits. One thing reserved for God alone is worship, and the devil has always sought that. If he can't be the one to receive worship, then he seeks to turn others away from giving true worship to the most high God. Praise and worship to the Lord is such a powerful tool against Satan. He can't stand to see God worshipped. Worship God today in spirit and in truth. The Father seeks those who will worship Him this way. He's waiting for you.

APRIL 20
GOD LIKES US
MARK 5:18-20

Mark 5:19 "Howbeit Jesus suffered him not, but saith unto him, Go home to thy friends, and tell them how great things the Lord hath done for thee, and hath had compassion on thee."

One of the ways God's goodness is revealed is through His mercy. We may describe mercy as "the readiness of God to relieve the misery of fallen creatures." Many times, mercy is called com-passion or lovingkindness. It is expressed toward the sinner because of the misery that sin has brought upon him.

God's mercy to the believer is revealed by His taking away the misery of sin's consequences through the New Covenant of our Savior, the Lord Jesus Christ. Mercy is not something merited or earned, but as the Apostle Paul states, "Not by works of righteousness which we have done, but according to HIS MERCY He saved us."

Our heavenly Father is the author, originator, and source of all mercy. "Mercy is condescend-ing love, reaching out to meet a need without considering the merit of the person who receives the aid." (Expository Dictionary of Bible Words [EDBW])

"Even when we were spiritually dead because of our sins, God's forbearance was working on our behalf. He was tolerant, patient and kind towards us. God abounded in excessive proportion with good will, compassion, and desire to help us. His disposition was kind, compassionate, and forgiving in His treatment of us. He wanted in abundant supply to alleviate our distress and bring relief from our sins. He did this by giving us life in place of death. It was with Christ that this salvation was secured. By grace, kindness, and favor we are saved. All of this was the result of God's extremely large degree of love wherewith He loved us, always seeking the welfare and better-ment of us. God likes us." (Don Krow)

APRIL 21
LOVE AND TRUST
MATTHEW 9:18-19

Matthew 9:18 "While he spake these things unto them, behold, there came a certain ruler, and worshipped him, saying, My daughter is even now dead: but come and lay thy hand upon her, and she shall live."

Jesus could have healed this girl by His spoken word, but He did as He was requested to do. This illustrates how the Lord ministers to us according to our faith. Jesus ministered to him at the level where his faith was and didn't rebuke his little faith (Jas. 1:5).

There is a human faith that is limited to believing only what we can perceive through our five senses. The supernatural, God-kind of faith goes beyond what we can see, taste, hear, smell, and feel. God's kind of faith calls those things which be not as though they were.

We exercise faith almost daily in such things as sitting on a chair and driving a car. But our faith is no better than the object in which it is placed. If I were to sit in a chair made of cardboard, I would go crashing to the ground. Regardless of how much faith I had, my faith would fall flat because the object of my faith was faulty. Hebrews 12:2, tells us that we are to be *"looking unto Jesus, the author and finisher of our faith."* We must transfer our faith from human self-reliance and independence, to reliance upon, adherence to, and trust upon Jesus Christ in all areas of our lives. Faith, in its simplest definition, is to trust, to rely, and to depend upon the resource of another. God's Word declares that the object of our faith, Jesus Christ, can never fail or disappoint us.

Love produces faith, or is what makes faith work. We naturally trust those who we know truly love us. A revelation of God's unconditional love for us will make faith just naturally abound in us. Are you struggling with faith? If so, you have a deficiency in understanding how much God loves you. Let Him reveal His love to you today.

APRIL 22
THE LAW OF FAITH
MATTHEW 9:18-20; MARK 5:21-34; LUKE 8:40-48

Luke 8:45 "And Jesus said, 'Who touched me?' When all denied, Peter and they that were with him said, 'Master, the multitude throng thee, and press thee, and sayest thou, Who touched me?'"

The multitudes were thronging Jesus. That is, they were compressing and crowding in on all sides. Therefore, it seems strange that He would ask, "Who touched me?" Many people were physically touching Jesus, but this woman touched His power by faith. Many people in the crowd probably needed healing, but this person is the only one mentioned who received. The difference was the touch of faith.

If it was simply Jesus' willingness to heal that determined whether the healing took place, then all of the sick in this multitude would have been healed. This instance illustrates that it's not prayer that saves the sick, but rather the prayer of faith that saves the sick (Jas. 5:15).

Healing is governed by law and not by a case by case decision from God based on His feelings toward us. This woman received her healing by the law of faith before Jesus knew anything about her. Impassioned pleas to God will not obtain the miracle we seek. Although Jesus is touched by our feelings, it requires faith. It's not because Jesus doesn't know our needs or hear our cries that miracles don't happen, but rather it's because very few know how the law of faith works.

One of the main differences between a God-kind of faith and a natural, human faith, which everyone has, is that human faith believes only what it can see, taste, hear, smell, or feel. God's kind of faith believes in things that cannot be seen. You must believe that you receive your answer, when you pray—not when you see the thing you've desired. Simply put, faith is our response to God's ability, made complete by our actions. Trust Him completely, and because you believe, your actions will follow.

APRIL 23
MAKE FAITH WORK
LUKE 8:43-48

Luke 8:46 "And Jesus said, Somebody hath touched me: for I perceive that virtue is gone out of me."

Is it possible that Jesus, who was God manifest in the flesh, and therefore all-knowing, did not actually know who touched Him? Yes! Although Jesus' spiritual man was divine, He took upon Himself a physical body with its limitations. Jesus drew on His divine ability through the gifts of the Holy Ghost, and so can we (Jn. 14:12; 1 Cor. 12:7). Before His resurrection, He operated as a man (sinless) by receiving from His Father through faith. Luke 8:47 says that the woman, "saw that she was not hid." It is evident that Jesus received a word of knowledge from the Holy Spirit and had singled out this woman. However, this was after He felt the power of God flow out of Him and heal her. The woman was healed before He discerned her by the law of faith.

The law of electricity has been here on earth since creation. Man has observed it in such things as lightning and static electricity, but it was not until someone believed that there were laws that governed the activity of electricity that progress began to be made in putting it to use. Likewise, you don't deny the existence of faith, but it is only when you begin to understand that there are laws that govern faith, and begin to learn what those laws are, that faith will begin to work for you.

APRIL 24
GET RID OF FEAR
MATTHEW 9:23-31; MARK 5:35-43; LUKE 8:49-56

Luke 8:50 "But when Jesus heard it, he answered him saying, Fear not: believe only, and she shall be made whole."

Jesus told Jairus to "believe only," implying that faith and fear can operate in us at the same time. This is also the reason James tells us not to be double-minded, or to waiver. (Jas. 1:5-8) Fear will negate faith. We can have thoughts of faith and thoughts of unbelief at the same time.

Fear and faith are opposing forces. Fear is actually faith in reverse. Fear is believing something or someone other than God. Therefore, fear makes us subject to Satan and his death just as faith makes us recipients of all that God has to offer. This is the reason Jesus told Jairus, "Fear not." Jairus' fear would have sealed his daughter's death.

Instead of trying to build huge amounts of faith to overcome our fears and unbelief, a simpler method is to remove our fears by cutting off their source. Then, our simple "child-like" faith that remains will do the job. It doesn't take big faith—just pure faith.

Where does fear come from? Second Timothy 1:7 says, *"For God hath not given us the spirit of fear; but of power and of love, and of a sound mind."* It doesn't come from God. The way that fear is able to come upon us is that we take our attention off of Jesus and put it on our situation.

Fear or doubt cannot just overcome us. We have to let it in. In the same way that faith comes by hearing the Word of God, fear comes by hearing or seeing something contrary to God's Word. We would not be tempted with fear or doubt if we didn't consider things that Satan uses to minister that fear and doubt. Satan tries to distract us with thinking about our problems. No problem is too big for God. We should cast our concern about the problem over on God and just keep our eyes on Jesus, the Word.

APRIL 25
THE GOSPEL IS THE POWER OF GOD
MATTHEW 9:35-38; 13:53-58; MARK 6:1-6

Matthew 9:38 "Pray ye therefore the Lord of the harvest, that he will send forth laborers into his harvest."

People are born again through the power of the Word of God, not through prayer. Prayer is very important, but it is not a substitute for the Gospel. Many people petition God for someone to be saved and can't understand why it hasn't happened yet. We don't have to ask the Lord to save anyone. He isn't willing that anyone should perish. He has already made provision for everyone's salvation.

So what do we pray concerning someone coming to the Lord? Jesus said to pray that the Lord send laborers across their path. They need to hear the Word. Also, we should bind the influence of the god of this world (Satan) who tries to blind them to spiritual truth (II Cor 4:4).

God is more motivated to save our loved ones than we are. We don't need to plead with Him, but rather we need to become a channel for Him to flow through to reach that person. We do that by sharing the good news (Gospel) with them and/or praying that others will come across their path who will do the same.

The Gospel is the power of God that releases the effects of salvation in our lives (Rom 1:16). If a person needs healing, it's in the Gospel. If deliverance is needed, it's in the Gospel. Prosperity, answered prayer, joy, peace, love—they are all found through understanding and believing the Gospel.

The Gospel is the good news that although we are sinners and worthy of God's wrath, God, in love, sent His Son to be our substitute, bearing our punishment, so that we could be made completely righteous in His sight. It's based only on our faith in this completed work of Christ and not our own performance. Now that's **GOOD NEWS**!

APRIL 26
GODLY SORROW LEADS TO REPENTANCE
MARK 6:7-12

Mark 6:12 "And they went out, and preached that men should repent."

"Repent" comes from the Greek word, "metanoeo," and literally means to have another mind. Repentance is a necessary part of salvation. Repentance may include Godly sorrow, but sorrow does not always include repentance. Repentance is simply a change of mind accompanied by corresponding actions.

There is a Godly type of sorrow and an ungodly type of sorrow. Godly sorrow leads to repentance. Ungodly sorrow, or the sorrow of this world, just kills. Our culture has rejected all negative emotions, but God gave us the capacity for these negative emotions, and there is a proper use for them. Ecclesiastes 7:3 says, *"Sorrow is better than laughter: for by the sadness of the countenance the heart is made better."* People should feel bad about sin. There should be sorrow over our failures. However, this sorrow should lead to repentance. Then, when forgiveness is received, our sorrow should be cast upon the Lord (Isa. 53:4).

The Lord's statements to His disciples, the night before His crucifixion, caused them sorrow (Mt. 26:21-22; Jn. 16:6). If they would have let that sorrow lead them to repentance, then they wouldn't have denied the Lord. Peter's sorrow after his denial of Jesus changed him, and certainly, he never regretted the tears he cried.

The sorrow experienced by those who do not turn to God produces only death. They grieve over their situation because they don't turn to God (that's repentance). Christians should only have sorrow until they repent. Once repentance has come, we need to appropriate the forgiveness and cleansing that are already ours through Christ. Godly sorrow that produces repentance leaves us with no regrets. The positive changes that our sorrows lead us to, changes our attitudes toward the things that caused us sorrow. Let the negatives in your life become positives through Jesus.

APRIL 27
ABOUT PERSECUTION
MATTHEW 10:16-26

Matthew 10:23 "But when they persecute you in this city, flee ye into another: for verily I say unto you, Ye shall not have gone over the cities of Israel, till the Son of man be come."

Persecution is an inevitable part of the Christian life. Persecution is from Satan and is designed to uproot God's Word in our lives by taking our eyes off Jesus. We should not think it is strange to be persecuted. "All that will live godly in Christ Jesus shall suffer persecution" (2 Tim. 3:12). We can actually rejoice because we are being persecuted for Jesus' sake, knowing that the Lord will be with us in the midst of the persecution and that there will be more than ample reward when we stand before Him (Heb. 11:26).

Persecution is an indication that the ones doing the persecuting are under conviction. They realize that they are not living what our words or actions are advocating; therefore, in defense of self, they attack the ones whom they perceive to be the source of their conviction. If this is understood, it makes persecution much easier to take. They aren't just mad at you; they are convicted. When the Gospel is presented in the power of the Holy Spirit, there will always be either a revival or a riot, but not indifference.

There are many forms of persecution. Having your life threatened because of your faith in Jesus is one way you can be persecuted, but it is not the most damaging. History shows that the Church has always flourished under persecution with increased numbers and zeal. During intense, life-threatening persecution, people's priorities get straightened out and the Lord assumes His rightful place. This always works for our good, regardless of what our outward circumstances might be. Remember it is not you that they are persecuting, but rather Christ in you.

APRIL 28
DEGREES OF DENIAL
MATTHEW 10:32-33

Matthew 10:33 "But whosoever shall deny me before men, him will I also deny before my Father which is in heaven."

This word "deny" can mean a variety of things from as little as "to assert the contrary of" to "to disavow; disown." For example, we can see that it must have been the lesser type of denial that was committed by Peter because God certainly forgave Peter's sin and continued using him. In Hebrews 6:4-6, the Lord states that there is no repentance from total denial of the Lord (Heb. 10:29). Therefore, even though Peter denied (asserted he did not know) the Lord, he did not disown or disavow the Lord.

No believer desires to deny the Lord, but failing to provide for spiritual health is the first step in that direction. Remembering this will help motivate us to seek the Lord as we know we should. It takes more than desire; it takes preparation. We have all been taught how to rely on ourselves, but we have to learn anew how to be strong in the Lord and in the power of His might (Eph. 6:10). Just as in the physical realm, muscles have to be exercised to become strong, so we have to exercise ourselves unto Godliness (1 Tim. 4:7).

Many people have been tormented by fear in thinking that they have denied the Lord because of some type of sin in their life. However, God looks on the heart (1 Sam. 16:7), and regardless of how offensive our actions or words might be, if there is still a place in our hearts where we honor Him, He will not deny us (2 Tim. 2:12-13).

APRIL 29
OPPOSITION TO THE GOSPEL
MATTHEW 10:34-42

Matthew 10:34 "Think not that I am come to send peace on earth: I came not to send peace, but a sword."

This statement seems like a contradiction to some prophecies concerning Jesus and some of Jesus' own statements concerning peace, as well as what was written of Him in the New Testament Epistles. However, the peace that Jesus purchased was peace between God and man. We have peace with God (Rom. 5:1). We are exhorted to take this peace and extend it to all men, but it is also made very clear that not all men will receive it.

Peace can only come when we relate to God on the basis of faith in what He did for us, instead of what we do for Him. A person who is thinking that he must perform up to some standard to be accepted by God will have no peace. That puts the burden of salvation on our shoulders, and we can't bear that load. We were incapable of living holy enough to please God before we were saved, and we are incapable of living holy enough to please God now that we are saved (Heb. 11:6). We were saved by faith, and we have to continue to walk with God by faith (Col. 2:6). Not understanding this has made many Christians, who love God, unable to enjoy the peace that was provided for them through faith in Jesus.

The Gospel will always produce opposition from those who don't receive it. This "sword of division," even among family members, is not God's will, nor is it God that causes it. But, it will inevitably come, and Jesus was simply preparing His disciples for that time. As much as we would like everyone to receive the good news, we must not think it is strange when even our loved ones don't receive it. Jesus was rejected by His own, and we will be also. We must remain faithful to continue preaching the Gospel, for there are others who will receive. Keep sharing the "Good News!"

APRIL 30
HE REWARDS EVEN LITTLE THINGS
MATTHEW 10:1-42, 11:1, MARK 6:7-13, LUKE 9:1-6

Matthew 10:42 "And whosoever shall give to drink unto one of these little ones a cup of cold water only in the name of a disciple, verily I say unto you, he shall in no wise lose his reward."

This verse shows that even our smallest acts of kindness will be rewarded. As revealed in 1 Corinthians 3:13, every man's work shall be tried to determine "what sort it is," not what size it is. Many people who have never done anything to gain the attention of the masses will shine bright in the day when the Lord passes out His rewards.

Some of the Lord's rewards for our actions come in this life, such as children, financial blessings, health, and many others. However, some of our rewards will not be realized until we stand before God. This is the case with the reward for enduring persecution.

Many of the rewards for ministering the Gospel will not come until we appear before the Lord. Rewards can be shared by those who aid others in their righteous tasks.

The unGodly who are not in the Kingdom of God will receive no rewards even though some of their actions might have been good. Rewards are only for those who have been cleansed from their evil deeds by the blood of the Lamb. Regardless of what these rewards shall be, there will not be any exalting of self over others. *"For who maketh thee to differ from another? And what hast thou that thou didst not receive? now if thou didst receive it, why dost thou glory, as if thou hadst not received it?"* (1 Cor. 4:7) The 24 elders in Revelation 4:10 are shown casting their crowns (which were rewards) down before the Lord and giving all their praise and worship to Him. It's all because of Him. Thank Him today for His goodness.

MAY 1
NO PEACE FOR THE WICKED
MATTHEW 14:1-12; MARK 6:14-29; LUKE 9:7-9

Luke 9:7 "Now Herod the tetrarch heard of all that was done by him: and he was perplexed, because that it was said of some that John was risen from the dead."

Others may have thought Jesus was John the Baptist risen from the dead, but as can be clearly seen by looking at Matthew's account and especially Mark's record, Herod was convinced of this personally. This illustrates Herod's own conviction of the sin John had rebuked, his guilt and torment over his even greater sin of beheading John, and his fear of John and the God he represented. As revealed in Mark 6:20, Herod once listened to John gladly. It is certain that John was preaching his favorite message of, "Repent ye: for the kingdom of heaven is at hand." For Herod to hear him gladly, he must have been under deep conviction from God.

Herod feared his wife and the opinions of others more than he feared God. Herod was not as Festus, who told Paul he was mad for speaking of the resurrection from the dead. Herod knew the truth personally, was exceedingly sorry, yet chose death—both John the Baptist's and his own spiritual death. Apparently, seen in this instance, Herod lacked peace after his fatal choice.

According to the world's mentality, peace is the absence of problems. However, God's peace is not dependent on circumstances. It is dependent only on God Himself who is the same yesterday, today, and forever (Heb. 13:8). A Christian can have great peace even in the midst of terrible problems because his faith is in God. *"Thou wilt keep him in perfect peace, whose mind is stayed on thee: because he trusteth in thee"* (Isa. 26:3). Let His peace rule in your heart today. Trust Him.

MAY 2
REST AND RE-FIRE
MATTHEW 14:13-21; MARK 6:30-44; LUKE 9:10-17; JOHN 6:1-14

Mark 6:31 "And he said unto them, Come ye yourselves apart into a desert place, and rest a while: for there were many coming and going, and they had no leisure so much as to eat."

Jesus often separated Himself from others so that He could spend time with the Father. Here, we see Jesus calling His disciples apart for rest and leisure. Many zealous Christians have neglected the needs of their physical bodies and have, therefore, cut their ministries short through death or severe illness. Likewise, many have failed to take the time to be still and know God (Ps. 46:10). This will also cut your ministry short through non-effectiveness. One of Satan's deadliest weapons against those involved in ministry is busyness. We must balance our time ministering to others with our time being ministered to by our Father. If the devil can't stop you from "getting on fire" for God, then he'll try to stop you by getting you "burned out."

Remember the reason Jesus and His disciples were going to this remote place was to get away from the multitude for awhile and rest. This rest was not optional, but rather a necessity. Jesus and His disciples were taking a much needed vacation. However, the multitude followed them and their vacation ended even before it began. Surely, Jesus and His disciples were just as disappointed as you or I would have been, but instead of getting angry or bitter, Jesus was moved with compassion.

Later on in the evening, Jesus went up onto a mountain and prayed until the fourth watch (3 to 6 a.m.). The Lord intends for us to take care of these physical bodies as can be seen by Jesus' actions in taking His disciples aside for rest. When this purpose was frustrated by the demands of the ministry, Jesus gave priority to the spirit man and stayed up all night praying and getting the spiritual rest He needed. We should follow His example and always put the needs of the spirit ahead of the needs of the flesh.

MAY 3
JESUS MEETS ALL OUR NEEDS
MATTHEW 14:15-18

Matthew 14:16 "But Jesus said unto them, They need not depart; give ye them to eat."

The disciples were using natural reasoning and recognized that they didn't have the ability to minister to the multitude's need for food. Jesus did have the ability and the willingness to minister to their needs, so the multitude did not need to depart. *All* of their needs could be met through Jesus.

The same thing is true today. Some disciples today are sending the multitudes to the world to meet their physical needs (finances, health, counseling, etc.) and proclaiming that God only meets spiritual needs. But, "they need not depart." The Lord is willing and able to heal our bodies, prosper us financially, or counsel us from His Word in any area of our life where we might have need.

Before we can be a blessing, we have to be blessed (Gen. 12:2). One of the purposes of God's prosperity in our lives is so that we can be a blessing to others. The Scriptures instruct us to walk in God's love towards all men, believers and non-believers alike. Jesus told us to love our enemies (Mt. 5:44). In Galatians 6:10, Paul places a priority on helping fellow Christians. This does not diminish our responsibility to show God's love to non-believers. Instead, Paul is simply saying "charity must start at home." It would be hypocritical to step over hurting brothers and sisters in the Lord to find unbelievers to minister to.

God didn't just give us something that He had; He gave Himself. What was God's motive for giving? It wasn't because of His need, but for ours. He was motivated out of love for us (Jn. 3:16). In the same way, we should be encouraged to give unselfishly of ourselves. Pray for divine appointments, to be used of God to touch someone's life today.

MAY 4
HE BLESSES WHAT WE ALREADY HAVE
JOHN 6:1-13

John 6:9 "There is a lad here, which hath five barley loaves, and two small fishes: but what are they among so many?"

Notice that Jesus didn't just turn some of the stones into bread (as Satan had tempted Him to do in Luke 4:3). We find only one instance in scripture where God created a supply to meet a need (Num. 11:21-23). Usually, the Lord simply blesses what we set our hands to do. The resources were totally inadequate to meet the need in this instance, but when the Lord blessed it, there was more than enough.

Jesus didn't just teach the disciples; He trained them also. He was constantly trying to involve them in these miracles. In just a matter of days, He again asked His disciples what they could do to feed the multitude of 4000 men. It was like He was saying, "You missed this question when I asked you how we could feed the 5000 men. Now, here are less people and more food. What would you suggest this time?"

Instead of remembering the previous miracle, they acted like they had never seen Jesus feed the multitude and they looked at their own resources again (Mt. 15:32; Mk. 8:1). Likewise, we all too often try everything we can do first and forget God's supernatural power until all we can do is pray. Many people have missed their miracle because they never took that first step of faith and used what they had. This young lad was certainly credited with part of this miracle for offering what he had. When in need, we should seek God's direction for something to set our hand to, and then trust Him to bless it and multiply the results of our work.

MAY 5
GOD'S OPTIONS OR OURS?
MATTHEW 14:22-33

Matthew 14:27-28 "But straightway Jesus spake unto them, saying, Be of good cheer,
it is I; be not afraid. And Peter answered him and said, Lord,
if it be thou bid me come unto thee on the water."

It is important to analyze Peter's statement. Peter was overwhelmed when he saw Jesus walking on the water, and he wanted to do the same. While there is really nothing wrong with his desire, the request he put before Jesus was totally wrong. He didn't ask the Lord if he wanted him to walk on the water, or if his faith was up to it. Instead he said, "If it be thou, bid me come unto thee on the water." What was Jesus going to say? "It isn't me. Don't come."

There are no other examples of someone walking on water in the Word of God. Jesus had a definite reason for walking on the water; however, Peter simply wanted to see if he could do it. God will permit us to do things that are not His perfect will for us.

Many times we hinder our own prayers by the way we ask God for things. We say, "Do you want me to do 'a' or 'b'?" The Lord may not want us to do either one. We should offer Him a third choice—"c": none of the above. We should trust God's wisdom and even allow Him to select the options.

MAY 6
ABOUT HUMILITY
JOHN 6:15

John 6:15 "When Jesus therefore perceived that they would come and take him by force, to
make him a king, he departed again into a mountain himself alone."

Jesus *"was in all points tempted like as we are, yet without sin"* (Heb. 4:15). The temptation for Jesus to submit to the crowd and exalt Himself must have been there, but He didn't respond to it. He came to do the Father's will and not His own will (Jn. 6:38). He immediately withdrew from everyone and spent all night in prayer with His Father. Prolonged prayer is an antidote for the temptation of pride and will work a God-type of humility in your life.

In Galatians 2:20, Paul is preaching a death to self, but it is very important to notice how this death takes place. Paul said he was dead through what Jesus did. He experienced this death by simply reckoning what had already happened through Christ to be so (Rom. 6:11).

There are people today who have taken the "dying to self" doctrine to an extreme, and instead of being free of self, they are totally self-centered. They constantly think of self. It may be in all negative terms, but it is still self-centered. A truly humble person is one who is Christ-centered. Dying to self is not a hatred of self, but rather a love for Christ more than self.

There are false religions that preach a denial of self. We need to be not just dead to self, but alive to God. A focus on the denial of self without the enthronement of Christ leads to legalism. True humility is not a debasing of self, or a hatred of self or our accomplishments. It is simply an awareness that all that we have and are, is a gift from God. Therefore, only a person who acknowledges God can operate in true humility.

MAY 7
WORD POWER
MATTHEW 14:29

Matthew 14:29 "And he said, Come. And when Peter was come down out of the ship, he walked on the water, to go to Jesus."

This one word "come" was spoken by the one who made all things (Jn. 1:3) and it had just as much power in it as the words that were spoken at creation. This is where the power came from for Peter to walk on the water. Likewise, any word spoken to us by God carries in itself the anointing and power it takes to fulfill that word, if we will release it by believing it and acting on it.

We need to not only know God's power, but the greatness of God's power, and then the exceeding greatness of God's power. This exceeding greatness of God's power is towards us. That means that it is for us and our benefit. Some people get glimpses of God's power, but very few have the revelation that it is for us and at our disposal. It doesn't do us any good to believe that God has power if we don't believe that it will work for us. This great power of God is effectual only for those who believe. *We must believe to receive, or if we doubt, we do without.*

Despite all the criticism that Peter may have received in this instance, he did walk on the water. There were eleven other disciples in the boat and although they clearly saw Jesus and Peter walking on the water, they still did not participate. One of the important steps in receiving a miracle from God is to leave the security of your natural resources (get out of your boat) and put yourself in the position where there has to be a miracle from God to hold you up. God is no respecter of persons (Rom. 2:11). Any of the disciples could have walked on the water, if they would have asked and gotten out of the boat.

MAY 8
ENTER DOUBT, EXIT FAITH
MATTHEW 14:30-31

Matther 14:30 "But when he saw the wind boisterous, he was afraid; and beginning to sink, he cried, saying, Lord, save me."

The reason Peter began to sink was because of his fear. In verse 31 Jesus used the word "doubt" in reference to Peter's fear. Fear is simply negative faith or faith in reverse. Where did this fear come from? Second Timothy 1:7 says, *"For God hath not given us the spirit of fear; but of power and of love, and of a sound mind."* It didn't come from God. This fear was able to come upon Peter because he took his attention off Jesus and put it on his situation.

Fear or doubt cannot just overcome us. We have to let it in. If Peter had kept his attention on Jesus, the author and finisher of his faith (Heb. 12:2), he wouldn't have feared. In the same way that faith comes by hearing the Word of God (Rom. 10:17), fear comes by hearing or seeing something contrary to God's Word. We would not be tempted with fear or doubt if we didn't consider things that Satan uses to minister fear and doubt. The wind and waves didn't really have anything to do with Peter walking on the water. He couldn't have walked on the water apart from Jesus even if it had been calm. The circumstances simply took Peter's attention off of his Master and led him back into carnal thinking. Likewise, Satan tries to distract us with thinking about our problems.

Peter's faith didn't fail him all at once, as can be seen that he only "began" to sink. If there had been no faith present, he would have sunk all at once and not gradually. This illustrates that the entrance of fear and the exit of faith do not happen instantly. There are always signs that this is happening. If we will turn our attention back to Jesus, as Peter did, He will save us from drowning. No problem is too big for God. We should cast our care about the problem over on God and just keep our eyes on Jesus, the Word.

MAY 9
SENSITIVITY TO THE RIGHT THINGS
MARK 6:45-52; JOHN 6:15-21

Mark 6:52 "For they considered not the miracle of the loaves: for their heart was hardened."

Most of the time, we think of a person with a hard heart as being someone who is in terrible rebellion to God. While it is true that a rebellious person does have a hard heart, in this instance, the Word is referring to the disciples' hearts being hardened. They were, "sore amazed in themselves beyond measure, and wondered" at Jesus walking on the water.

The word "hardened" as used here, means "to make calloused, unyielding or cold in spirit, or insensitive to." The disciples were not God haters, but rather they had become so sensitive to the natural world and its limitations that they were overwhelmed to see Jesus supersede these laws. Therefore, they had hard hearts.

If they had kept in mind the miracle they had just seen Jesus perform (the feeding of the five thousand), then they wouldn't have been amazed to see Jesus walking on the water toward them. After all, He had constrained them to get into the ship and was therefore responsible for them. He was just a short distance away from them, and was in the same storm himself, so they knew He was aware of their situation. They should have expected Jesus to come and save them, even if He had to walk on the water to do it.

Many of us are more sensitive to fear and doubt than we are to the truths of God's Word. This is because we have thought more on things that minister fear and doubt. We can take these laws about hardening our hearts and use them in a positive way. We can actually harden our hearts to doubt by considering only God's Word. It is a possible and obtainable goal to become just as sensitive to God and faith as we have been to Satan and doubt. Meditate on God's Word today.

MAY 10
SALVATION: A RELATIONSHIP
MARK 6:53-56
Mark 6:54 "And when they were come out of the ship, straightway they knew him,"

The word "know" can mean many things from as little as "to perceive with the senses or the mind," to a much deeper meaning of "a thorough experience with." This knowing, then, is not just intellectual, but a personal, intimate understanding. Jesus defines eternal life as knowing God the Father and Jesus Christ. Eternal life is having an intimate, personal relationship with God the Father and Jesus the Son. This intimacy with God is what salvation is all about. Forgiveness of our sins is not the point of salvation. This intimacy with the Father is. Of course, Jesus did die to purchase forgiveness for our sins because unforgiven sins block us from intimacy with God. Sin was an obstacle that stood between God and us. It had to be dealt with and it was. Anyone who views salvation as only forgiveness of sins and stops there is missing out on eternal life.

Salvation was intended to be presented as the way to come back into harmony with God. Instead, it has often been presented as the way to escape the problems of this life and later the judgment of hell. It is possible to get born again with that kind of thinking, but more often than not, people who get saved through that type of ministry view the Lord as someone to help them through times of crisis and not someone to know in an intimate way. Jesus died for us out of love (Jn. 3:16)—a love that longed to have intimate communion with man.

Most non-believers are so occupied with their "hell on earth" that they don't really think or care about their eternal future. They are fed up with religion. They are looking for something that will fill the emptiness inside. Only an intimate relationship (eternal life) with our Father can do that. We need to tell them.

MAY 11
SELF SEEKING NOT GOD SEEKING
MATTHEW 14:34-36; MARK 6:53-56; JOHN 6:22-39

John 6:26 "Jesus answered them and said, Verily, verily, I say unto you, Ye seek me, not because ye saw the miracles, but because ye did eat of the loaves, and were filled."

Jesus knew the hearts of all men; therefore, He did not commit Himself to this crowd. Just the day before, these same people tried to take Him by force and make Him their king, but He withdrew and spent the night in prayer.

This crowd looked like they were seeking Jesus, but they were actually trying to use Jesus to seek their own end. It is true that there are many personal benefits to be reaped through serving the Lord, but the benefits are never to become our object. In all things, Christ must have the preeminence (Col. 1:18).

Jesus exposed the true intentions of the people's hearts by preaching a strong message of commitment. Those who were self-centered were offended and left while those who were willing to lay down their lives to experience God's abundant life remained. Commitment to God Himself (not what He can produce) is what always separates the true worshippers of God from the false.

As Jesus began to explain in these verses that He was the only way to the Father (Jn. 14:6) and that they would have to come through Him, the people grew angry. It always angers the flesh to think that all our righteous acts can't save us, but Jesus made it clear that our only part in salvation is to believe. Believe what? Believe on Jesus and His sacrifice—not ours. Salvation is a gift and cannot be purchased (Rom. 10:2-3).

Many times, we get so intent on seeking God in one area that we forget the greatest miracle of all, which is the love and redemption given to us from God through His Son. God loves us so much!

MAY 12
DEAD WORKS
JOHN 6:24-29

John 6:28 "Then said they unto him, What shall we do, that we might work the works of God?"

All throughout history, mankind has been seeking ways to do the works of God. All people have a knowledge within them of the reality of God (Rom. 1:18-20), and a desire to be right with Him. However, just as with these Jews, few agree with the Lord as to how to do it. These Jews were willing to do something to obtain salvation, but they were not willing to commit themselves to Jesus and accept His gift.

This is one of the major differences between Christianity and the religions of the world. Religion is willing to make sacrifices to obtain right standing with God, but Christianity recognizes our complete inability to ever do enough to save ourselves and calls for total faith and reliance on what Jesus did for us.

No one deserves salvation. It cannot be earned by what the Bible calls *"dead works"* (Heb. 6:1; 9:14). Dead works include all religious activities, good deeds, or charity that people may do as a means of being justified before God. Faith towards God and what He has done through Christ Jesus is the only means of receiving His free gift of salvation. He only asks us to believe.

MAY 13
BREAD OF HEAVEN
JOHN 6:31-35

John 6:34 "Then said they unto him, Lord, evermore give us this bread."

It is probable that these Jews were expecting Jesus to rain down manna on them the way God did before in the wilderness. After all, anyone who could feed five thousand men with one small lunch should be able to produce manna. They were still thinking of physical food.

The word "manna" means "what is it?" The children of Israel said, "It is manna: for they wist (or knew) not what it was" (Ex. 16:15). Manna was a nutritious food that appeared on the ground every morning shortly after the children of Israel left Egypt and began their 40-year wandering in the wilderness. Moses called it, "Bread which the Lord hath given you to eat." The Lord, in speaking to Moses, called it "Bread from heaven." It was small and round, like coriander seed, and was white in color or yellowish, like bdellium. The people, after gathering it, ground it in mills or beat it in a mortar, baked it in pans and made cakes out of it. It tasted like wafers made with honey or fresh oil. It was gathered every morning and had to be used that day or it would stink and have worms. An exception was on the sixth day when it could be gathered for the Sabbath and wouldn't spoil (Ex. 16:22-26).

Although they were looking for pieces of bread to materialize, which would have been a great miracle; it would have been insignificant compared to the miracle of God being manifested in the flesh (1 Tim. 3:16). They were talking to the greatest miracle that God had ever performed, but they were blind to it. Many times, we get so intent on seeking God in one area that we forget the greatest miracle of all, which is the love and redemption given to us from God through His Son.

MAY 14
REVELATION KNOWLEDGE
JOHN 6:40-45

John 6:45 "It is written in the prophets, And they shall be all taught of God. Every man therefore that hath heard, and hath learned of the Father, cometh unto me."

The Old Testament prophets prophesied of a new covenant where we would all be taught of God. This is speaking of revelation knowledge that comes from within, through our spirits. Under the old covenant, God dealt with the Jews through the outer man. He did this because an old covenant man (who was not born again) could not perceive the spiritual truths revealed in the new covenant by the Spirit (1 Cor. 2:14). This difference between the old and new covenants is the reason why there had to be two covenants.

The Old Testament man was comparable to a child in his ability to grasp spiritual truth. It is impossible to explain spiritual truth to a young child, yet a child must be restrained from submitting to evil. So, the Word of God teaches us to use the "rod of correction" (Prov. 13:24; 19:18; 22:15). The child may not understand resisting the devil, yet when the devil tries to entice him to steal, he will say "No!" because he fears he will get the rod if he does steal. Likewise, Old Testament saints were restrained from sin by a fear of the wrath and punishment of God. This curbed sin, but it also hindered them from receiving the goodness and love of God (1 Jn. 4:18).

Under the New Testament, which Jesus is speaking of in this verse, the punishment for our sins was laid on Him. We no longer serve God out of fear of punishment like we once did when we were "children" under the law, but we serve Him out of love; because He has sent the Spirit of His Son into our hearts, making us His sons. We serve Him because our nature has been changed through the new birth. Today, be taught of God through the indwelling presence of Christ.

MAY 15
RECEIVING CHRIST
JOHN 6:47-59

John 6:56 "He that eateth my flesh, and drinketh my blood, dwelleth in me, and I in him."

Many thought that Jesus was speaking of cannibalism, but He was speaking of the spiritual man. Just as the physical man receives life from the food he eats, so the spiritual man receives life as he partakes of Jesus, the life of men (Jn. 1:4; 10:10; 14:6), or the "Bread of Life." Just as the life of a root is found in the soil, a branch in the vine, or a fish in the sea, so the believer's true life is found to be in union with Christ.

The Bible presents salvation as a life transforming experience. Change is one of the distinguishing characteristics of a true believer. Yet, failure to understand that this change takes place in our spirits first, and then is reflected in the outward thoughts and actions proportional to the way we renew our minds, has caused much confusion. This change has to take place in our born-again spirits. Why is that? If you were overweight before you got saved, you will be overweight after you get saved, unless you go on a weight loss program. Your body doesn't instantly change. Also, your soulish or mental realm doesn't instantly change. How you thought about things before you got saved will be how you think after you get saved, until you start renewing your mind. The only part of you that is left is your spirit. It is your spirit that is instantly changed at salvation. It is perfect (Heb. 12:23). It cannot sin (1 Jn. 3:9). Everything that is true of Jesus is true of our born-again spirits. Your spiritual salvation is complete. At salvation, you receive the same spirit that you will have throughout eternity. It will not have to be changed or cleansed again. It has been sealed with the Holy Spirit (Eph. 1:13) and is therefore sanctified and perfected forever (Heb. 10:10, 14; 12:23). Jesus lives in the spirits of believers. All that He is will be available to you if you will depend on Him instead of your own abilities.

MAY 16
SEPARATING THE TARES FROM THE WHEAT
JOHN 6:60-69

John 6:61 "When Jesus knew in himself that his disciples murmured at it, he said unto them,
Doth this offend you?"

This scripture, as well as Matthew 15:12, reveals that people will be offended by the Gospel; however, as much as possible, we should make sure that it is not us who are offensive. We cannot labor under the deception that everyone will receive the Gospel, even if the truth was presented properly. We know that Jesus represented His Father perfectly, yet most people rejected His message.

In these two instances, when Jesus realized He had offended the listeners, He didn't apologize and try to make concessions to gain their acceptance. Instead, He got harder. This hard message of commitment is not only beneficial to those who receive it, but it serves a dual purpose in that it exposes the "tares among the wheat."

It is important to be aware that the children of the wicked one are placed among the true believers. We should be very careful about putting just anyone who professes Christianity into any position of authority (1 Tim. 3:10). Our best defense is to preach the Word of God without watering it down. False brethren will not endure sound doctrine (2 Tim. 4:3). They leave when the Word, which is sharper than any two-edged sword, begins to expose the thoughts and intents of their hearts. There will still, however, be those who are deceived and unaware that they are not born again, remaining among the church until the end of this world.

As long as Jesus was in the world in His physical body, He was lighting the way to the Father. He now shines through our lives. It is our responsibility to be a witness. The purpose of a light is to dispel the darkness. "Let your light so shine before men. . ."(Matt. 5:16).

MAY 17
THE SPIRIT AND THE WORD ARE ONE
JOHN 6:40-71; 7:1

John 6:63 "It is the spirit that quickeneth; the flesh profiteth nothing: the words that I speak unto you, they are spirit, and they are life."

Jesus is stating that in the spirit, not the flesh, is where life comes from. These people were so dominated by their physical lives that they were missing all the spiritual significance of His words. Although God's Word does benefit our physical man, the Word is spiritual and must be understood through the spirit. God's Word is spirit and it takes our spirits to illuminate its truths to our minds.

The Word of God is not just paper and ink. Jesus is the Word, and He existed in spiritual form long before any words were inspired by the Holy Ghost to be written down. The Bible is simply a physical representation of Jesus and spiritual truth. It is inspired of God; therefore, is totally accurate and reliable, yet until we receive the Spirit expressed in these words, the Bible will not profit us. This is why many people have read the Word, maybe even memorized it, yet aren't reaping its benefits.

Just as the physical man receives life from the food he eats, the spiritual man receives life as he partakes of Jesus, the "bread of life." Jesus plainly stated that the words He spoke were spiritual—not physical.

If we want to know what spiritual truth is, we must believe the Bible, for it is spirit and life. If we want to be led by the Spirit, then we must follow God's Word. If we want to hear from the Spirit of God, then we must listen to what God says in His Word. The Spirit (Holy Spirit) and the Word (Jesus) are one (Jn. 1:1).

MAY 18
THE LAW IS NOT OF FAITH
MARK 7:1-7

Mark 7:2 "And when they saw some of his disciples eat bread with defiled, that is to say, with unwashen, hands, they found fault."

Man looks on the outward appearance (what the scribes and Pharisees were concerned with), but the Lord looks on the heart (1 Sam. 16:7). Jesus looked on men's hearts. The Old Testament laws concerning washing served a secondary purpose of hygiene, but as stated in Colossians 2:16-17 and Hebrews 9:1,9-10, their real purpose was to shadow or illustrate spiritual truth. Defiled food may hurt our bodies, but it cannot reach our spirits (Jn. 3:6). The scribes and Pharisees missed the principle of spiritual purity taught by the Old Testament ordinances and became obsessed with strict adherence to their rituals. While they relentlessly enforced the laws dealing with the physical realm, they had become completely corrupt in the spiritual realm.

"The law is not of faith." When combined with Romans 14:23 which says, *"...whatsoever is not of faith is sin,"* this statement must have been near blasphemy to the legalistic Jews, just as it is to legalistic Christians today. It is sin for the New Testament believer to try to relate to God by attempting to keep the Old Testament law. The law itself is not sin (Rom. 7:7), but it is sin to try to use the law for justification with God. This was never the purpose of the law.

Under the law, a person got what he deserved. Under faith, the New Testament believer receives grace because of what Jesus did for him. Any departure from faith, especially a departure back to the Old Testament law, voids the work of Christ (Gal. 2:21) and is the worst sin of all. Only faith in Jesus Christ has the key that unlocks the door to the law's harsh imprisonment of guilt and condemnation. With a great price He has purchased your freedom. Walk in it today and enjoy His Life.

MAY 19
TAKING OFF THE MASKS
MARK 7:6-9

Mark 7:6 "He answered and said unto them, Well hath Esaias prophesied of you hypocrites, as it is written, This people honoureth me with their lips, but their heart is far from me."

This is the biblical definition of a hypocrite, "Someone whose words and heart (actions) don't agree." A hypocrite may act the part of a Christian or he may talk like Christ, but he won't do both. When both confession and action from the heart are consistent with God's Word, there is salvation (Rom. 10:9-10).

The word "hypocrite" comes from the Greek word "hupokrites," meaning, "the playing of a part on the stage; an actor." It was a custom for Greek and Roman actors to use large masks when acting to disguise their true identity. Hence, hypocrisy became, "the feigning of beliefs, feelings, or virtues that one does not hold or possess; insecurity" (American Heritage Dictionary).

The dictionary defines "dissimulate" as, "to disguise under a feigned appearance." The Greek word means, "without hypocrisy, unfeigned." It has become customary in our society to conceal our real feelings behind a hypocritical mask. Although we should be tactful and not purposely say things to offend people, there is a time and a place for speaking the truth, even if it isn't popular.

In Leviticus 19:17, the Lord said, *"Thou shalt not hate thy brother in thine heart: thou shalt in any wise rebuke thy neighbour, and not suffer sin upon him."* This verse is saying that if we fail to rebuke our brother when we see sin approaching, then we hate him. Many people have concealed their true feelings about evil under the pretense of, "I just love them too much to hurt their feelings." The truth is, they just love themselves too much to run the risk of being rejected. That's hypocrisy. Motives, not actions, are usually what makes a person a hypocrite. Let God's love be your motivation today and everyday.

MAY 20
TRADITION NEUTRALIZES
MARK 7:1-13

Mark 7:13 "Making the word of God of none effect through your tradition, which ye have delivered: and many such like things do ye."

Deuteronomy 4:2 clearly states, *"Ye shall not add unto the word which I command you, neither shall ye diminish ought from it . . . ."* This same thought is repeated in the New Testament in Revelation 22:18-19 with very stiff penalties. Religious man is very swift to observe the part about not diminishing any of God's commandments, but there seems to be an unwritten law that adding to them is okay. Every denomination has its own set of "do's and don'ts" that aren't found in scripture, and like those of the hypocritical Pharisees, their unwritten laws usually have to do with outward appearance. We need to remember that adding to God's commandments is just as bad as taking away from them. We need to speak when the Bible speaks, and be silent when the Bible is silent.

The commandments of God and the traditions of men are not the same thing and must always be clearly distinguished. Any attempt to place them on the same level will always result in making the Word of God to none effect. You have to either lay aside the commandment of God to keep the traditions of men or you have to lay aside the traditions of men to keep the commandments of God (Ex. 20:3). Church liturgy is tradition, as well as many of the "do's and don'ts" taught by churches today. We can neutralize the positive power of God's Word toward us, by elevating man's traditions above God's Word. God's Word is still true (Rom. 3:3-4), and will not return to Him void (Isa. 55:11).

The Word will not profit anyone who doesn't believe it, but God's Word itself doesn't lose any power. If some do not believe God's Word, does that make God's Word of no effect? The answer to this question is a resounding "no!" God's Word still has its power to save, and it will profit you when you mix it with faith.

MAY 21
OUR HEARTS CONTROL OUR BODIES
MATTHEW 15:1-20; MARK 7:1-23

Mark 7:15 *"There is nothing from without a man, that entering into him can defile him: but the things which come out of him, those are they that defile the man."*

All of the Old Testament dietary laws were shadows (or pictures) of spiritual truths that would become realities in the New Covenant. These Pharisees (as well as many Christians today) missed the spiritual significance of these laws and saw only the physical act.

The real spiritual meaning that these Old Testament dietary laws symbolized was that we were supposed to be holy (separated) unto God in everything—even in what we eat. Under the Old Testament law, it was forbidden to eat or to touch certain animals, not because there was anything wrong with the animals, but to illustrate the point of being separated unto God and to serve as a constant reminder of this separation. Under the New Testament, we see that no animal is, or ever was, unclean of itself. The Old Testament designation of certain animals as unclean was purely symbolic, and this is why Jesus could make this statement.

Jesus' statements here refer to more than just the clean and unclean beasts of the Old Testament. He said nothing that enters into a man through his mouth can defile him. This statement cannot be interpreted, however, as condoning any type of abuse to our bodies such as gluttony, drug abuse, etc. Rather, Jesus is simply explaining that the condition of the heart of man should be given preeminence over the physical body. The heart of a man controls the body of a man, not the other way around. Sin doesn't make our hearts corrupt, but a corrupt heart makes us sin. God looks on our hearts, and our cleanliness or defilement in His sight is dependent solely on whether we have been made clean in our spirits by the blood of the Lamb. The blood of Jesus cleanses us from all unrighteousness.

MAY 22
CHANGE YOUR MIND
MARK 7:17-23

Mark 7:21 *"For from within, out of the heart of men, proceed evil thoughts, adulteries, fornications, murders."*

These verses (21-23) further establish the truth that our hearts include more than just our spirits. Even Christians still struggle with things like pride and foolishness, which Jesus said come out of the heart. It's certain that our born again spirits are not the source of these sins; therefore, the heart encompasses more than the spirit.

The word "spirit" is used in different ways in scripture. The most frequent usage refers to either the Spirit of God or the spirit of man. In that context, it denotes the person of the Holy Spirit or identifies a part of our three-part being (1 Th. 5:23). The word "spirit" can also describe a mental disposition (Strong).

In Ephesians 1:17, Paul is praying that what is already true in our spirits will become our "mental dispositions." He's praying for a release into the physical realm of what is already present in our spiritual being.

The Christian life is not an attempt to get more faith, or more anointing, or to get closer to the Lord. We already have these things in their fullness. We just need a revelation of what is already ours. Understanding this takes a lot of frustration and doubt away. It's much easier to release something you already have than to try and get something you don't have. Why would anyone doubt whether he could receive what he already has? Through Christ, we are already blessed with all spiritual blessings. All we have to do is appropriate what is already ours, through the renewing of our minds. If you will change your thinking to believe what God says in His Word about who you are and what you have, then this agreement between your spirit and soul will form a majority, and your flesh will experience the life of God that has been deposited in your spirit.

JESUS TRIED HER FAITH
MATTHEW 15:21-39; MARK 7:24-37; 8:1-10

Mark 7:27 "But Jesus said unto her, Let the children first be filled: for it is not meet to take the children's bread and cast it unto the dogs."

It is very clear in scripture that Jesus was sent to fulfill God's covenant to the Jews. However, it was equally clear that Jesus would open up faith unto the Gentiles. Jesus certainly knew this, and had already ministered to numerous Gentiles without the apparent disdain that we see here with the Syro-Phoenician woman. Jesus could not have been forced into ministering to this woman's daughter if it was not His will to do so; therefore, His silence and rough answer to this woman must have been designed to accomplish a positive result.

Humility is an important ingredient of faith. This woman was a stranger to the covenants of promise and had no right to demand anything. Jesus' silence and then comparison of her to a dog would certainly have offended an arrogant person, and it is possible that for this very reason, Jesus tried her faith. Jesus didn't need to do this with the centurion in Luke 7:6-7 because the centurion had already humbled himself.

An integral part of faith is seeking God alone with your whole heart. If we are concerned with what people think and gaining their approval (or honor), we will never take a stand in faith for anything. After all, we might be criticized for it. This one thing has probably stopped as many people from receiving from God as anything else. You cannot be a man-pleaser and please God at the same time. Satan uses persecutions to steal God's Word, thereby stopping our faith. To see faith work, you must say with Paul, "Let God be true, but every man a liar" (Rom. 3:4).

THE MINISTRY OF THE HOLY SPIRIT
MARK 8:11-13

Mark 8:12 "And he sighed deeply in his spirit, and saith, Why doth this generation seek after a sign? verily I say unto you, There shall no sign be given unto this generation."

The Greek word used here for "sighed deeply" means an intense grieving, inaudible prayer, or groan. This is intercession of the Holy Spirit, with groanings that cannot be uttered. Some Spirit-filled Christians believe this means groanings that cannot be uttered in normal speech and that this refers to speaking in tongues. However, this actually refers to a type of intercession different than speaking in tongues.

In John 11:33 and 38, Jesus groaned in the Spirit twice, and in those cases there were *no* words uttered. It was exactly as the Scripture states, a groaning *in the Spirit*. Everyone who has the indwelling presence of the Holy Spirit has or will have this happen to him. Paul was referring to this in Galatians 4:19 when he spoke of travailing in birth for the Galatians. This groaning of the Holy Spirit is not just grief, but a groan of anger and resistance against Satan's devices in our lives. Many times, Christians don't discern this because they think it is just their own grief over the situation; however, this is the Holy Spirit desiring to intercede with us against our problems.

Jesus drew on this ministry of the Holy Spirit. John 11:33 and 38 says that Jesus groaned in the Spirit twice when He raised Lazarus from the dead. What infirmity did Jesus have that He needed this ministry of the Holy Spirit? Jesus had no sin, but He did have an infirmity. It was His physical mind. Even a sinless human mind could not comprehend raising a man from the grave after four days. If Jesus needed the Holy Spirit to help Him when He didn't know how to pray, then this should certainly be an important ministry of the Holy Spirit in our lives.

JESUS CHALLENGES THE SADDUCEES
MATTHEW 16:1-4

Matthew 16:1 "The Pharisees also with the Sadducees came, and tempting desired him that he would show them a sign from heaven."

The Sadducees were a Jewish sect (Acts 5:17), of both a political and religious nature, that was best known for its opposition to the more popular party (the Pharisees), because of differences in various doctrinal and political beliefs. Sadducees rejected the oral tradition of the Pharisees who made a mountain of burdensome legislation and accepted only the written law. We are told they believed there was "no resurrection, nor angel, nor spirit" (Acts 23:8). From Josephus, we learn that the Sadducees believed that the soul perishes with the body (Antiq. XVIII. 1.4), and can receive neither penalties nor rewards in an afterlife (WarII. 8.14).

The most significant mention of the Sadducees in the Gospels concerns their interview with Jesus in Jerusalem. They tried to trap Jesus with a crafty question concerning the resurrection. In His answer, Jesus accused them of not knowing the scriptures, nor the power of God (Mt. 22:29). He then proceeded to quote from the Pentateuch (the first five books of the Bible) out of Exodus 3:6 in support of the doctrine of the resurrection. The Sadducees became alarmed and decided to take action (Jn. 11:47), as Jesus posed a threat to their security and position (as in the cleansing of the temple; Mk. 11:15-18). Confronted with Jesus and His claims, the Sadducees were able to unite with their traditional enemies, the Pharisees, for the purpose of disposing Jesus. Both parties worked together for the arrest and trial of Jesus by the Sanhedrin. These religious leaders were only aware of external actions and were ignorant of the issues of the heart. Religion (man trying to approach God) will always differ with Christianity (God coming to man) in this respect. "Man looketh on the outward appearance, but the Lord looketh on the heart" (1 Sam. 16:7).

SYMPTOMS OF A HARD HEART
MATTHEW 16:1-12; MARK 8:11-21

Mark 8:17 "And when Jesus knew it, he saith unto them, Why reason ye, because ye have no bread? perceive ye not yet, neither understand? have ye your heart yet hardened?"

Just a few days before this instance, hard hearts caused Jesus' disciples to be amazed when they saw Jesus walk on the water to them. Here, Jesus' statements reveal some of the characteristics of someone with a hard heart.

First, a hard heart keeps us from perceiving spiritual truths. This is why everyone in a church service hears exactly the same message, yet some will receive it while others won't. It's not the Word that is the variable, but rather the condition of the hearts. A hard heart stops spiritual perception.

Second, a hard heart stops us from understanding spiritual truth. When a person doesn't understand God's Word, Satan finds no resistance when he comes to steal it.

Third, a hard heart keeps us from remembering. This isn't to say that we can't recall facts or scriptures. As related in Mark 8:19-20, the disciples remembered the *facts* of the two miraculous feedings, but they had forgotten any spiritual lessons they might have learned. Likewise, some people can quote scripture or remember what the sermon was about, but they can't perceive the spiritual life in the message or retain what they did perceive.

A hard heart blinds us to any spiritual perception and keeps us thinking only in the natural realm. Small faith and a hard heart are the same. Hebrews 3:12-13 parallels an evil heart of unbelief to a hard heart. It takes great faith to keep your heart sensitive to God. Seek Him with your whole heart today.

MAY 27
PETITION NOT REPETITION
MATTHEW 16:13-15; MARK 8:11-25; LUKE 9:18-20

Mark 8:24-25 "And he looked up, and said, I see men as trees, walking. After that he put his hands again upon his eyes, and made him look up: and he was restored, and saw every man clearly."

It was unusual for Jesus to inquire about the results of His ministry as He did in verse 23. It was even more unusual that Jesus laid hands on this man a second time. This is the only example in the New Testament where Jesus had to minister to any need more than once to affect a total healing.

Many people request things from God and then look at their circumstances to see if God answered their prayers. That is walking by sight and not by faith. If they can't "see" God's answer, then they pray again asking for the same thing. This is not the way Jesus taught us to pray and receive. We can be certain that Jesus didn't lay hands on this man a second time because He thought His Father hadn't heard Him the first time. Since the man received partial sight, it is evident that God's healing power was at work in him. Jesus was not petitioning His Father again for healing.

Through His spirit, Jesus knew that unbelief was hindering a perfect manifestation of God's power in this man, and He simply gave him another "dose" of the anointing power of God. Satan may hinder, but he cannot overcome someone who continues resisting him. Believe that you received when you prayed and continue to apply the power of God. Press in to such a degree that you can confront anything that is contrary to what you have asked, and overcome it. Perseverance in prayer is the key to overcoming Satan—not God.

MAY 28
JESUS, THE CHIEF CORNERSTONE
MATTHEW 16:13-19

Matthew 16:18 "And I say also unto thee, That thou art Peter, and upon this rock I will build my church; and the gates of hell shall not prevail against it."

Some people have mistakenly interpreted this passage to say that Peter was the foundation on which Christ would build His Church; however, that would violate many scriptures that refer to Jesus as the "chief cornerstone." Ephesians 2:20 does mention the apostles as being part of the foundation stones of Christ's church, but it doesn't single Peter out above any of the other apostles. This same scripture once again mentions Jesus as the "chief cornerstone."

There are two different Greek words used for "Peter" and "rock" respectively in verse 18. The word used for "Peter" means "rock" but signifies a piece of rock like a pebble. In contrast, the word translated as "rock" signifies a massive rock which certainly refers to Jesus, the "chief cornerstone." Some have suggested that the foundation rock referred to was a confession that Peter made saying that Jesus was "the Christ, the Son of the living God" (Mt. 16:16). Although it is true that to enter God's kingdom, we do have to confess that Jesus is Lord (Rom. 10:9-10), in light of the Old Testament prophecies and New Testament references to Jesus being the "chief cornerstone," this passage of scripture must be referring directly to Jesus as the "rock" upon which He will build His church.

One of the greatest differences between New Testament believers and Old Testament believers is that New Testament saints are the temple of God. God Himself actually indwells us. God does not dwell in a building made by man's hands. He now lives in the hearts of those who make Jesus their Lord (Rom. 10:9). The cornerstone of our lives in God must be an ever-increasing revelation of His Son. If we had a real understanding of the reality of Christ in us (Col. 1:27), it would drastically change our attitudes, emotions, and actions.

MAY 29
GOD'S WILL ABOVE OURS
MATTHEW 16:16-26; MARK 8:30-37; LUKE 9:21-27

Luke 9:23 "And he said to them all, if any man will come after me, let him deny himself, and take up his cross daily, and follow me."

Self-denial is an important part of the Christian life. Jesus sacrificed His life for us and He demands that we die to ourselves that we might experience the new life He has provided. We do this first by recognizing that we can't save ourselves by our own efforts, and second, by trusting God, not self, for salvation. Then daily, we need to deny our own wisdom and seek God's wisdom and direction for our lives.

Self-denial is only good when we are denying ourselves for the singular purpose of exalting Jesus and His will for us in some area of our lives. Some have made a religion out of self-denial and find pleasure in their denial—not in Jesus' lordship. This leads to legalism and bondage, which Paul condemned as will worship (Col. 2:23). We are told not only to deny ourselves, but to "deny ourselves, take up our cross, and follow Jesus."

The cross is what Jesus died on. There are circumstances in our lives which, like the cross of Jesus, give us the opportunity to die to ourselves each day. These are not things like sickness, poverty, etc., for which Jesus' atonement provided redemption, but rather things like persecution (which we are not redeemed from) and the constant battle between our flesh and our born again spirits. The cross that we must bear is to take God's Word (which is His will) and exalt it above our own will in each situation every day.

MAY 30
RECOGNIZE THE REAL ENEMY
MARK 8:30-33

Mark 8:33, "But when he had turned about and looked on his disciples, he rebuked Peter, saying, Get thee behind me, Satan: for thou savourest not the things that be of God, but the things that be of men."

Jesus was not implying that Peter and Satan were one-and-the-same, but was referring that Satan had inspired Peter's statement. This type of metaphor was used elsewhere in scripture such as when God spoke to the serpent in the garden of Eden (Gen. 3:15), as though addressing Satan. The serpent was merely the vehicle of communication Satan used to tempt Adam and Eve, while Peter was the vehicle Satan used to tempt Jesus. Ephesians 6:12 reveals that our warfare isn't with people, but against the spiritual powers who inspire and use people. Jesus recognized that Peter's reaction to His prophecy about His death was motivated by His enemy, Satan, so He went right to the source.

Every Christian is at war. There is a perpetual struggle against Satan and his kingdom from which there are no "leaves" or "discharges." Our enemy goes about as a roaring lion, seeking whom he may devour (1 Pet. 5:8). Those who resist the devil will see him flee (Jas. 4:7).

Some of us believe that anger will put others in their place. But *"the wrath of man does not work the righteousness of God"* (Jas. 1:20). Anger against people makes us play right into the hand of the devil. The way to overcome the spiritual powers that come against us through people is to turn the other cheek (Mt. 5:39). This makes the demons flee in terror. We cannot win a spiritual battle with carnal weapons. We must realize who the real enemy is and fight with the spiritual weapons the Lord has given us. It is supposed by many that the higher echelons of the devil's spiritual authority take more power to rebuke or remove. That's not true. There is no demonic power, including the devil himself, that will not flee at the name of Jesus when faith is put in that name. What a wonderful name!

MAY 31
HIS PURPOSE REVEALED
MATTHEW 16:20-28

Matthew 16:21 "From that time forth began Jesus to show unto his disciples, how that he must go unto Jerusalem, and suffer many things of the elders and chief priests and scribes, and be killed, and be raised again the third day."

Despite the abundant and clear prophecies about His death and resurrection, Jesus' disciples didn't understand or remember Jesus' words until after His resurrection (Lk. 24:5-9). Luke records twice that Jesus' sayings about His resurrection were hidden from the disciples. It is interesting to note, however, that the chief priests and Pharisees remembered Jesus' prophecies about His resurrection (Mt. 27:63) when His disciples didn't.

One of the great truths of the Bible is that Jesus died for our sins, not for His own. Jesus was totally sinless. This is one of the major differences between Christianity and the religions of the world. No other religious leader has ever claimed to be sinless, therefore no other religious leader is even in the same class with Jesus. Also, no other religious leader has ever given his life in sacrifice to atone for the sins of others. It wouldn't have done any good if one had. Since the religious leaders were sinners themselves, their lives weren't worth any more than any other sinner. Since Jesus was the sinless Son of God, His life was worth more than all of humanity throughout the ages.

Every detail of Christ's death, burial, and resurrection was already prophesied in scripture before it happened. All the events of Jesus' life, death, and resurrection had fulfilled scripture. God's Word is the ultimate authority and only through His Word can we receive faith to be born again. We must preach the Word, not experiences. Experiences are only useful to illustrate that God's Word is true. Jesus is alive from the dead. His tomb is empty. Jesus provided us with the ultimate verification of His authority. He arose from the dead.

JUNE 1
ALIVE UNTO GOD
MATTHEW 17:1-8; MARK 9:1-8; LUKE 9:28-36

Matthew 17:2 "And was transfigured before them: and his face did shine as the sun, and his raiment was white as the light."

It is interesting to compare Jesus' transfiguration with that of Moses'. Jesus' face shone as the sun and His garment was as white as the light. This certainly exceeded what Moses experienced, yet Jesus' face did not continue to shine when He came down off the mountain as Moses' face did.

Moses' face reflected the glory of God, but Jesus was the glory of God (Jn. 1:14; Heb. 1:3). Moses put a veil over his face to conceal the glory of God (Ex. 34:29-35), so that the people would not be afraid to come near him. Jesus' body was His veil that concealed His true glory within. During His transfiguration, He pulled back the veil of His flesh, and we simply caught a glimpse of His glory that he had with the Father before the world was (Jn. 17:5). At Jesus' death, the veil of His body was "rent in two" giving us direct access to the glory of God (Heb. 10:19-20).

We need to be conformed to the death of Christ. That is, reckoning ourselves dead to sin and all its effects upon us in the same way that Christ is dead to sin and all its effects upon Him. Many people focus on the death to sin and omit, or at least put second, being alive unto God. It is assumed that if we will just die to sin, then life with Christ will come automatically. That's no more true than physical death automatically producing physical resurrection. God doesn't need dead people. He needs people who have risen from the dead spiritually. People who know who they are "in Christ." The victorious New Testament believer is not just living for the Lord, but the risen Christ is actually living through him. There are over a hundred scriptural references to the indwelling presence of the Lord in the life of a believer. Look into the Word, and see what God has to say about you.

JUNE 2
BUILD FAITH: DESTROY DOUBT
MATTHEW 17:14-20; MARK 9:9-27; LUKE 9:37-42

Matthew 17:20 "And Jesus said unto them, Because of your unbelief: for verily I say unto you, If ye have faith as a grain of mustard seed, ye shall say unto this mountain, Remove hence to yonder place; and it shall remove; and nothing shall be impossible unto you."

The disciples' unbelief in this instance was not a disbelief in God's power to produce deliverance, but rather a natural kind of unbelief that came from a hard heart that was more sensitive to what it saw than to what it believed. Jesus said that a very small amount of faith (a "mustard seed") is sufficient to remove a mountain, if no unbelief is present to hinder it.

Jesus was disappointed that His disciples had not been able to cast this devil out. Most people would have not criticised these disciples. After all, it wasn't normal to have power over evil spirits. However, Jesus had already given these disciples power and authority over all devils. These disciples had also already used this power and authority successfully on previous occasions, making them more accountable than others. They weren't just normal men any longer. They had a supernatural ability and calling.

We also receive power from on high when the Holy Ghost comes upon us, and it becomes our normal Christian service to use this power to witness to others. We can always look around and find plenty of Christians who are not using this power, but 2 Corinthians 10:12 says that comparing ourselves among ourselves is not wise. Most Christians are living so far below what God intended for them that when someone begins to live a normal Christian life (according to God's standard), they think he's abnormal. We will be successful when we not only build our faith, but destroy our doubts.

JUNE 3
FASTING DRIVES AWAY DOUBT
MARK 9:28-29

Mark 9:29 "And he said unto them, This kind can come forth by nothing, but by prayer and fasting."

Prayer and fasting do not drive demons out. If the name of Jesus and faith in His name won't do the job, then fasting and prayer won't either. Jesus is saying that fasting and prayer are the only ways of casting out this type of unbelief.

An unbelief that comes as a result of ignorance can be done away with by receiving the truth of God's Word (Rom. 10:17; 2 Pet. 1:4). However, the unbelief that hindered the disciples in this case was a natural type of unbelief. They had been taught all of their lives to believe what their five senses told them. They were simply dominated by this natural input more than by God's supernatural input (God's Word). The only way to overcome this unbelief that comes through our senses is to deny our senses through prayer and fasting.

Fasting accomplishes many things. One of the greatest benefits of fasting is that through denying the lusts of the flesh, the spirit man gains ascendancy. Fasting was always used as a means of seeking God to the exclusion of all else. Fasting does not cast out demons, but rather it casts out unbelief. Fasting is beneficial in every aspect of the Christian life—not only in casting out devils.

The real virtue of a fast is in humbling ourselves through self denial (Ps. 35:13; 69:10), and that can be accomplished through ways other than total abstinence. Partial fasts can be beneficial, as well as fasts of our time or pleasures. However, because appetite for food is one of man's strongest drives, fasting from food seems to get the job done the quickest. Fasting should be a much more important part of seeking God in our lives.

JUNE 4
ONE HUNDRED TIMES ZERO
MATTHEW 17:24-27

Matthew 17:27 "Notwithstanding, lest we should offend them, go thou to the sea, and cast an hook, and take up the fish that first cometh up; and when thou hast opened his mouth, thou shalt find a piece of money; that take, and give unto them for me and thee."

This was quite a miracle. Not only was the money supplied for their taxes, but it was the exact amount needed, and it was from the first fish that was caught.

Although this sets the precedent that God can supply our needs in a miraculous way, it's important to remember that God doesn't counterfeit money. He didn't create money in the fish, but rather he had the fish miraculously find and swallow the exact Roman coin that Peter needed. It's a mistake to just pray and then wait on God to rain the money down from heaven. As Luke 6:38 says, God uses men (and sometimes fish) to give finances to us. He can do it in a very unexpected, supernatural way, but it will involve people and existing currency. We need to believe that the Lord hears and answers our prayers and then pray for the people He's going to use to deliver the answer. This could be our employer, the person who buys our goods, or any number of people.

The Lord also blesses what we set our hands to do. When in need, we should seek God's direction for something to set our hands to and then trust Him to bless it and multiply the results of our work. But 100 times zero is zero. Many people have missed their miracle because they never took that first step of faith and used what they had. God can give you a creative idea today that will bless you and make you a blessing to others. Seek and you will find.

JUNE 5
HUMILITY BEFORE HONOR
MATTHEW 18:1-5; MARK 9:30-37; LUKE 9:46-48

Matthew 18:4 "Whosoever therefore shall humble himself as this little child, the same is greatest in the kingdom of heaven."

It is interesting that Jesus used a little child to illustrate humility. Although it is true that little children have a purity and humility that is many times missing in adults, they certainly are not selfless. A child comes into the world totally self-centered, wanting what he wants when he wants it. Parents are to train children out of this self-centeredness.

One of humility's dominant characteristics is a God-dependency and not a self-sufficiency. The truth of humility being the key to greatness or success is not new. Jesus gave this truth new meaning by walking in humility as no one ever had before.

This path of self-denial to greatness is exactly the opposite of the world's path of exalting self at everyone else's expense. The path of humility could not possibly work if there was no God. We would simply be trampled underfoot. Humility is a step of faith—faith that God is the judge and that promotion comes from Him (Ps. 75:6-7). God will resist the proud, but give grace unto the humble (1 Pet. 5:5). Humility is trusting in God and not in ourselves. This is why it is easy to be humble when we've failed, and conversely, hard to be humble when we've achieved great success. This is precisely why Paul commanded Timothy not to put a novice into a position of leadership in the church. Pride is self-sufficiency and self-exaltation while humility is self-denial and dependence upon God.

God's kingdom is founded upon this principle of humility before honor. God's kind of love is selfless as can be seen by Jesus' own actions. Pride is the only reason that strife comes (Prov. 13:10); so remember, humility is the key to walking in love with our brothers and sisters in the Lord.

JUNE 6
ANGELIC PROTECTION
MATTHEW 18:10-11

Matthew 18:10 "Take heed that ye despise not one of these little ones; for I say unto you, That in heaven their angels do always behold the face of my Father which is in heaven."

We have angels assigned to us. Hebrews 1:14 further reveals that their purpose is to minister to us (on our behalf). In the Old Testament, Psalm 91 teaches on the ministry of angels to God's people.

Some have realized this truth and have taken it even further to say that we are supposed to speak to our angels and they will obey our commands. There is no instruction in scripture to do this nor is there any example of it being done. Many of the angels' protective duties described in Psalm 91 are preventative, and we certainly could not effectively command these activities.

Rather, these angels are dispatched exactly as this verse describes—by looking at the Father's face. God Almighty controls them for us; however, we do have a part to play. In Psalm 91 it is those who dwell in the secret place of the Most High that are able to benefit from angelic activity (v. 1). Verse two further instructs us to say that the Lord is our refuge and fortress and that we trust in Him.

It is the combination of our faith in God and His faithfulness to us that releases the angels on our behalf. If it was solely up to God, His provision would be the same for everyone because of His mercy and grace. However, we have to receive God's grace by faith (Eph. 2:8). As you seek the Lord, become aware of His ministering spirits that were created to minister to you. Speak forth your faith in this area, and He will send forth His angels on your behalf.

JUNE 7
GOD LIKES US
MATTHEW 18:12-14

Matthew 18:14 "Even so it is not the will of your Father which is in heaven, that one of these little ones should perish."

One of the greatest truths of the Bible and also one of the hardest to comprehend, is that we are the objects of God's love. God didn't just pity us or feel some sense of moral obligation to save us. He saved us because of His infinite love for us (Jn. 3:16).

God loves people. He even loves those who have gone astray. As Jesus said in a similar parable (Lk. 15:7), "I say unto you, that likewise joy shall be in heaven over one sinner that repenteth, more than over ninety and nine just persons, which need no repentance."

Once we experience the life-changing power of Christ, there is a tendency to become harsh and impatient with others who continue to live their lives without Him. We sometimes forget that it was the love and goodness of God that brought us to repentance (Rom. 2:4), and we become condemning and judgmental toward the lost. This is not the attitude that Jesus had, nor the attitude He wants us to have.

"Even when we were spiritually dead because of our sins, God's forbearance was working on our behalf. He was tolerant, patient and kind towards us. God abounded in excessive proportion with good will, compassion, and desire to help us. His disposition was kind, compassionate, and forgiving in His treatment of us. He wanted in abundant supply to alleviate our distress and bring relief from our sins. He did this by giving us life in place of death. It was with Christ that this salvation was secured. By grace, kindness, and favor we are saved. All of this was the result of God's extremely large degree of love wherewith He loved us, always seeking the welfare and betterment of us. God likes us." (Eph. 2:4-5 paraphrased by Don Krow). God loves YOU!

JUNE 8
DISCIPLINE BRINGS LIFE
MATTHEW 18:15-19

Matthew 18:18-19 "Verily I say unto you, Whatsoever ye shall bind on earth shall be bound in heaven: and whatsoever ye shall loose on earth shall be loosed in heaven. Again I say unto you, That if two of you shall agree on earth as touching any thing that they shall ask, it shall be done for them of my Father which is in heaven."

Verses 18 and 19 have many applications, but taken in context, they are specifically referring to church discipline. Some might think that church discipline is only symbolic and carries no real weight; however, Jesus is making it clear that in the spiritual realm, discipline that is directed by the Holy Spirit has much power.

The scriptural commands concerning church discipline are designed to help restore the brother or sister who is in sin just as much as they are designed to protect other members of the body from that sin. If the person being disciplined repents, the objective has been achieved and no further action should be taken. Church discipline is two-fold. It consists of withdrawing both our fellowship and our intercession.

Proper intercession can actually keep Satan at bay, although an individual is living in sin. This is good if the person uses this freedom to repent and come back to God. But, if the person takes this freedom from the wages of sin to commit more sin, there comes a time when this form of intercession ceases to be beneficial. In that case, intercession against Satan's attacks should be withdrawn, and we should actually retain that person's sins unto him so that he can no longer get by without experiencing the death that sin brings (Rom. 6:23). As he starts reaping what he has sown, it hopefully will cause him to turn back to the goodness of God that he once enjoyed. This is the binding and loosing being referred to in this verse. Heaven and earth are affected by our binding and loosing.

JUNE 9
LIMITLESS FORGIVENESS
MATTHEW 18:21-35

Matthew 18:33 "Shouldest not thou also have had compassion on thy fellowservant, even as I had pity on thee?"

Peter thought he was being very generous by offering to forgive his brother seven times in one day, but Jesus said he should forgive him 490 times in one day. It would be impossible to have someone sin against you 490 times in one day. Jesus is actually saying that there should be no limit to our forgiveness.

When we are offended or hurt, we often feel justified in holding a grudge. The Old Testament law expressed this when it stated, "Eye for eye, tooth for tooth" (Ex. 21:23-25). Until the offense was paid, people did not feel free to forgive; however, God dealt with all men's offenses by placing sin upon the perfect Savior who was judged in place of every sinner of all time. To demand that others now earn our forgiveness is not Christ like. Jesus died for every man's sins, extending forgiveness to us while we were yet sinners, and we should do the same.

The main thrust of this parable is that when people wrong us, we should remember the great mercy that God has shown to us and respond likewise. Any debt that could be owed to us is insignificant compared to the debt we were forgiven. We should have compassion on others as Christ had on us.

If God expects us to forgive our brother who has trespassed against us 490 times in one day (actually an unlimited number of times), certainly He who *is* love will do no less with us.

The forgiveness that we have received from the Lord is infinitely greater than any forgiveness we could ever be asked to extend toward others.

JUNE 10
HOLY GHOST TEACHER
JOHN 7:14-15

John 7:15 "And the Jews marvelled, saying, How knoweth this man letters, having never learned?"

Jesus received His wisdom and knowledge by direct revelation from the Spirit of God rather than by the teachings of man. Jesus had been learning, but not through man. The Holy Ghost was His teacher. Jesus had to be taught the things of God. This looks contrary to Colossians 2:3, which says that all the treasures of wisdom and knowledge are hidden in Jesus. If Jesus was God manifest in the flesh, why would He have to learn or be taught?

The harmony between these apparently opposite statements is that Jesus' spirit man was 100 percent God and had all of the wisdom and understanding of God in it, but it was manifest in natural flesh. It wasn't sinful flesh, but it was flesh nonetheless, and had to be educated. Jesus was not taught by man, but He was taught by the direct revelation of the Holy Spirit. The knowledge was within Him but it had to be drawn out.

At the new birth, a born-again man's spirit "is renewed in knowledge after the image of him that created him" (Col. 3:10). "We have the mind of Christ" (1 Cor. 2:16), and "an unction from the Holy One, and ye know all things" (1 Jn. 2:20). All of these things are a reality in our spiritual man. However, just as Jesus had to be taught, so we must draw this wisdom and knowledge out of our spirits and renew our minds with it (Rom. 12:2). This is one of the main ministries of the Holy Spirit to the believer. Through the new birth, we have received the mind of Christ in our spirits and are in the process of growing in wisdom by drawing this knowledge out of our spirits and renewing (or reprogramming) our minds. This wisdom has to be drawn out by faith, time spent in the Word, and prayer.

JUNE 11
REBIRTH
JOHN 7:16-19

John 7:19 "Did not Moses give you the law, and yet none of you keepeth the law? Why go ye about to kill me?"

These Jews prided themselves on their observance of the law, but they were keeping the letter of the law and missing its true intent. The greatest of all the Old Testament laws was to love God and then to love your neighbor as yourself. The Jews were violating these laws by having hatred in their hearts toward Jesus and wanting to kill Him. They denied that they desired to kill Him, but the scriptures declare that they had already plotted or tried to kill Him three times.

They also knew much about God. It was required of the Jewish men to memorize large portions of the Torah (the first five books of the Bible). Their whole society revolved around God's moral standards and countless religious observances. However, they did not know God.

There is a difference between knowing about someone and really knowing him. Likewise today, millions of people are acquainted with knowledge about Jesus. They may even be moral and observe religious ceremonies, but if they don't personally experience knowing Jesus, they are not saved and will not make it to heaven. Even the devils believe and tremble, but they aren't saved.

Our spiritual man became dead unto (separated from) God through sin. Just as we didn't accomplish our physical birth, we cannot produce this spiritual rebirth. We are totally incapable of saving ourselves; therefore, we need a Savior. We simply believe on the Lord Jesus Christ and we are saved. Salvation is not a reformation, but rather a regeneration, a new birth, a new creation, that can only be accomplished by a creative miracle of the Holy Spirit. You must be born again.

JUNE 12
THE HEART MATTERS
JOHN 7:21-24

John 7:22 "Moses therefore gave unto you circumcision; (not because it is of Moses, but of the fathers;) and ye on the sabbath day circumcise a man."
The covenant of circumcision was given to Abram in Genesis 17:9-14. In verse 14, the Lord said that any man who did not carry this sign of the covenant in his flesh was to be killed. This placed a great importance on the act of circumcision. Paul says in Romans 4:3-13, that Abraham had already been justified by faith before he was circumcised. It was Abram's faith that saved him at least 13 years before the Lord commanded Abram to be circumcised. The Jews had focused on the outward act of obedience instead of the inward act of faith that caused Abram to be obedient. This was the source of the contention between Jesus and the religious leaders too. They were emphasizing all the outward acts that the Lord had commanded and were totally disregarding the motives of the heart. Jesus was saying that if an individual would cleanse his heart, then his actions would inevitably change too.

The truth of salvation by faith had been lost in Judaism, and even though many of the Jews had come to put faith in Jesus as their Savior, they were trying to mix faith and keeping the commandments, as a requirement for salvation.

The condition of a person's flesh is not the important thing. It doesn't matter if that flesh is circumcised or holy. It is the condition of the spirit that matters to God. Today, the act of circumcision is not the issue, but acts of holiness are still deemed by many as essential for receiving salvation. This same legalistic thinking lives on today in the doctrine of water baptism, church membership, and other acts of holiness that some preach are necessary for salvation. Faith alone in the love of God, as expressed through Jesus, is the only thing that God demands for justification. Religious rites mean nothing. The only thing that counts is becoming a new creation.

JUNE 13
EFFORTLESS FRUIT
JOHN 7:37-41

John 7:38 "He that believeth on me, as the scripture hath said, out of his belly shall flow rivers of living water."
These rivers of living water are referring to the Holy Spirit and the effects He produces in the life of a believer. Galatians 5:22-23 says, *"The fruit of the spirit is love, joy, peace, longsuffering, gentleness, goodness, faith, meekness, temperance."* These qualities should flow out of us like an artesian well. They should not have to be pumped. They will flow as we conform our thinking to God's Word.

Jesus speaks of bearing fruit in John 15 and declares that *". . . without me ye can do nothing"* (Jn. 15:5). This fruit is the product of the Holy Spirit, not our efforts. However, since *"he that is joined unto the Lord is one spirit"* (1 Cor. 6:17), then this fruit of the Spirit is also what our born-again spirits produce. Our spirits always have these attributes regardless of what we feel in our emotions. Failure to understand this has caused many Christians to think they would be hypocrites to express joy when the truth is, they are depressed. However, it's only our soulish part that gets depressed. Our spirits are always bearing the fruit of *"love, joy, peace, etc."* For a person who seeks to walk in the Spirit, it is actually hypocritical to let his soulish emotions dominate his spiritual emotions. The truth is, our spirits are never depressed, just our souls. Those who understand this have the choice of letting their souls depress them or letting the Holy Spirit, through their born-again spirits, release the joy and peace spoken of here.

The "fruit" is not produced by the believers, but by the Holy Spirit, as we live in union with Him. Our part is to yield and trust; God's part is to produce the fruit.

JUNE 14
AMAZING GRACE
JOHN 8:1-11

John 8:4-5 "They say unto him, Master, this woman was taken in adultery, in the very act. Now Moses in the law commanded us, that such should be stoned: but what sayest thou?"

This was possibly the most potentially damaging temptation the scribes and Pharisees ever presented to Jesus. Much of Jesus' widespread popularity with the people was because of His examples of and teachings about God's mercy and forgiveness towards sinners. This was received with great enthusiasm by the people who, before this time had been presented with only a harsh, legalistic, judgmental picture of God.

The scribes and Pharisees had often tried to portray Jesus as condoning or practicing sin because of His association with sinners and His ministry to them when it violated Jewish traditions, such as the Sabbath. However, Jesus had successfully turned every attack into a victory for the side of grace and mercy.

This time, the Jews felt that they had Him cornered. If Jesus held to His teachings of forgiveness and refused to stone this woman, He would be in direct rebellion to the law of Moses. This would give these Jews legal grounds to kill Jesus. On the other hand, if He stoned the woman as the law declared, the people would forsake Him. It looked like they had Him trapped either way He went.

As always, the foolishness of God is wiser than men, and Jesus rose to the occasion. He did not condone the sin nor disregard the law of Moses. He simply told the one who was without sin to cast the first stone. As the Holy Ghost began to convict them of their own sin, they all had to leave; therefore, they could not fault Jesus for not stoning the woman. Jesus was justified in His forgiveness of this woman because He was operating under the dispensation of grace. Think about God's grace today.

JUNE 15
MYSTERY OF THE TRINITY
JOHN 8:12-27

John 8:19 "Then said they unto him, Where is thy Father? Jesus answered, Ye neither know me, nor my Father: if ye had known me, ye should have known my Father also."

The scriptures teach Jesus' oneness with the Father. This oneness is more than singleness of purpose and actually denotes "a single one to the exclusion of others" as in the statement, "There is one God" (1 Tim. 2:5). This truth is so well established in scripture that some people make no distinction between the Father, Son, and Holy Spirit, but believe they are simply one God expressing Himself in three different ways. However, in this passage, Jesus makes a distinction between Himself and His Father. He uses Himself and His Father as two different witnesses to fulfill the requirement of Deuteronomy 17:6. Jesus would have been deceiving these Jews if there was no distinction between His Father and Himself, yet they are one (Jn. 10:30; 1 Jn. 5:7). This is a great mystery, yet a well established truth in scripture.

One of the great statements of the Old Testament from Deuteronomy 6:4 says, "The Lord our God is one Lord." We do not have three Gods, but one God, clearly identifiable as three persons. This is a great mystery that has not been adequately explained. Scriptures reveal the truth of the Trinity, but make no attempt to explain it. We simply accept this revelation as it is, until we know all things, even as we are known (1 Cor. 13:12).

Jesus said the witness of His Father was the greatest testimony of who He was. Everyone can hear the Father's testimony of Jesus through the scriptures. Moses and all the Old Testament prophets spoke of the coming of Jesus, and Peter said the written Word of God was a more sure word of prophecy than the audible voice of God. Read the Word today.

JUNE 16
JESUS PAID IT ALL
JOHN 8:12-30

John 8:28 "Then said Jesus unto them, When ye have lifted up the Son of man, then shall ye know that I am he, and that I do nothing of myself; but as my Father hath taught me, I speak these things."

This is the second of three times that Jesus spoke of Himself being "lifted up" (first- Jn. 3:14; third-Jn. 12:32-33). As the scripture explains in John 12:33, this was a reference to crucifixion as the means of His death. The lifting up is speaking of being lifted up from the earth and suspended on a cross in crucifixion. The Jews understood that Jesus was speaking of death.

The crucifixion didn't just happen. It was planned by God. Does this mean that God bears all responsibility and those who were actually instrumental in the rejection and crucifixion of Jesus are not guilty? Not at all. Jesus came to the earth to die in our place and thereby purchase redemption for us. That was His plan, but He didn't force anyone to fulfill it. His ministry and message placed Him in direct opposition to the devil and his followers. Their hatred for Jesus caused them (of their own free will) to crucify Jesus. God, in all His wisdom, simply knew what man would do and He determined to use their rejection of His Son to accomplish His will. He never controls our will to accomplish His.

If a person truly understands the message of the cross, then he understands grace. Jesus didn't just make a token sacrifice for us. He paid it all. There's no sacrifice that we can make that will add to or replace the sacrifice of Christ. He did it all, and we can thank Him forever.

JUNE 17
SONSHIP OR SLAVERY
JOHN 8:34-36

John 8:34 "Jesus answered them, Verily, verily, I say unto you, Whosoever committeth sin is the servant of sin."

The devil has been deceiving the world about sin since the Garden of Eden when he told Eve that through sin she could be like God. Time has proven, not only to Eve, but to each one of us, that this is not true. Sin brings death—not life. Jesus is making it clear that sin enslaves. We become slaves not only to the sin itself, but to the author of sin: the devil. We are either servants of God through obedience or servants of the devil through sin.

Jesus is likening the bondage that sin produces to slavery, while comparing the freedom that comes through serving God to being a beloved son. No one would doubt that being a son is better than being a slave. Likewise, obeying God is better than yielding to sin. True freedom is found only in serving God. There is a false freedom that Satan has been promoting since the Garden of Eden. He has deceived all of us at one time or another into thinking that God is a tyrant who really doesn't want us to enjoy life and consequently has told us not to do certain things. Because we believe this lie, we disobey God (or sin) in the name of freedom.

However, the Word of God and personal experience conclusively prove that the wages of sin is death (Rom. 6:23). Jesus is stripping sin of any glamour with which the devil may disguise it. Sin brings bondage. The only true freedom is found in Jesus. Jesus not only dealt with the original sin that contaminated the human race, but He also dealt with each individual act of sin. Even if an individual could stop all sinning, he could not change his sin nature with which he was born. That's the reason we must be born again.

JUNE 18
ABRAHAM'S CHILDREN
JOHN 8:33-38

John 8:37 "I know that ye are Abraham's seed; but ye seek to kill me, because my word hath no place in you."

The Jewish people were direct descendants of Abraham. However, as with so many biblical truths, there was much more to the Abrahamic covenant than what a casual glimpse would reveal. In truth, these Jews were not actually a part of the spiritual children of Abraham.

The Holy Spirit revealed through the Apostle Paul in Galatians 3:16 and 29 that God's covenant was to Abraham and his singular "seed" or descendant, which was Christ. No one ever became an heir of God's promises through his natural birth. Before Jesus gave Himself as an offering for our sins, the Old Testament saints were justified by faith in God's promises concerning the Messiah who was yet to come. After Jesus' death and resurrection, New Testament saints are justified by faith in what Jesus has already accomplished. No one has ever been saved because of who his parents are.

Those who have been born again through faith in Jesus have been circumcised in their hearts (Col. 2:11-12) and are the true Jews. They aren't Jews in nationality or religion, but are the true people of God. Gentiles who are united with Christ in the new birth are now God's people. Anyone who is saved through faith in Jesus is now Abraham's seed and an heir according to the promise (Gal. 3:16, 22, 26-29). This leaves no doubt that the church is now God's chosen people on earth. This does not mean that God has forsaken the Jews. There are still prophesies that apply to the physical nation of Israel that will be fulfilled. However, the New Testament church, composed of Jews and Gentiles, is now God's kingdom on earth. We are all His.

JUNE 19
THE OLD MAN IS GONE
JOHN 8:39-47

John 8:44 "Ye are of your father the devil, and the lusts of your father ye will do: he was a murderer from the beginning, and abode not in the truth, because there is no truth in him. When he speaketh a lie, he speaketh of his own: for he is a liar, and the father of it."

All of us were born into sin; therefore we were by nature, children of the devil. That's the reason we sinned. Our sins don't corrupt our natures, but our corrupt natures make us sin. That's why we must be "born again" and become new creatures (or a new creation) in Christ.

The scriptures teach that everyone was born with a sin nature or old man. For the Christian, the old man is dead. We do not have a nature that is driving us to sin. If that it is the case, then why do we seem so bound to sin even after we experience the new birth? The reason is because our old man left behind what Romans 6:6 calls a body. Just as a person's spirit and soul leave behind a physical body at death, so our old man left behind habits and strongholds in our thoughts and emotions. The reason a Christian tends to sin is because of an unrenewed mind, not because of a sin nature.

Our old man ruled our thinking before we were born again. He taught us such things as selfishness, hatred, and fear. He also placed within us the desire for sin. The old man is now gone, but the negative parts of his body remain. Until renewed, our minds continue to lead us on the course that our old man charted.

To experience the resurrection life of Jesus, we have to know that our old man is dead. Then, through the renewing of our minds, we destroy the body that the old man left behind. The end result is that we will not serve sin any longer.

JUNE 20
WHAT PLEASES GOD
JOHN 8:53-56

John 8:56 "Your father Abraham rejoiced to see my day: and he saw it, and was glad."
Jesus is referring to the day when men would be justified by putting faith in God and not in their own works. Abraham had this truth revealed to him (Rom. 4:13), and he believed it and was himself justified by faith (Rom. 4:3-4,9).

Hebrews 11:6 says, *"But without faith it is impossible to please him."* It was Abraham's faith that pleased God. The Lord promised Abraham that his seed would be as numerous as the stars in the sky and the sand on the seashore and Abraham believed God. That pleased Him so much that he counted Abraham righteous right then, even though Abraham had not yet fulfilled the rite of circumcision and was not living a holy life.

According to Leviticus 18:9, it was an abomination (Lev. 18:26) for a man to marry a half sister. Sarah, Abraham's wife, was his half sister (Gen. 20:12). Therefore, Abraham's marriage to Sarah was not what pleased God. Abraham had already lied about Sarah not being his wife so that he could save his own neck. He was willing to let a man commit adultery with his wife with no objections from him. Immediately after this instance is when the Lord counted Abraham's faith for righteousness (Gen. 15:6). Abraham tried to accomplish God's will in the flesh with Hagar (Gen. 16), and then repeated the terrible sin of denying that Sarah was his wife again (Gen. 20).

Anyone who really studies the life of Abraham and the favor that he found with God would have to conclude that it was Abraham's faith that pleased God. It's the same with any of us. The only thing that we can do to please God is put faith in Jesus as our Savior.

JUNE 21
GOD MADE FLESH
JOHN 8:57-59

John 8:58 "Jesus said unto them, Verily, verily, I say unto you,
Before Abraham was, I am."
Jesus didn't seek to clarify the Jews' misunderstanding of His previous statements. Instead, He made a new statement, that those who didn't believe that He was God in the flesh (1 Tim. 3:16), could not possibly understand. "Before Abraham was, I am." He not only said that He existed before Abraham, but He was again associating Himself with the great "I AM" statement of Exodus 3:14. This statement could leave no doubt that Jesus was claiming deity in the highest sense of the word.

Jesus proclaimed, "I am." This is how Jehovah identified Himself to Moses in Exodus 3:14. When spoken under the anointing power of God, Jesus' pronouncement: "I am he," knocked all of those who came to arrest Him backwards to the ground (Jn. 18:5-6). Jesus was the great "I AM THAT I AM" of Exodus 3:14 manifest in the flesh!

When the Jewish authorities heard Jesus call God his "own" Father, they immediately understood that Jesus claimed for Himself deity in the highest possible sense of that term. That claim was either blasphemy to be punished by death, or Jesus was who He claimed to be.

The purpose of the fourth Gospel is clearly stated, "That ye might believe that Jesus is the Christ, the Son of God; and that believing ye might have life through his name" (Jn. 20:31). The object of John's Gospel was to show that Jesus is, "the true God" (1 Jn. 5:20) who was "made flesh" (Jn. 1:14).

JUNE 22
SICKNESS IS NOT FROM GOD
JOHN 9:1-4

John 9:2 "And his disciples asked him saying, Master, who did sin, this man, or his parents, that he was born blind?"

The disciples asked a question that still puzzles many people today. Why is a child born with a physical defect? Is it a judgment of God upon the parents for some sin, or is it possibly God's judgment upon the child for sins that God knows he will commit?

Jesus Himself had previously linked sickness with sin. In this instance, however, Jesus said this blindness was not caused by this man's or his parents' sins.

This has led many people to interpret the rest of this verse as saying that God made this man blind just so that He could heal him and be glorified thereby. From this thinking, many doctrinal teachings have risen about how sickness and other problems in our lives are actually blessings from God, intended to bring glory to God and correction to us. This reasoning, however, does not line up with the other truths of God's Word.

It was not God who made this beggar blind. This man was not born blind because of any one person's sins, but because sin in general had corrupted the perfect balance that God had created in nature. Therefore, some maladies happen, not as a direct result of an individual's sins, but as an indirect result of sin in general.

Deuteronomy 28 settles forever the question of whether sickness, poverty, and oppression are really blessings in disguise. God says that sickness and poverty are curses—not blessings from God. Christ redeemed us from these curses of the law so that now the blessings may come upon us through Him (Galations 3:13). God's curses have been placed on Jesus and removed from those who accept Jesus' sacrifice. You are blessed!

JUNE 23
LOVE CONQUERS FEAR
JOHN 9:6-27

John 9:27 "He answered them, I have told you already, and ye did not hear: wherefore would ye hear it again? will ye also be his disciples?"

This man showed great courage in confronting these religious leaders. Even Peter later backed down for fear of this same group of men (Lk. 22:54-62). Certainly one thing that gave him this boldness was that he knew what Jesus had done for him. Even beyond the physical healing, he knew that Jesus had healed him because He loved him. It's our security in the Lord's love for us that gives us the strength to face rejection from others. As Proverbs 28:1 puts it, "The righteous are bold as a lion." The antidote for fear of men is a large dose of the love of God.

One of the greatest truths of the Bible and one of the hardest to comprehend, is that we are the objects of God's love. God didn't just pity us or feel some sense of moral obligation to save us. He saved us because of His infinite love for us (Jn. 3:16). An experiential understanding of God's love is the key to being filled with all the fullness of God (Eph. 3:19).

Paul prays in Ephesians 3:19, that we would experience the love of God which passes mere knowledge about it. How can we know the love of God if it passes knowledge? This sounds like a contradiction. It's not. The knowing is experiencing it. The end result of having understanding and experiential knowledge of God's love is that we will be filled with all the fullness of God. God's love is the key that opens the door to everything that God is. God is love (1 Jn. 4:8).

It's not just a casual acquaintance with God's love that we need, but an intimate understanding and experiential knowledge of the depths of God's love. Just as a tree's roots provide stability and nourishment for the tree, so our revelation of God's love is the foundation upon which everything else we receive from God is built.

JUNE 24
IT'S WHO YOU KNOW
JOHN 9:28-30

John 9:30 "The man answered and said unto them, Why herein is a marvellous thing, that ye know not from whence he is, and yet he hath opened mine eyes."

The "acid test" of whether someone is of God is by his actions. Jesus' actions were so miraculous and overwhelmingly consistent with God's Word that any reservations about whether He was of God should have been set aside. But, as in Mark 7:13, the Pharisees and some of the teachers of the law had exalted their own traditions above God's Word, thereby making the Word of God of no effect in their own lives. Just as in this instance nearly two thousand years ago, theologians today are sometimes the last to accept a move of God if it violates their traditional beliefs. "The common people heard him gladly" (Mk. 12:37). "Knowledge puffeth up, but charity edifieth" (1 Cor. 8: 1).

In spiritual matters, a person can educate himself in theology to the degree that it does more harm than good. It is possible to win a theological battle and yet lose the war for a person's heart. Arguments over points of theology often distract from the more important issues. There is no premium on ignorance, but love is infinitely superior to knowledge. We should learn all we can, but we must make our knowledge a servant to love. "The greatest of these is love" (1 Cor. 13:13).

If anyone's quest for knowledge leads him away from knowing God, then it would have been preferable for him to stay ignorant. What we know is not as important as who we know (speaking of the Lord). Our most important goal in life must be to love God and be known of Him.

JUNE 25
ABOUT THOSE PHARISEES
JOHN 9:34

John 9:34 "They answered and said unto him, Thou wast altogether born in sins, and dost thou teach us? And they cast him out."

Much of the Pharisees' problem was spiritual pride, as is evident by this statement. They were so blinded by their arrogance that they couldn't believe that anyone who hadn't been through their "seminary" could teach them anything.

The name "Pharisees" comes from a Hebrew word meaning "separate." This term was applied to this sect because of its extreme devotion to the Mosaic law and commitment to leading a separated life. This was a reaction of the devout Jews who came back to Jerusalem from the Babylonian captivity, and saw the pagan customs and influences of the Babylonians everywhere. Not only their religion, but their identity as a nation was being threatened. The Pharisees were patriots as well as religious zealots, who in the beginning served a very needed function in the Jewish nation that was struggling for survival. However, over the centuries, the Pharisees had departed from the Mosaic law and had written their own interpretations of the law—interpretations that they held to be God-inspired and equal to that of Moses. In Jesus' day this group was characterized by hypocrisy and self-righteousness. They, as a whole, persecuted Jesus and His followers and received the Lord's most stinging rebukes.

The Pharisees, like many people today, were ignorant of achieving right standing (righteousness) with God through the simple act of receiving His forgiveness by faith. They were trying to earn salvation by their own acts. No one can fulfill God's commands (Rom. 3:23) except Jesus (Heb. 4:15). Therefore, to be righteous, we must put our faith in what He has done for us.

JUNE 26
JESUS FOUND HIM
JOHN 9:35

John 9:35 "Jesus heard that they had cast him out; and when he had found him, he said unto him, Dost thou believe on the Son of God?"

It is one thing to seek God; it is quite another thing to have God seek you. Jesus sought this man out when others had forsaken him. The acceptance of Jesus is worth more than everything this world has to offer. This is what enables the believer to endure and even leap for joy amidst persecution. When our sufferings in Christ abound, then the consolation of Christ abounds much more. Notice that this man's parents, who knew the truth, but refused to share it for fear of persecution, did not have Jesus seeking them out (Jn 9:22). They chose the company of the hypocritical scribes and Pharisees, which is exactly what they got.

Even though believers are redeemed and delivered from many afflictions that were a result of sin and its power, we are still called to partake in what the scriptures call the "sufferings or afflictions of Christ" (2 Cor. 1:5; Col. 1:24). However, these afflictions are not sickness and poverty as some religious teachings suggest. These afflictions are described as the "fellowship of sufferings" that the believer will encounter for doing the will of God, or the sufferings brought on by one's allegiance to Christ.

Persecution for righteousness' sake is not something that we can rebuke (2 Tim. 3:12). We must remember that as we live godly lives, suffering will follow. The Apostle Peter reminds us that these trials of our faith will result in praise, honor and glory at the appearing of Jesus Christ (1 Pet. 1:7). Jesus' comfort, strength, help, and love are ready to overflow into every trial that we face, if we will only look to Him (Heb. 12:2).

JUNE 27
HEARING GOD'S VOICE
JOHN 10:1-21

John 10:2-3 "But he that entereth in by the door is the shepherd of the sheep. To him the porter openeth; and the sheep hear his voice: and he calleth his own sheep by name, and leadeth them out."

This verse promises all who are God's sheep that they not only can, but that they do hear His voice. Many born-again people doubt the truth of this statement based on their experiences. They don't think they can hear God's voice; however, the Word of God is true—not our experiences.

The harmony between what this verse says and what our experiences say is that it is our new born-again spirits that hear God's voice. Although God has spoken and still does speak in an audible voice at times, very few people experience this. God speaks to your inner person (spirit) and your inner person hears Him. The problem comes when we aren't sensitive to, or controlled by our spirits, but are walking in the vanity of our minds. The Bible calls this walking in the flesh instead of the Spirit (Gal. 5:16-18).

Man is a spirit, soul, and body. Our spirits are as perfect as they will ever be in heaven. If we will change our thinking so that we believe what God says in His Word about who we are and what we have, then this agreement between our spirits and souls forms a majority and our flesh will experience the life of God that has been deposited in our spirits.

Prayer, Bible study, fasting and fellowship are ways of refocusing our mind's attention away from the voice of this world and back to the voice of our Shepherd who is constantly communicating with our spirits. If we fail to renew our minds, we can live our entire time on earth without experiencing the abundant life that Jesus provided for us. Listen, and you will hear His voice speak to you through His Word today.

JUNE 28
LIFE OF GOD
JOHN 10:7-10

John 10:10 "The thief cometh not, but for to steal, and to kill, and to destroy: I am come that they might have life, and that they might have it more abundantly."

The Greek word translated "life" here is "zoe" and it means life in the absolute sense or life as God has it. Everyone who is breathing has life in the sense of physical existence, but only those who receive Jesus can experience life as God intended it to be. Jesus came to not only save us from the torment of eternal hell, but to give us this "zoe" or God-kind of life in abundance. The life of God is not awaiting us in heaven, but is presently possessed by every born-again person in his spirit. We can release this "zoe" life and enjoy it now by losing our natural lives and finding this supernatural life. The way we lose our lives is to deny any thoughts, emotions, or actions that are contrary to the Word of God, which is life ("zoe" in Jn. 6:63). When we line our thoughts, emotions, and actions up with the instructions of God's Word, then we will find this "zoe" life manifest in our bodies and souls as well.

The Word is spiritual and must be understood through the spirit (1 Cor. 2:14). The Bible is simply a physical representation of Jesus and spiritual truth. It is inspired of God; therefore, it is totally accurate and reliable, yet until we receive the spirit that these words express, the Bible will not profit us (Heb. 4:2).

If we want to know what spiritual truth is, we must believe the Bible, for it is spirit and life. If we want to be led by the Spirit, then we must follow God's Word. If we want to hear from the Spirit of God, then we must listen to what God says in His Word. The Spirit (Holy Spirit) and the Word (Jesus-Jn. 1:1) are one (1 Jn. 5:7).

JUNE 29
GROW IN GRACE
LUKE 9:54-56

Luke 9:55 "But he turned, and rebuked them, and said, Ye know not what manner of spirit ye are of."

Jesus was constantly being accused of breaking the law of Moses. He taught different lessons than what was taught in the law of Moses (Mt. 5:21-48), and now He rebukes His disciples for desiring to do what an Old Testament prophet did with God's blessing and power. However, Jesus didn't come to destroy the law, but to fulfill it.

Jesus came not to destroy men's lives, but to save them (Jn. 3:16; 10:10). "God was in Christ, reconciling the world unto himself, not imputing their trespasses unto them" (2 Cor. 5:19). Jesus was just in doing this because He bore our sins (Isa. 53:4-6) and the accompanying wrath of God (Mt. 27:46; Heb. 2:9). Jesus didn't reject God's judgment against sin; He bore it (2 Cor. 5:21). Therefore, He was able to extend the grace and mercy of God to those who would have been doomed under the law of Moses (Acts 13:38-39).

The Old Testament law was like a judge passing sentence upon sin. Jesus became our advocate (lawyer). Even more than that, He became our substitute, bearing "our sins in his own body on the tree" (1 Pet. 2:24). He didn't destroy God's judgment; He fulfilled it in Himself so that we could go free. This forever changed God's dealings with sinful man. In light of what Jesus has done in the New Covenant, we would be rebuked for trying to release God's wrath upon others as was done in the Old Covenant. Likewise, if Jesus would have been on the earth in His physical body, reconciling the world unto Himself in the days of Elijah, then Elijah would have been rebuked for his actions, as recorded in 2 Kings 1:9-15. There is a difference between Old Testament law and New Testament grace. "For the law was given by Moses, but grace and truth came by Jesus Christ" (Jn. 1:17). Grow in grace.

JUNE 30
THE COST OF LIVING FOR CHRIST
MATTHEW 8:18-22; LUKE 9:51-62

Luke 9:58 "And Jesus said unto him, Foxes have holes, and birds of the air have nests; but the Son of man hath not where to lay his head."

This verse has often been used to support the misconception that Jesus and His disciples lived in poverty. However, in this instance, the reason why Jesus had nowhere to lay His head was because of persecution. The Samaritans, because of a religious prejudice, had just refused Him hospitality and a place to stay as He journeyed to Jerusalem. Persecution is part of the cost of living a Christian life. Jesus was communicating to this man that not having a place to stay at times was part of that cost.

There are many forms of persecution. Having your life threatened because of your faith in Jesus is one way you can be persecuted, but it is not the most damaging. History shows that the Church has always flourished under persecution with increased numbers and zeal. During intense, life-threatening persecution, people's priorities get straightened out and the Lord assumes His rightful place. This always works for our good, regardless of what our outward circumstances might be.

A far more deadly form of persecution is men simply speaking evil of you or separating you from their company. It's more deadly because it's more subtle. Many who would never directly deny the Lord will fall into self-pity or strife because of someone's criticism. This will render one just as ineffective as a negative reaction to having one's life threatened would.

It helps to recognize that it is not you that they are persecuting, but rather Christ in you. You are actually becoming a partaker of His sufferings and will share His rewards. With this in mind, we can actually shout and leap for joy in persecution!

JULY 1
SHARING GOD'S LOVE
LUKE 10:1-2

Luke 10:2 "Therefore said he unto them, The harvest truly is great, but the laborers are few: pray ye therefore the Lord of the harvest, that he would send forth laborers into his harvest."

It is commonly thought that an evangelist is someone who has a passion to lead people to the Lord. But every believer should have a passion for souls. When presenting the Gospel, we are not just presenting a theory about God, but the factual account of God's dealings with man as revealed through His Word, with the ultimate witness being the bodily resurrection of Jesus. Our personal witness of the reality of Jesus being alive in our lives brings Christ from theory to reality.

The early Christians had experienced the love of Christ in an intimate and life transforming way. This motivated them to reach their known world with the Gospel of Christ more than any generation of Christians has done since. They didn't have the benefits of our modern technology, but they did have the benefit of being full of the love of Christ. Experiencing the love of Christ causes us to be filled with the fullness of God (Eph. 3:19) and makes us a witness that the world cannot resist (Jn. 13:35).

Today, much of the emphasis of the Church is placed on techniques of evangelism or spiritual warfare. We motivate people to witness through feelings of guilt or punishment if they don't. Much of our evangelism has become as dead and non-productive as that of the cults who knock on doors and argue people into their way of thinking. The early Christians had a much greater impact on their world because they were full of, and motivated by, the love of God. The Church today needs a revival of their personal relationship with the Lord. When we can say with Paul that the love of Christ constrains us, then we will impact our world for the Lord, too. You can't give away what you don't possess. We need to personally know the love of Christ in an experiential way before we try to share it with others.

JULY 2
GOD'S PEACE
LUKE 10:5-6

Luke 10:5 "And into whatsoever house ye enter, first say, Peace be to this house."

Peace is the result of casting our care upon the Lord through prayer and thanksgiving. However, many people are asking God to give them peace so that their cares will leave. It doesn't work that way. Through faith we cast our cares on the Lord and then God's peace comes. Christians who are lacking God's peace have not taken their cares to the Lord and left them there. All Christians have peace. It is a fruit of the Spirit that is always present in our born again spirits. Cares will blind us to God's peace. When we eliminate the cares, peace flows.

Being carnally-minded doesn't just tend towards death, it is death. Likewise, being spiritually minded doesn't just tend towards life, it is life and peace. A person who says he is spiritually-minded, yet is experiencing death is deceived. If we would just dominate ourselves with the spiritual truths of God's Word, we would receive only life and peace.

True peace that comes from God, only comes through grace and faith. No one who seeks to obtain right standing with God by his own effort will ever have God's peace. Human peace is only experienced in the absence of problems. Those who only know human peace don't experience it very often and to a lesser degree. God's peace is independent of circumstances and is infinitely greater in supply than any problem we could ever have. God has given us His supernatural peace to enjoy. What a blessing!

JULY 3
POWER IN THE NAME OF JESUS
LUKE 10:17-18

Luke 10:17 "And the seventy returned again with joy, saying, Lord, even the devils are subject unto us through thy name."

It was the power in the name of Jesus, plus the disciples' faith in that power, that made the demons subject unto them. This can clearly be seen in Acts 19:13-17, where certain Jews called on the name of Jesus in an effort to cast demons out of a man. They used the name of Jesus, but it didn't work because they had not put faith in that name.

These Jews were vagabonds who used incantations to affect deliverance for people who were demon possessed. The first century historian, Josephus, wrote of an exorcism that he witnessed in the presence of Vespasian and many of his soldiers. The exorcist supposedly followed a ritual passed down from King Solomon to affect the deliverance. There is no doubt that men throughout all history have tried to resist demonic spirits, but as this example proves, only Jesus and those who have received His life are successful.

Those who relegate demonic spirits to the realm of superstition do not believe in the entire Word of God. The Gospels alone contain over 90 references to the devil or devils (demons). The Apostle Paul said when writing to these people in Ephesus, "We wrestle not against flesh and blood, but against principalities, against powers, against the rulers of the darkness of this world, against spiritual wickedness in high places" (Eph. 6:12). The devil and demons do exist, but all believers in Jesus share in His total victory over them.

The name of Jesus is not magic. It does not work like a charm. As Peter said, "His name, through faith in his name" (Acts 3:16), is what brings results.

JULY 4
FREEDOM FROM TEMPTATION
LUKE 10:19-20

Luke 10:19 *"Behold, I give unto you power to tread on serpents and scorpions, and over all the power of the enemy: and nothing shall by any means hurt you."*

Although these are examples of God's protection from harm caused by the physical creation, this scripture is also speaking of mastery over the spiritual realm of the enemy (Satan). This scripture does not say that Satan cannot inflict any harm. The scriptures abound with examples and warnings of the enemy's damage on the godly and the ungodly alike (2 Cor. 2:11; 2 Tim. 2:26; 1 Pet. 5:8-9). However, he cannot harm us when we are walking in faith in Christ's redemptive work.

There are no unique temptations. The devil likes to make us think there are. If he can convince us that no one understands, no one has ever had this problem before, then he can isolate us and take away our hope. But any temptation we face is just some variation of the same old thing. It may come in a different sized box, be wrapped in a different paper and have a different bow, but the contents are the same. Understanding this diffuses much of the power of temptation.

Even though temptation is universal to mankind, we are not left on our own. God is faithful. Jesus was tempted in all points as we are, yet he overcame every time (Heb. 4:15). Part of His ministry is to specifically aid us in overcoming temptation (Heb. 2:17-18). Most of us have experienced times when we thought we couldn't resist another minute. Either we were wrong, or we were on the verge of a breakthrough. The Lord promised that He would not allow us to be tempted above what we are able to bear. So, at those times when you can't stand another minute, stand two and this promise will pull you through.

JULY 5
FOCUS ON JESUS
LUKE 10:20-25

Luke 10:20 *"Notwithstanding, in this rejoice not that the spirits are subject unto you; but rather, rejoice because your names are written in heaven."*

We were never instructed to have a Ph.D. in demonology; however, some people justify focusing on Satan and his activity to an inordinate degree. This will actually encourage demonic activity and become a device that Satan can use against us.

As Paul said, we should not be *"ignorant"* of Satan's devices; we need to know that the devil and demons exist. We need to recognize when we are facing demonic activity, but we need to keep our focus on the Lord. Some people who are excessive in spiritual warfare actually spend more time talking to the devil each day than they do talking to God. That's not right.

The best defense against the devil is to be so God-centered that we give no place to Satan. People who are very sensitive to the devil's presence usually are so at the expense of being sensitive to the Lord's presence. David said, *"If I make my bed in hell, behold, thou art there"* (Ps. 139:8). Any time Satan's oppression is there, God's presence is there too (Heb. 13:5). It's just a matter of which one we focus on. Focusing on the devil is a trick of the devil.

Our total ability in the Christian life is found in Christ. It is not our ability that makes us strong, but our availability to Christ that enables us. Paul said, *"For when I am weak, then am I strong"* (2 Cor. 12:10). He was saying that when he recognized his inability, and relied on the Lord, is when the Lord's strength flowed through him. We can do all things THROUGH CHRIST.

JULY 6
SAVED BY GRACE
LUKE 10:25-29

Luke 10:28-29 "And he said unto him, Thou hast answered right: this do, and thou shalt live. But he, willing to justify himself, said unto Jesus, And who is my neighbor?"

Just as with this lawyer, pride causes many people to resist the truth of justification by faith in the grace of God. This lawyer loved himself and the public recognition his holy acts brought him. He was not willing to love God first and his fellow man ahead of himself. His was not a sincere question, but rather an evasive question, seeking to shun responsibility. This man was seeking to be justified in the sight of God through his actions. He knew he had not loved everyone as he loved himself, so he tried to interpret the scripture (Lev. 19:18) in a way that would conform to his actions. He wanted to define "neighbor" as just his close friends whom he had treated well. Self-justification always produces excuses, while repentance and faith towards God produces obedience.

The basis of our salvation is grace—that is, God's undeserved, unmerited favor towards us as expressed in providing redemption through Christ Jesus. The means of God saving us is through faith. Through faith we accept God's free gift of salvation which was provided by grace. So we are saved *"by grace...through faith."* Notice that we are not saved by grace alone. We are saved by grace through faith. Faith grants us admission to God's grace. Without faith, God's grace is wasted and without grace, faith is powerless. Faith in God's grace has to be released to receive what God has provided through Christ.

Just as sodium and chloride are poisonous by themselves, so grace or faith used independently of each other are deadly. But when you mix sodium and chloride together in the proper way, you get salt, which you must have to live. Likewise, putting faith in what God has already provided by grace is the key to victorious Christian living.

JULY 7
WHO CROSSES YOUR PATH?
LUKE 10:29-37

Luke 10:29 "But he, willing to justify himself, said unto Jesus, And who is my neighbor?"

This question, "Who is my neighbor?" can be used by Satan to deceive us in more than one way. Not only can he deceive men into thinking they have fulfilled the command to "love thy neighbor as thyself," when they haven't, but he will also try to apply this command in a way that condemns those who are seeking to fulfill it, by making them think they are not doing enough.

We cannot meet the needs of every single person in the world. Jesus wasn't teaching that. This wounded man was directly in the path of these three men. The priest and the Levite had to walk around him. Jesus is simply teaching that we should take advantage of the opportunities we have. Just because we can't help everyone is no excuse not to help anyone.

Jesus, through this parable, defined a neighbor as any fellow human being that crosses our path and is in need of our assistance. The Samaritan went to the full extent of his ability and beyond, to help the man. The priest and Levite did nothing.

There was a racial and religious hatred between Jews and Samaritans. Devout Jews would not associate with or even talk to a Samaritan. The priest and the Levite who passed by this wounded man were his fellow ountrymen, yet they didn't help him. This Samaritan, who was considered by religious Jews to be of another nationality, was the true neighbor. Jesus made it clear that you could not define "neighbor" on the basis of geographic origin or your familiarity with someone. A neighbor is anyone who God puts in your path.

JULY 8
SEEK FIRST THE KINGDOM
LUKE 10:38-42

Luke 10:40 "But Martha was cumbered about with much serving, and came to him, and said, Lord dost thou not care that my sister hath left me to serve alone? bid her therefore that she help me."

There are only three instances in scripture that give us information about Martha. From these accounts, we can see that Martha had a brother named Lazarus, whom Jesus raised from the dead, and a sister named Mary. Martha had misplaced her priorities on this occasion and was corrected by Jesus. Later, at a supper for Jesus in the home of Simon the leper, Martha was once again serving while Mary, her sister, was worshipping Jesus by anointing His feet with costly perfume.

Martha was the first one to run and meet Jesus when He came to their home after the death of Lazarus. It was at this time that Martha said she knew Jesus could have prevented Lazarus from dying and that, even then, she knew He could raise him from the dead. She made a confession of faith in the deity of Jesus, every bit as strong as Peter's, which received a blessing from Jesus.

Martha was not wrong in serving Jesus and His disciples. Other women ministered to Jesus in this way without being corrected. Serving was a good thing, but Martha had put it in the wrong place. Her problem was priorities—not what she was doing. It was a great honor to have Jesus in her home and to hear His personal words for them. Martha should have given this the same priority that Mary did.

Just like Martha, many people today are occupied with things that keep them from hearing the words of Jesus. It is easy to recognize and turn from things that are obviously sin, but even good things that we are involved in must be prioritized so that nothing takes the place of seeking first the Kingdom of God.

JULY 9
PRAYER POWER
LUKE 11:1-4

Luke 11:1 "And it came to pass, that, as he was praying in a certain place, when he ceased, one of his disciples said unto him, 'Lord, teach us to pray, as John also taught his disciples.'"

When you consider that Jesus was the greatest miracle worker who ever walked the earth and the greatest preacher who ever lived, it is amazing that His disciples asked Him to teach them to pray. Why didn't they ask Him to teach them how to work these miracles or how to preach and amaze the people with their doctrine?

It's because Jesus' prayer life was even more powerful than His miracles or His doctrine. Indeed, it was His union with the Father that gave Him His power to work miracles and His authority to speak as no man had ever spoken before. Jesus said repeatedly that it was His Father who was doing the miracles through Him and that His doctrine was not His own, but the Father's.

The same holds true today. Jesus said in John 15:5, that without Him, we can do nothing. There are many things that we should do in addition to praying, but there is nothing that we can effectively do without prayer. Prayer is one of the main ways of abiding in Him (Jn. 15:7). Therefore, our requests should be like these disciples': "Lord, teach us to pray."

We should come expecting to receive answers to prayer. The Father is ready and willing to answer our prayers. Just ask and you shall receive.

JULY 10
OUR LOVING FATHER
LUKE 11:11-13

Luke 11:11 "If a son shall ask bread of any of you that is a father, will he give him a stone? or if he ask a fish, will he for a fish give him a serpent?"

The most loving father in the world cannot compare to our heavenly Father and the love He has for us. Although many times, we find it easier to believe in the willingness of a father, mother or mate to help us than in the willingness of God to use His power on our behalf. Relatively few people really doubt God's ability, but doubt His willingness to use His ability on their behalf, which causes them to do without. Jesus is assuring us that God's love, and His willingness to demonstrate that love, is far greater than we can ever experience in any human relationship.

The Lord didn't just save us out of pity or a sense of obligation as our Creator; He saved us because He loved us (Jn. 3:16). It was the *"good pleasure of his will"* for us to become adopted sons (Eph.1:5). We are wanted and accepted by our Father. What a wonderful thing this is! It would have been more than any of us deserve to be forgiven by God. Then to be given certain rights and privileges would have been more than we could have expected. The Lord even went further than that. He has actually accepted us. The dictionary defines "accept" as, "to receive gladly; to receive into a place or a group" (NAHD). The Lord does not just tolerate us. He actually loves us. He even likes us. He rejoices over us with joy (Zeph. 3:17).

JULY 11
BE FILLED
LUKE 11:13

Luke 11:13 "If ye then, being evil, know how to give good gifts unto your children: how much more shall your heavenly Father give the Holy Spirit to them that ask him?"

The Holy Spirit is a gift (Acts 2:38). You cannot be good enough to earn the gift of the Holy Spirit, but you do have to ask for it. This is speaking of the baptism of the Holy Ghost, which is subsequent to the born again experience.

The Holy Spirit resides in our spirits and once He comes, He doesn't leave (Jn. 14:16). There is an initial filling when the Holy Ghost first comes; however, His control and influence over our souls and bodies does fluctuate proportionally to how well we renew our minds to His will (Rom. 12:2). In that sense, we can be more full of the Holy Ghost than at other times, although in our spirits the presence and power of the Holy Spirit does not come and go. Therefore, even after we receive the baptism of the Holy Ghost, there will be times when our souls and bodies stray from the leadership of the Holy Spirit, and we need, once again, to be filled with the Holy Spirit.

In Ephesians 5:18, believers are commanded to ". . . be not drunk with wine. . . but be filled with the Spirit." Being filled with the Holy Spirit is in the present tense, making it a continual command for the believer. In the book of Acts, the same people who were filled with the Holy Spirit on the day of Pentecost were filled again. Most people don't get drunk on just one drink. Likewise, being filled with the Holy Spirit is not just a one-time experience. There is an initial filling of the Holy Spirit, but many subsequent fillings. Just as drunkenness can change a person's personality and make him act totally different, so being filled with the Holy Spirit can make us act just like Jesus. Be filled with the Spirit today.

JULY 12
GROW IN GRACE
LUKE 11:37-41

Luke 11:38 "And when the Pharisee saw it, he marveled that he had not first washed before dinner."

A sure sign of the error of legalism is misplaced priorities, as we see here with these Pharisees. It is not recorded in Scripture that the Pharisees marveled at the wonderful works of Jesus. They were too busy looking for something to criticize (Mk. 3:2). They did marvel at Jesus not washing his hands. This is a classic example of "straining at a gnat and swallowing a camel" (Mt. 23:24).

Those who seek to earn righteousness through keeping the law are consumed with "doing," while those who receive righteousness by faith are simply confessing what has already been done. This is a simple, yet profound difference. If we are still "doing" acts of holiness to get God to move in our lives, then we are still operating under a "law" mentality that is not faith (Gal. 3:12). When we simply believe and confess what has already been provided through Christ, that's grace.

A person who is living under the law, and a person who lives under grace should have similar actions of holiness, but their motivations are completely opposite. The legalist has his attention on what he must do, while the person living by faith has his attention on what Christ has already done for him. For instance, the Scriptures teach us to confess with our mouths and believe with our hearts and we will receive from God. The legalist thinks, *I can get God to heal me by confessing, "By his stripes I am healed."* However, the person who understands God's grace will not confess the Word to get healed. He will confess, "By his stripes I am healed," because he really believes it has already been done.

Analyzing our mind-set is the simplest way of discerning whether we are operating in true biblical faith, or in a legalistic counterfeit. If the motive for our actions is to be accepted by God, that's legalism. If we live wholly out of faith and gratefulness for what God has already done, that's grace. Grow in grace!

JULY 13
HOLINESS IS A FRUIT
LUKE 11:42-44

Luke 11:42 "But woe unto you, Pharisees! for ye tithe mint and rue and all manner of herbs, and pass over judgement and the love of God: these ought ye to have done and not to leave the other undone."

When Jesus said, *"and not to leave the other undone,"* it is clear that He is not arguing against doing what is right. God's Word stresses holiness in our actions. The Pharisees' error that caused Jesus' rebuke was that they believed their actions could produce a right relationship with God. A proper relationship with God can only come by humbling ourselves and putting faith in a Savior, who is Jesus. God cleanses our hearts by grace through faith (Eph. 2:8), and then we have our fruit unto holiness (Rom. 6:22). Holiness is a fruit, not a root of salvation.

In a similar instance found in Matthew 23:26, Jesus told the Pharisees, "Thou blind Pharisee, cleanse first that which is within the cup and platter, that the outside of them may be clean also." True Christianity comes from the inside out. A good heart will change a man's actions, but a man's actions cannot change his heart.

One of religion's favorite doctrines is that if you will just act right, you will be right. Nothing could be further from the truth. You must be born again. If you are born again, then holiness is a by-product and not the way to a relationship with God.

This is the heart of the Gospel. Every major religion of the world has a moral standard it enforces, but only Christianity offers salvation through a Savior. Presenting holiness in any way other than as a result of salvation is denying Jesus as our Savior and places the burden of salvation on us. Improper emphasis on achieving holiness or salvation through one's own actions can damn that person. We must trust Jesus completely.

JULY 14
JESUS, THE WISDOM OF GOD
LUKE 11:46-49

Luke 11:49 "Therefore also said the wisdom of God, I will send them prophets and apostles, and some of them they shall slay and persecute."

This phrase, "Therefore also said the wisdom of God," is a part of Luke's narrative and not the words of Jesus. Luke is saying that Jesus is the wisdom of God, a truth well-established in scripture.

There is no way to access the wisdom of God except through Jesus. Until a person receives Christ, he is missing the only source of true wisdom. Men and women are incapable of receiving the wisdom of God, but those who submit themselves to God have access to the wisdom of God on their own, through the Holy Spirit. We must be dependent upon the Holy Spirit to receive the wisdom of God in our lives.

A Christian who has not received the baptism of the Holy Spirit can have some revelation knowledge, but it will be limited. One of the greatest evidences that an individual has received the baptism of the Holy Spirit is the tremendous amount of God's wisdom that becomes available to him.

The truths of the Gospel, and the power of God that these truths release, can only be imparted through the anointing of the Holy Spirit. Human wisdom, regardless of how eloquent it is, cannot convey the life of God. Much of the preaching of the Gospel today is done in man's wisdom. It's impressive to the carnal mind, but it leaves the spirit starving for the touch of God. The greatest need among ministers today is not to have more of the world's education, but to receive the revelation knowledge of the Holy Spirit. Only words spoken by the Spirit of God can reach the spirit of man. Spiritual thoughts have to be spoken with spiritual words (1 Cor. 2:13).

JULY 15
HYPOCRISY IS...
LUKE 12:1-3

Luke 12:1 "In the mean time, when there were gathered together an innumerable multitude of people, insomuch that they trode one upon another, he began to say unto his disciples first of all, Beware ye of the leaven of the Pharisees, which is hypocrisy."

This is the biblical definition of a hypocrite: "Someone whose words and heart (actions) don't agree." A hypocrite may act the part of a Christian or talk like Christ, but he won't do both. Hypocrisy is defined by the dictionary as, "The feigning of beliefs, feelings, or virtues that one does not hold or possess; insincerity"(American Heritage Dictionary). In the Greek, the word is "hupokrisis" and means "the playing of a part on the stage."

Hypocrisy is often said to be doing something even though you don't want to or feel like doing it. It is true that God demands that our motives and reasons for doing things be right, but this does not mean that we always want to, or delight in, doing something. To do what God wants you to do, or to do unto others what you would want them to do unto you, is not hypocrisy (Mt. 7:12)—even if you don't feel like doing it. It is hypocrisy only when your motive for doing it is wrong and you're not genuinely seeking the welfare and benefit of others. Remember, Jesus didn't feel like going to the cross, but He went anyway to seek the welfare and benefit of the world.

Agape love is described as, "the love (that) can be known only from the actions it prompts." This is not the love of complacency or affection, that is, it is not drawn out by any excellency in its objects (Rom. 5:8). Christian love (agape), whether exercised toward the brethren, or toward others, generally is not an impulse from feelings. It does not always agree with our natural inclinations. It (agape) seeks the welfare of all (Rom. 15:2), and works no ill to any (Rom. 13:8-10). "Agape love seeks opportunity to do good to all men . . . ." Let God's love flow through you today.

JULY 16
THE GOODNESS OF GOD
LUKE 12:4-5

Luke 12:5 "But I will forewarn you whom ye shall fear: Fear him, which after he hath killed hath power to cast into hell; yea, I say unto you, Fear him."

Second Timothy 1:7 says, "God hath not given us the spirit of fear; but of power, and of love, and of a sound mind." First John 4:18 says, "There is no fear in love; but perfect love casteth out fear: because fear hath torment. He that feareth is not made perfect in love." These scriptures may look like they are contradictions to Jesus' statement here; however, they are not.

There are two kinds of fear. The American Heritage Dictionary defines fear as "a feeling of alarm or disquiet caused by the expectation of danger, pain, disaster, or the like; terror; dread; apprehension." It also defines fear as "extreme reverence or awe, as toward a supreme power."

It is this reverence or awe that God's Word teaches saints to have towards God. Hebrews 12:28 says that there is a godly fear with which we are supposed to serve God and thereby implies that there is an ungodly fear that is not acceptable in serving God.

Satan has always used this ungodly dread or terror to torment godly people. Those who have been born again should have no dread or terror of God unless they are planning to renounce their faith in Jesus as their Savior. We have a covenant that guarantees us acceptance with God (Eph. 1:6), as long as we hold fast to our profession of faith in the atoning blood of our Savior, Jesus Christ.

For an unbeliever, the fear of the Lord is a great deterrent from sin. However, for those of us who have received the grace of God, it is His goodness that causes us to fear him and depart from sin. His goodness is awesome!

JULY 17
STEWARDS OF GOD'S GRACE
LUKE 12:42

Luke 12:42 "And the Lord said, Who then is that faithful and wise steward, whom his Lord shall make ruler over his household, to give them their portion of meat in due season?"

A steward is a person who has been entrusted with administering someone else's wealth or affairs. The possessions a steward controls are not his own and he does not have the freedom to do with them as he wishes. He is supposed to carry out the desires of the one who made him a steward.

A banker is a steward. He has been entrusted with other people's money. He is free to invest that money wisely in a way that will benefit his depositors and stockholders, but would be sent to jail if he took all that money and simply consumed it on himself. A steward is accountable (Lk. 16:2) to someone else for the use of that person's money. The money does not belong to him even though it is in his possession.

This parable, and other scriptures (1 Cor. 4:1; Ti. 1:7; 1 Pet. 4:10), describes every believer as a steward of God's grace. The wealth, talents, and abilities we possess, as well as the revelation of God's love that we've been given, are not our own to do with as we please. We have received these things from God and are therefore accountable to Him for the use or misuse of these gifts. Keeping this in mind is essential for fulfilling our obligation to God as stewards of His "manifold grace."

JULY 18
NO EXCUSES
LUKE 12:45-48

Luke 12:48 "But he that knew not, and did commit things worthy of stripes, shall be beaten with few stripes. For unto whomsoever much is given, of him shall be much required: and to whom men have committed much, of him they will ask the more."

This verse is one of the clearest references in scripture about varying degrees of God's judgment according to the knowledge of the person who committed the sin. The whole fourth chapter of Leviticus is written to deal with sins committed in ignorance. Jesus said in John 9:41, "If ye were blind, ye should have no sin: but now ye say, We see; therefore your sin remaineth." Also, Romans 5:13 says, "sin is not imputed when there is no law."

Paul said, in 1 Timothy 1:13, that he obtained mercy because he had sinned "ignorantly in unbelief." The sin he was speaking of was blasphemy, which Jesus taught was unforgivable if done against the Holy Ghost. Therefore, we see that ignorance in Paul's case entitled him to a second chance. If he would have continued to blaspheme after he saw the truth, he would surely have paid the price. This is not to say that a person who doesn't have a complete revelation of God's will is innocent regardless of his actions. Leviticus 5:17 makes it clear that an individual is still guilty even if he sins through ignorance. Romans 1:18-20 reveals that there is an intuitive knowledge of God within all people to the degree that they even understand the Godhead. This same chapter goes on to explain that people have rejected and changed this truth, but that God did give it and they are without excuse.

No one will be able to stand before God on judgment day and say, "God is not fair." He has given every person who has ever lived, regardless of how remote or isolated he may have been, the opportunity to know Him.

JULY 19
AVOID STRIFE
LUKE 12:56-59

Luke 12:58 "When thou goest with thine adversary to the magistrate, as thou art in the way, give diligence that thou mayest be delivered from him; lest he hale thee to the judge, and the judge deliver thee to the officer, and the officer cast thee into prison."

Jesus had just spoken about relationships before He gave this parable of delivering ourselves from the judge. The warning is clear that we should do everything within our power to avoid strife (Rom. 12:18). However, the consequences of failing to settle the differences are more than just physical prison or punishment.

Strife can produce spiritual and emotional prisons. James 3:16 says, "Where envying and strife is, there is confusion and every evil work." Depression, fear, loneliness, bitterness, sickness, financial problems, and many other things can become prisons from which we will not be delivered until we reconcile.

The dictionary states that to reconcile means "to re-establish friendship between; to settle or resolve, as a dispute" (American Heritage). The key to reconciliation is effectively dealing with the enmity, ill will, hatred, or hostility that has caused the dispute. There are several approaches to reconciliation that may be applied. For instance, if we've offended someone by an unkind word that we've spoken, we can apologize. If we owe money to someone, we can pay the debt. If we've done something to someone, we can make the necessary restitution. In every case, reconciliation lies in dealing effectively with the root cause of the enmity.

The enmity between man and God was sin. God took the initiative to remove this barrier through the means and agency of Jesus Christ, thus leaving Him and man as friends once again. Thank God for His great love!

JULY 20
WE MUST RECEIVE
LUKE 13:10-17

Luke 13:16 "And ought not this woman, being a daughter of Abraham, whom Satan hath bound, lo, these eighteen years, be loosed from this bond on the Sabbath day?"

This sickness was the work of Satan—not the work of God. Jesus said it had bound her, not blessed her, for 18 years. The teaching that says that sickness is actually a blessing in disguise, because the Lord is working His plan in one's life, is not found in scripture. As Acts 10:38 says, Jesus "went about doing good, and healing all that were oppressed of the devil," not "oppressed of God."

There are 17 times in the Gospels when Jesus healed all of the sick that were present. There are 47 other times when He healed one or two people at a time. Nowhere do we find Jesus refusing to heal anyone. Jesus said that He could do nothing of Himself, but only what He saw the Father do. His actions are proof enough that it is always God's will to heal!

Jesus provided for physical healing as well as forgiveness of sins. The very word "save" (Gk.-"sozo") is translated "made whole" in reference to physical healing in Matthew 9:22, Mark 5:34, and Luke 8:48. James 5:15 says "the prayer of faith shall save (Gk.-"sozo"-) the sick." Many scriptures mention the healing of our bodies in conjunction with the forgiveness of our sins. Healing is a part of our salvation, just as much as the forgiveness of our sins.

It is God's will that no one should perish, but many do because of their unbelief. Likewise, it is God's will that we all be healed, but not all are healed because of failure to believe. It is a mistake to assume that whatever God wills will automatically come to pass. We play a part in receiving from God. Believe His Word today.

JULY 21
GOD'S GREAT LOVE FOR US
JOHN 10:24-25

John 10:25 "Jesus answered them, I told you, and ye believed not: the works that I do in my Father's name, they bear witness of me."

There were many ways in which Jesus already revealed who He was. His miraculous works certainly revealed who He was. Jesus had also clearly revealed that He was the Christ, both in the synagogue at His hometown of Nazareth, and when speaking to the Samaritan woman at Jacob's well.

Jesus, in His pre-existent state, was in the form of God. *"In the beginning was the Word and the Word was with God, and the Word was God"* (Jn. 1:1). Jesus was God, manifest in the flesh (1 Tim. 3:16). However, Jesus did not demand or cling to His rights as God, but laid aside His Divine rights and privileges in order to take the form of a servant and be made in the likeness of men. He further humbled Himself by becoming obedient to the Father, even to the point of death.

This was the supreme sacrifice that identified Jesus totally with humanity and enabled God to redeem mankind. By dying a criminal's death upon the cross, Jesus fulfilled the Old Testament prophecy in Deuteronomy 21:23 and bore our curse in His own body. This redeemed us from that curse and opened wide God's blessing of justification through faith in Christ and the promise of His Holy Spirit (Gal. 3:13-14).

Jesus left His state of being recognized and worshipped by all the hosts of heaven as the Supreme God, to become a man who was despised and rejected. The Creator became the creation; the Lord became the servant; the Highest became the lowest. All of this was done because of God's great love for us.

JULY 22
NO DENIAL OF DEITY
JOHN 10:30-39

John 10:34 "Jesus answered them, Is it not written in your law, I said, Ye are gods?"
Some people have tried to interpret this scripture to say that Jesus was disclaiming deity by associating Himself with the gods spoken of in Psalm 82:6. However, Jesus is not saying that He is a god only in the sense that the scriptures, spoke of men with divine authority as gods (Ex. 4:16; 7:1; 22:28; Ps. 82:1). In the verses before this, Jesus proclaimed His oneness with the Father and in His statements after this, He says that the Father is in Him and He is in the Father, making clear His claim to deity. Also, the Jews were not pacified by His answer, but they tried again to stone Him. If they would have understood His statements to mean that He was not proclaiming His deity, they would have left Him alone.

The comparison that Jesus is making is between the scriptures clearly stating that the Christ was God (Isa. 9:6), and the scriptures saying that rulers were gods (this refers to having divine authority—not deity). Jesus accepted their position and authority, because of the infallibility of the scriptures, and they should have done the same with Him. The scriptures prophesied His coming and the works that He would accomplish, and He fulfilled these prophecies as no one else could. His works proved He was the Messiah prophesied through scripture.

Jesus had already manifested supernatural power by His ability to walk through the midst of those who were trying to kill him and He eventually does the same thing here. But first, He refers back to Psalm 82:6. In this passage, God was speaking to the rulers of His covenant people—the Jews, and He called them gods. Jesus was saying, "If those in authority were called gods, how can you fault me for claiming to be the Son of God when I have fulfilled so many scriptures?"

JULY 23
WHO IS SAVED?
LUKE 13:22-27

Luke 13:23-24 "Then said one unto him, Lord, are there few that be saved? And he said unto them, Strive to enter in at the strait gate: for many, I say unto you, will seek to enter in, and shall not be able."
Jesus said that many will seek to enter salvation and will not be able to. There are many reasons for this, but it is not because God refused salvation to anyone. *"The grace of God that brings salvation has appeared to all men . . ."* (Ti. 2:11) and God *"is not willing that any should perish, but that all should come to repentance"* (2 Pet. 3:9).

There is effort involved in obtaining salvation. The effort is not for the purpose of earning salvation. That is a free gift (Rom. 5:15); but we do have to fight the good fight of faith (1 Tim. 6:12). Faith in Jesus' goodness is what saves us—not our own goodness. Satan is constantly trying to destroy our faith. We have to earnestly contend for the faith. True salvation is not just mental assent, but a real heartfelt commitment.

Many people today think that going to church and associating with Christians will provide them with salvation. Some people think that they are Christians because their parents were. Salvation is having a personal relationship with the Lord. You cannot inherit salvation through the natural birth process. "You must be born again."

We can rest assured that all those who hunger and thirst after righteousness shall be filled (Mt. 5:6). "Whosoever shall call upon the name of the Lord shall be saved."

Luke 14:16, 23 "Then said he unto him, A certain man made a great supper, and bade many: . . . And the lord said unto the servant, Go out into the highways and hedges, and compel them to come in, that my house may be filled. "

The man who made the supper symbolizes God who has invited "whosoever will" to come to Him. The parable teaches that it is not God who fails to offer salvation to everyone, but rather it is the invited guests who reject God's offer.

These people had feeble excuses just like the excuses of those today who don't accept God's offer of salvation. Therefore, the Lord's marriage supper of the Lamb will be furnished with "undesirables" from the world's point of view, not because God rejects the upper class, but because they reject Him. Those who have an abundance of this world's possessions don't tend to recognize their need for God as much as those who are without.

Jesus' parable could also be applied to the Jewish nation. God offered salvation to the Jews, but as a whole, they refused Him. Therefore, the Lord sent His servants to the Gentiles to fill His kingdom.

This parable proves that the Lord is not advocating us to use force to convert people to Christianity, because this man accepted the decision of those who rejected his invitation. Therefore, it must be understood that the Lord is admonishing us to compel them to come in by our persuasion or entreaty. The word "compel" denotes aggressiveness, even in persuading of people. The Church, as a whole, and all of us as individuals, are not supposed to simply hang out our "shingle" and wait for the world to come to us. We are supposed to be aggressively going into all the world with the Good News. We have an urgent command to be a witness because the time before our Lord's return is short.

Luke 14:28 "For which of you, intending to build a tower, sitteth not down first, and counteth the cost, whether he have sufficient to finish it?"

The parable of the man building a tower is a continuation of the teaching regarding what it takes to be a disciple of Jesus. This parable stresses commitment. "Jailhouse religion," where a person is only sorry he got caught and is trying to get out of a bad situation, will not produce true discipleship. It takes a forsaking of all to be Jesus' disciple. Jesus is simply saying, "count the cost."

Jesus' teaching on discipleship emphasizes commitment. Just as a king wouldn't engage in war without thoroughly considering all the possible outcomes, so no one should attempt to become a disciple of Jesus without counting the cost. It would be better not to start following Jesus than to start and then turn back.

When a person first comes to Jesus, it is impossible to know everything that following Jesus might entail. No one, however, should be fearful of making a total commitment because of some imagined problem that may never come to pass. There should be a willingness to forsake everything to follow Jesus. Once we make that decision, then Christ begins to live through us (Gal. 2:20), and we find a strength that is not our own, but equal to whatever test we may encounter.

JULY 26
HARD KNOCKS OR GOD'S WORD?
LUKE 15:11-17

Luke 15:17 "And when he came to himself, he said, How many hired servants of my father's have bread enough and to spare, and I perish with hunger!"

God's Word makes it clear that the wages of sin is death (Rom. 6:23). Romans 1:18-20 reveals that even those who don't know God's Word have an intuitive knowledge of right and wrong and God's judgment against sin. Therefore, for anyone to live in sin, as depicted by this prodigal son, they have to be deceived. This is exactly what the Bible says is the case in 2 Corinthians 4:4. When Jesus said, *"He came to himself,"* He was referring to the deception being removed and the son's spiritual eyes being opened.

Like this story of the prodigal, tragedy often brings people out of deception and back to their senses. It's not that God sends the tragedy. God spoke through the prophet Jeremiah, *"Thy way and thy doings have procured these things unto thee"* (Jer. 4:18). However, tragic situations do clearly illustrate that "it is not in man that walketh to direct his steps" (Jer. 10:23), and they cause us to look somewhere else for help. Although turning to God is always beneficial, regardless of what provides the motivation, hard knocks are not the best teacher.

Paul said in 2 Timothy 3:16-17, *"All scripture is given by inspiration of God, and is profitable for doctrine, for reproof, for correction, for instruction in righteousness: That the man of God may be perfect, thoroughly furnished unto all good works."* God's Word was given for reproof and correction and if we will submit to it, we can "be perfect, thoroughly furnished," without having to experience tragedy first.

JULY 27
NEGATIVES BECOME POSITIVES
LUKE 15:18-19

Luke 15:18 "I will arise and go to my father, and will say unto him, Father, I have sinned against heaven, and before thee."

This is a good example of true repentance. This son did not claim any goodness of his own or try to justify his actions, but he humbled himself and appealed to the mercy of his father. Likewise, we cannot approach God in self-righteousness, but we have to humble ourselves, put all of our faith in a Savior, and turn from our wicked ways (2 Chr. 7:14). That is true repentance.

Repentance is a necessary part of salvation. Repentance may include godly sorrow, but sorrow does not always include repentance. Repentance is simply a change of mind accompanied by corresponding actions.

There is a godly type of sorrow and an ungodly type of sorrow. Godly sorrow leads to repentance. Ungodly sorrow, or the sorrow of this world, just kills. Our culture has rejected all negative emotions, but God gave us the capacity for these negative emotions and there is a proper use for them. People should feel bad about sin. There should be sorrow over our failures. However, this sorrow should lead to repentance, then when forgiveness is received, our sorrow should be cast upon the Lord (Isa. 53:4).

The sorrow experienced by those who do not turn to God produces only death. They grieve over their situation because they don't turn to God (that's repentance). Christians should only have sorrow until they repent. Once repentance has come, they need to appropriate the forgiveness and cleansing that are already theirs through Christ (1 Jn. 1:9). The positive change that our sorrows led us to, changes our attitude toward the things that caused us sorrow. Negatives become positives through Jesus.

JULY 28
THE FATHER'S LOVE
LUKE 15:20

Luke 15:20 *"And he arose, and came to his father. But when he was yet a great way off, his father saw him, and had compassion, and ran, and fell on his neck, and kissed him."*

For this boy's father to have seen him "a great way off," would imply that the father had been eagerly awaiting his son's return. Certainly, in the spiritual application of this parable, our heavenly Father is longing to cleanse and receive the sinner, if he will just repent and come to Him for forgiveness.

Jesus was using this parable to rebuke the Pharisees for their harsh, self-righteous, unforgiving attitude towards sinners. The older brother in this parable was symbolic of the Pharisees. Like this brother, the Pharisees had not lived an outward life of rebellion and they thought that others who didn't measure up to their standards were surely hated by God. But, "God so loved the world," and "Christ Jesus came into the world to save sinners." Just as this older brother was self-centered and jealous, the Pharisees were not operating in the love of God towards sinners because they were so in love with themselves. They resented Jesus giving the sinners what they thought they deserved.

If relationship with his father had been the real desire of the older brother, he would have rejoiced to see his father's joy at the return of his son. The repentant prodigal son had learned the vanity of things and he had come home to a relationship with his father that neither he nor his older brother had known before.

The scribes and Pharisees, like the older brother, had gotten caught up in serving self through their religious actions. The publicans and sinners who repented were supplying their Father with what He really wanted—relationship. Relationship with the Father was always available to the scribes and Pharisees, but they chose the temporal praise of men rather than relationship with God.

JULY 29
ALL THE WRONG REASONS
LUKE 15:25-28

Luke 15:28 *"And he was angry, and would not go in: therefore came his father out, and entreated him."*

If this elder son had considered his brother, he would have rejoiced at his return even as his father did. Rather, he was totally self-centered (that's pride) and became angry. This illustrates Proverbs 13:10; *"only by pride cometh contention."*

How can we esteem others better than ourselves when in truth we really think we are better than others? Some people are better athletes than others. Some are better businessmen than others. Some are better speakers than others, and so forth. First, we need to recognize that our accomplishments don't make us better than others. There is a difference between what we do and who we are. Better performance does not make a better person. A person's character can be severely wanting even though his performance is good. A classic example of this is found in the Pharisees of Jesus' day. They did the right things for all the wrong reasons. Inside they were corrupt. So our evaluation of others needs to change. God judges by looking on the inside, not the outside (1 Sam. 16:7). We need to esteem others on a different basis than what most of us do.

Second, to esteem someone better than ourselves simply means to value him more than we value ourselves. To some, that may seem impossible, but it isn't. It is exactly what Jesus did. If Jesus, who was God in the flesh (1 Tim. 3:16), could humble Himself and value our good above His own welfare, then we should certainly be able to do the same. It can happen when we die to self and live for God.

JULY 30
BLESSED TO BE A BLESSING
LUKE 16:1-18

Luke 16:1 "And he said also unto his disciples, There was a certain rich man, which had a steward; and the same was accused unto him that he had wasted his goods."

The unjust steward was covetous. He had not been faithful to his master or to his master's debtors. He had wasted his master's goods on himself. When found out, his self-serving nature considered the options, and decided there had to be a change. He decided to use his lord's money to make friends so that when he was fired he would have someone to help him.

His master was apparently wealthy enough that he didn't take offense at the steward's discounting of the debts owed to him, but rather he commended the steward. He didn't commend his dishonest ways, but he was commending the fact that he had finally used his lord's money to plan for the future instead of wasting it on himself. Although the steward was motivated by what he would ultimately gain, there was prudence in his actions. This was lacking before.

In this sense, the children of this world (lost men), are wiser than the children of light (born again men), because they plan for the temporal future. Jesus is telling us to use money (the unrighteous mammon) to make friends that would receive us into "everlasting" habitations. The use of the word "everlasting" denotes that Jesus is now talking about our eternal future. The people who have been saved and blessed by our investments in the kingdom of God will literally receive us into our everlasting home when we pass on to be with the Lord.

Our material possessions have been given to us by God, so we are actually stewards of His resources. The Lord gave us this wealth to establish His covenant on this earth—not so we could consume it upon our own lusts. You have been blessed to be a blessing!

JULY 31
THE RIGHT RIGHTEOUSNESS
LUKE 16:14-15

Luke 16:15 "And he said unto them, Ye are they which justify yourselves before men; but God knoweth your hearts: for that which is highly esteemed among men is abomination in the sight of God."

Justification is not something to be earned, but a gift to be received. Seeking to earn salvation is the only sin that will prevent a person from being saved. You cannot submit yourself to the righteousness of God which comes as a gift through faith, as long as you are seeking to establish your own righteousness.

Most people are unaware that there are two kinds of righteousness. Only one type of righteousness is acceptable to God. There is our righteousness, which is our compliance with the requirements of the law. This is an imperfect righteousness because human nature is imperfect and incapable of fulfilling the law. There is God's righteousness, which only comes as a gift and is received by faith. God's righteousness is perfect. Our righteousness is as filthy rags (Isa. 64:6). A person who believes that he must earn God's acceptance by his holy actions is not believing in God's righteousness, which is a gift. It has to be one or the other; we cannot mix the two. Righteousness is not what Jesus has done for us plus some minimum standard of holiness that we have to accomplish.

Right standing before a holy God is not to be achieved in the keeping of the law, but in humble trust in the person and work of Jesus Christ. No one who is trusting in his own righteousness can have the benefit of Christ's righteousness. The righteousness that gives men relationship with God is the RIGHTEOUSNESS OF GOD, and it comes freely through faith in Jesus Christ (Rom. 3:22). It is true that the way we obtained this righteousness is by putting faith IN what Christ has done for us. When we place our faith in Christ, then the righteousness that Jesus obtained by His faith becomes ours. We are possessors of Christ's righteousness, which His faith produced.

AUGUST 1
FREED FROM THE LAW
LUKE 16:16-17

Luke 16:16 "The law and the prophets were until John: since that time the kingdom of God is preached, and every man presseth into it."

The Bible teaches that there are different dispensations or divinely ordered ways of God dealing with mankind throughout the ages. A dispensation is simply a period of time in which God deals with mankind in a certain way.

The Old Testament law was only a temporary dispensation and ruled from the giving of the law (Ex. 20) until the ministry of John the Baptist. When Christ came, He put an end to the law for righteousness (Rom. 10:4). Anyone who advocates the keeping of the law for the purpose of right standing with God is going back to an Old Testament system of law that has been abolished and is making the work of Christ void in his life.

The New Testament believer is under the dispensation of God's grace. We are not under the law. That doesn't mean the law has passed away. It is easier for heaven and earth to pass away than for the smallest part of the law to fail. The law hasn't failed. It has been fulfilled (Mt. 5:17). Christ fulfilled every jot and tittle of the law for us and imputes to us that righteousness is not based on our performance, but on our faith in Him. The law was never given for the purpose of justification. It was totally powerless to save. It only showed us our need and pointed us to a Savior.

The law was not made for a righteous man and it still serves a purpose for those who are not born again. For those who do not accept Jesus as their Savior, the wrath of God, which the law produces, abides on them. In this present age, Jesus has come not to condemn men, but to bring them grace and truth. Those who do not believe on the Son are presently under the wrath of the Old Testament law, and unless they repent, will suffer the wrath of God eternally. Thank God for His grace today.

AUGUST 2
OUR DEBT WAS PAID
LUKE 16:17

Luke 16:17 "And it is easier for heaven and earth to pass, than one tittle of the law to fail."

The jot was not only one of the smallest letters of the Greek alphabet, but also one of the most insignificant, being sometimes deleted at the writer's pleasure. The tittle was only a mark or a point on a line that helped distinguish one letter from another. The tittle corresponds to our period or apostrophe. The point that Jesus is making is that even the tiniest detail of the law would not pass away.

Christ fulfilled every jot and tittle of the law. The law was ordained to life, but no one could keep it. So God Himself became flesh. He did what no sinful flesh had ever done. He kept the law thereby winning the life of God as the prize for keeping the law. This granted Him eternal life, but before He could give it to us, we still had a debt that had to be paid. This is similar to someone receiving the death penalty for some hideous crime, then some billionaire leaves his whole estate to him. It would do the condemned man no good. But if that same billionaire could somehow take that man's place and die for him, then he could go free and enjoy his new wealth. That's what Jesus did for us. He took our sins and gave us His righteousness.

Jesus did much more than just obtain eternal life for us; He also paid all the wages of our sins (Rom. 6:23). God literally placed the condemnation, or judgment that was against us, upon His own Son. Jesus' perfect flesh was condemned so our defiled flesh could go free. What a trade! Since Jesus bore our sentence (condemnation), we don't have to bear it. The debt has already been paid.

AUGUST 3
COMFORT IN ETERNITY
LUKE 16:19-31

Luke 16:22 "And it came to pass, that the beggar died, and was carried by the angels into Abraham's bosom: the rich man also died, and was buried;"

This story clearly teaches that there is life after death. It shows that there is no "soul sleep" where our souls are awaiting the resurrection of our bodies, but we go into a conscious eternity immediately. It also shows that there are only two destinations possible after death. We either go to a place of torment for the wicked or a place of blessing for the righteous. There is no "limbo" or "purgatory" and there is no second chance, illustrating the finality of our eternal destiny once we die.

Abraham's bosom is a symbolic term designating a place of comfort for the righteous dead. It was located in the heart of the earth, in the same region as hell, where the ungodly dead go. The rich man's body was in the grave and yet this scripture speaks of him lifting up his eyes and seeing Lazarus in Abraham's bosom. Our soul mirrors our physical shape so closely that it is recognizable. It is probable that one's soulish body is an exact duplicate of one's physical body.

Part of this man's torment was from the flames. However, he was also tormented by the thought of his loved ones' lives on earth and their eternal destiny. Surely his helplessness to warn them would make his misery worse. Also, the fact that he could see Lazarus and Abraham in a place of total blessing and comfort would keep him from ever adjusting to his situation.

In the light of Jesus' words, we can see that hell will be much more than just a place of physical torment. Those who are consigned to that place will also be tormented with the thoughts of what could have been if they had trusted Jesus. The greatest witness that anyone could ever receive is the witness from God's Word. The Gospel is the "power of God unto salvation." Share the Word today.

AUGUST 4
VENGEANCE IS GOD'S
LUKE 17:2

Luke 17:2 "It were better for him that a millstone were hanged about his neck, and he cast into the sea, than that he should offend one of these little ones."

God takes the persecution of His children personally. In Acts 9:4 when Jesus appeared to Saul on the road to Damascus and spoke to him about his persecution of the saints, Jesus said, "Saul, Saul, why persecutest thou me?" Saul was not directly persecuting Jesus, but he was persecuting His saints. Yet Jesus said, "Why are you persecuting me?" Judgment against those who persecute God's children will not always come in time to prevent their harm, but as this warning makes very clear, God will avenge His own (Rom. 12:19).

Letting God be the one who defends us is a matter of faith. If there is no God who will bring men into account for their actions, then turning the other cheek would be the worst thing we could do. But if there is a God who promises that vengeance is His, and He will repay, then taking matters into our own hands shows a lack of faith in God and His integrity.

We are not to take matters into our own hands and defend ourselves. "Vengeance is mine; I will repay, saith the Lord" (from Dt. 32:35-36; Rom. 12:19; Heb. 10:30). Striving to vindicate self actually shows a lack of faith in God keeping this promise. It also indicates spiritual "nearsightedness" which is only looking at the present moment instead of seeing things in view of eternity.

Even as Christ did not come to condemn the world and is not holding men's sins against them, even so, we have been given the same ministry of reconciliation. For those who do not receive the love we extend to them, but rather take advantage of us because of our "turning the other cheek," God will repay.

AUGUST 5
THE FAITH TO FORGIVE
LUKE 17:5

Luke 17:5 "And the apostles said unto the Lord, Increase our faith."
It is very interesting to note that the apostles asked Jesus to increase their faith after He spoke of forgiveness. They observed all of the wonderful miracles Jesus performed and yet that never inspired them to ask for greater faith. Truly, walking in love and forgiveness with each other takes as much faith as any miracle we will ever believe for.

The basis of forgiveness is the love and mercy of God. It is only because God first loved and forgave us that we can love and forgive others. If we aren't walking in the forgiveness of God, we won't minister it to others. He forgave us before we repented or asked for forgiveness.

The scriptures admonish us to forgive as Christ has forgiven us. God offered His forgiveness towards us while we were yet sinners. Therefore, forgiveness was offered to all, unconditionally. But only those who receive the offered forgiveness through repentance and faith are received as sons of God. Likewise, we are to forgive others their trespasses, just as God has forgiven us our trespasses. We forgive whether the other person repents or wants our forgiveness. We cannot restore such a person to complete relationship until there is repentance on his part. Failure to distinguish between forgiveness and restoration, which have different conditions, has caused some people to make themselves vulnerable to unscrupulous people and suffer tragic results. In marriage, we should forgive our mates for anything, even adultery. Although if there is no true repentance on your mate's part, it would be foolish to trust him or her in a sexually tempting situation. We should forgive a business partner for stealing from us whether or not he repents, but that doesn't mean we ought to put ourselves in a position to let him do it again. Complete restoration is dependent on repentance. Walk in forgiveness today.

AUGUST 6
THE MEASURE OF FAITH
LUKE 17:1-10

Luke 17:5 "And the apostles said unto the Lord, Increase our faith."
There are many scriptures that speak of varying degrees of faith. However, the scriptures also speak of Jesus increasing in wisdom (Lk. 2:52), which certainly refers to His physical intellect drawing more and more on the perfect wisdom of God that was already in Him at birth. It is in this way that we also increase in faith.

At salvation, the believer is given the supernatural faith of God. We had to use the very faith of God (not human faith) to believe the Gospel (Eph. 2:8). That faith came to us through hearing the Word of God (Rom. 10:17), and once we are born again, it becomes an abiding fruit of the Spirit within us.

Every believer is given the same measure of faith at salvation, but not all believers use what God has given them. Therefore, it is correct to speak of growing in faith and having great faith or little faith, but it is important to understand that this is speaking of how much faith we use or manifest—not how much faith we were given. All believers were given "the" same measure of faith.

Jesus' example of the grain of mustard seed underscores the truth that our faith is sufficient if we will just use it without the hindrance of unbelief. He then continues with the parable of the servant serving his master, to illustrate that our faith is not the problem, but rather our use of it. We are using it to serve ourselves instead of our master who is God.

Living by faith is not something special that only the "super-saints" are supposed to do. The Lord expects all of His children to live a supernatural life of faith. He gave you everything you need to do this, just let Him live through you.

AUGUST 7
TURN FROM SIN
JOHN 11:5

John 11:5 "Now Jesus loved Martha, and her sister, and Lazarus."
It is interesting to note that special mention is made of Jesus loving Martha. This is after the incident recorded in Luke 10:38-42, where Martha is caught up with serving instead of worshipping Jesus. Her priorities are still not in order. Jesus was not rebuking Martha, but rather exhorting her for her own profit. When the Lord deals with problem areas in our lives, it is always for our profit—not punishment, and we should not take it as rejection. This is one way to discern God's correction from the devil's—Is it condemning?

God convicts us of sin, but He doesn't condemn us. Conviction is solely for our profit with no malice, while condemnation includes punishment. Satan is the one who condemns the Christian, but the Holy Spirit has given us the power to escape that condemnation. The way the Lord convicts a believer is through the inner ministry of the Holy Spirit. This is always done in a positive manner that encourages us to turn from sin rather than the negative way of condemning us for having committed the sin.

A Christian who still walks in condemnation is being condemned by the devil or is condemning himself. Only those who are living in the power of the Holy Spirit escape condemnation. Compare this to the law of gravity. Gravity is a law that never quits exerting its power, but it can be overcome. Through the laws of aerodynamics, man can actually fly and send spaceships beyond the Earth's gravitational force, but it takes power to do this. If the power is shut off, the law of gravity is still at work and will cause the aircraft to fall.

Likewise, the law of sin and death still exists. If a Christian shuts off the power of the Spirit of life and begins to walk in the power of his own flesh, Satan will use this law of sin and death to condemn him and ensure he crashes. It's not God who condemns us.

AUGUST 8
WALK IN THE LIGHT
JOHN 11:9-10

John 11:9 "Jesus answered, Are there not twelve hours in the day? If any man walk in the day, he stumbleth not, because he seeth the light of this world."
Jesus compares His decision to return to Judaea to a man traveling during the day. Daytime travel doesn't guarantee a hazard-free trip, but the light does allow us to see the hazards. At nighttime, it's inevitable that we will stumble. Likewise, walking in the light of God's direction doesn't mean that there won't be problems, but the alternative of doing our own thing (walking in darkness) is guaranteed to get us into trouble.

Jesus was obeying the leading of His Father to return to Judaea. He could see exactly what was going to take place and He was going to walk in the light that His Father had given Him. Our decisions should not be based on whether we will be hurt in some way as a result of our actions, but we must discern God's will and do it regardless of the cost.

The misconception that, "If God is in it, there will be no problems," is not only wrong, but is dangerous. This kind of thinking has caused many people to back off from what God has told them to do when things don't go the way they expected. Our problems do not come from God; therefore, we should not pray for problems and embrace them as being "a blessing from God in disguise." Furthermore, when trials come, we should not be shocked (1 Pet. 4:12) and let problems or the lack thereof confirm or deny God's will for us.

Jesus died for each one of us. Each one of us ought to live for Him. Offering ourselves to God is not just a onetime deal. We have to die daily to our own desires. This has to be a living, ongoing commitment to the Lord.

AUGUST 9
OUR RESURRECTED BODIES
JOHN 11:11-14

John 11:13 "Howbeit Jesus spake of his death: but they thought that he had spoken of taking of rest in sleep."

There are many scriptures where death is spoken of as sleep; however, the disciples thought Jesus was speaking of Lazarus as simply resting. Jesus eventually clarifies their misunderstanding by using the word "death," but that was not His first choice. This is because God's perspective is different than ours. Death is final to natural man, but not to God. There will be a resurrection.

In his second letter to the Corinthians Paul uses natural illustrations to explain the resurrection. He speaks of seeds that are buried in the ground and "die." Then they are resurrected as a plant. The plant and the seed bear no resemblance, but they are actually the same. The plant is just in a resurrected state. Likewise, our physical bodies will die, but they will be resurrected just as surely as seeds produce plants.

In the same way that a seed is different than the plant that it produces, our resurrected bodies will be different. Our glorified bodies will be similar to our physical bodies in appearance. This can be said because of what the scriptures reveal about Jesus' glorified body. He still looked human; He ate food, had the print of the nails in His hands and feet, and He said He had flesh and bones. Yet He could appear and disappear. Our resurrected bodies will be immortal (i.e. not subject to death). Our resurrected bodies will be like Jesus' resurrected body.

In the same way that our present physical bodies are a miraculous creation, so our glorified resurrected bodies will have their own glory. We can rest assured that God never serves dessert first. If this physical body is wonderful, our resurrected body will be even better.

AUGUST 10
CONFESS GOD'S TRUTH
JOHN 11:14

John 11:14 "Then said Jesus unto them plainly, Lazarus is dead."

Jesus spoke of Lazarus being asleep instead of dead because that is really a much better description. Death, to their carnal minds, would be final; whereas the word "sleep" would not. When the disciples misunderstood what He was saying, He clarified the situation by saying plainly, "Lazarus is dead." This looks like a contrary statement to what Jesus was going to do (raise Lazarus from the dead), and indeed it would have been if He had left it at that. He went on to say in verse 15, "I am glad for your sakes that I was not there, to the intent ye may believe." This was referring to Lazarus being raised from the dead and it turned Jesus' statement of a negative fact into a positive confession of faith.

Many people have been confused over this issue. Many times people will refuse to speak of, or acknowledge any situation that is contrary to a promise that God has given them. It is certainly desirable to avoid talking about our problems and there is scriptural precedent for this (2 Ki. 4:20,26). In this instance, Jesus avoided using a word to describe Lazarus' situation that would have instilled fear into His disciples' hearts, but when dealing with people who didn't understand, He didn't deny the natural facts.

A true, positive confession doesn't deny natural truth. It just refuses to stop at the natural realm and speaks forth the greater spiritual truth. This is what Jesus did and we should follow His example. Therefore, it is not wrong to acknowledge a physical problem such as sickness, just as long as we acknowledge to an equal or greater degree the spiritual truth, "by whose stripes ye were healed" (1 Pet. 2:24). Don't deny that problems exist, just deny those problems the right to continue to exist in your life, by confessing your faith in God.

AUGUST 11
LIVE FOREVER IN HIM
JOHN 11:26

John 11:26 "And whosoever liveth and believeth in me shall never die.
Believest thou this?"

Some people have interpreted this as saying that it is possible to never die. Therefore, there are people today who are believing that they will live physically until the second coming of Jesus, even if that is thousands of years away. Although it is understandable how someone could interpret this verse in that manner, it is doubtful that this is what Jesus truly meant.

First, a doctrine as profound as this would certainly be well documented in other scriptures. Other scriptures may sometimes be quoted as supporting this claim, but they would not lead a person to this conclusion by themselves. There would already have to be a prejudice in favor of this stand within a person to lead him to interpret these scriptures in this light. That is not a sound method of Bible interpretation. Also, there is not a single scriptural example of anyone who obtained this. That should make anyone suspect of this teaching. Enoch or Elijah might be cited as examples, but they were translated so that they didn't die. They are not still in their physical bodies on this earth.

There have been periods in church history where certain truths were suppressed, such as the Baptism of the Holy Spirit or healing, and then revived through a move of God. But there was always a remnant of the church that continually experienced these blessings of God. That cannot be shown to be true with this belief—that a believer can remain on the earth in his physical body until Jesus comes. Therefore, this passage of scripture concerning never dying is generally accepted as referring to eternal life that we receive at salvation. The promise of never dying spiritually is made many times in scripture and it is promised to every believer.

AUGUST 12
GROANING IN THE SPIRIT
JOHN 11:33

John 11:33 "When Jesus therefore saw her weeping, and the Jews also weeping which came with
her, he groaned in the spirit, and was troubled."

The Greek word that is translated "groaned" expresses that Jesus was deeply moved, but not necessarily with sorrow. It was more a groan of anger at Satan who had caused all the grief Jesus was seeing around Him. Jesus came to "destroy him that had the power of death, that is, the devil" (Heb. 2:14), and He was grieved to see the pain that His enemy had inflicted on those He loved.

This is the type of groaning that the Holy Spirit does for us. It is not just the Holy Spirit sympathizing with us, but it is the Holy Spirit doing battle for us when we don't know how to pray. In this case, it was the Holy Spirit doing battle through Jesus against death and the doubt of those present, that would have kept Lazarus in the grave.

Everyone who has the indwelling presence of the Holy Spirit has or will have this happen to them. This groaning of the Holy Spirit is not just grief, but a groan of anger and resistance against Satan's devices in our lives. Many times Christians don't discern this because they think it is just them grieved with their situation. It is the Holy Spirit desiring to get into intercession with us against our problems.

Although the groaning is unutterable, you can discern it, and many times people react with audible groans or other outward acts. This has led to religious doctrines and traditions that are unscriptural and offensive to many people. There is nothing wrong with us reacting to the inner working of the Holy Spirit as long as we don't confuse our reactions with the Holy Spirit's actions. This intercession cannot be uttered. The genuine groaning in the Spirit is priceless.

AUGUST 13
FOCUS ON THINGS ABOVE
JOHN 11:44

John 11:44 "And he that was dead came forth, bound hand and foot with graveclothes: and his face was bound about with a napkin. Jesus saith unto them, Loose him, and let him go."

Symbolically, Lazarus is like many Christians. The Bible speaks of us passing from death unto new life when we get born again. It is also true that in the physical and emotional realm, we bring our "graveclothes" from our old life with us (i.e. habits, attitudes, etc.), and we need to be "loosed" to fully enjoy our new life.

Our emotions and attitudes follow what we think. When we focus our attention on our problems, they are magnified out of proportion. When we neglect our problems and think on God's provision, the answer is magnified and the problem shrinks. Whatever we think upon is going to dominate us. If we think on depressing things, we'll be depressed. If we think on uplifting things, we'll be uplifted. If we think, "by His stripes, we are healed," we'll be healed. If we think on sickness, we'll be sick.

Godly contentment isn't dependent upon circumstances. That is totally opposite of the way most people think today. No one really desires depression, but very few feel any responsibility or authority to maintain positive emotions in the face of negative circumstances. They think emotions follow circumstances. That's not true. Emotions follow the way we think, and we can choose to think on things that are lovely, true, of good report, and so forth regardless of our circumstances. As we think, is how we respond emotionally.

Focus your attention on the invisible truths of the spiritual realm that are eternal, instead of the visible things of this physical world that will pass away.

AUGUST 14
GIVE THANKS DAILY
LUKE 17:11-18

Luke 17:18 "There are not found that returned to give glory to God, save this stranger."

Relatively few people who receive the goodness of the Lord return to give Him thanks for what He has done. That does not keep the Lord from doing what is right for us. He healed all ten of these lepers according to their request—not just the one who was thankful. However, there was only one out of the ten that was made "whole."

The Lord desires that we prosper in spirit, soul, and body. He wants us to be whole—not just healed. Part of the reason God meets our physical needs is to prove to us His willingness and ability to meet our emotional and spiritual needs. The Lord is concerned about our temporal needs (Mt. 6:30), but He is even more concerned about our eternal needs. All of these lepers needed physical healing and the Lord was moved with compassion and met their needs. He also desired to meet their spiritual needs, but only one out of the ten came back for that.

Being unthankful is always a sign that self is exalting itself above God. A selfless person can be content with very little. A self-centered person cannot be satisfied. Thankfulness is a sign of humility and cultivating a life of thankfulness will help keep "self" in its proper place.

Thankfulness to the Lord for what He is and what He has done is a very important part of the Christian life. One of the many benefits of thanksgiving and praise is that they keep us from being "self" oriented. Giving thanks is a totally unselfish action and is a key to relationship with the Father that makes us "whole" and not just "healed."

AUGUST 15
LIKE A THIEF IN THE NIGHT
LUKE 17:24-31

Luke 17:24 "For as the lightning, that lighteneth out of the one part under heaven, shineth unto the other part under heaven; so shall also the Son of man be in his day."

This scripture and the parallel scripture in Matthew 24:27 make it very clear that the second return of Jesus will be no secret to anyone. In Matthew's account, it is especially clear that this statement about the lightning was made so that we wouldn't be deceived by false Christs. Just as lightning is visible to everyone, so the second return of Jesus will be witnessed by the whole world. That's the reason we don't have to be fearful about missing His second coming and anxiously follow every report that Christ has come. These verses completely destroy the claims of the Bahai religion and others who claim that Jesus has secretly come back the second time.

Just as Jesus had warned His disciples not to be deceived by false Christs because His second coming would be visible to everyone, He also explains that until the very day of His coming, the world will continue on its present course. People will not discern the signs of His coming just as the people during Noah's day didn't realize their impending judgment. This corresponds exactly with Jesus' prophecies about His coming being like the appearance of a thief in the night. Jesus is emphasizing that the unbelievers will not recognize that He is coming until it is too late. He is stressing that His coming will take the world by surprise.

The Lord is pointing out the urgent need to be ready for His return. In the same way that a thief comes when people are the least prepared, so our Lord will return in a time when people are not looking for Him. There will be a condition of apathy in the latter days that will tend to lull even the faithful to sleep if they don't take heed to His words. He urges us to be watchful so we will be prepared.

AUGUST 16
GOD ANSWERS PRAYER
LUKE 18:1-2

Luke 18:2 "Saying, There was in a city a judge, which feared not God, neither regarded man:"

This is not an exact comparison of God to this unjust judge, teaching us that we should badger God until we weary Him and He grants us our request. Rather, Jesus is contrasting His willingness to answer our prayers with this unjust judge's unwillingness. The parable is a contrast, not a representation.

Not only do we have a God who is a just judge who will avenge His elect speedily, but we also have Jesus as our advocate or attorney who is always making intercession for us. However, we have an adversary (the devil) who is constantly accusing us and misrepresenting God (the judge). This causes men to give up (faint) and not even plead their case with God because they doubt that He will answer them anyway.

Jesus is saying that our Father is not an unjust judge that we have to pressure into doing what is right. Many times we put more faith in people and their willingness to do what is right than we do in God. Satan has deceived us about the willingness of God to answer our prayers and Jesus is countering that deception with this parable. Jesus is encouraging us to pray (petition God) and not doubt His willingness to grant our requests. To teach that we must pester God until He gives in to our pressure is not good theology.

This widow's actions were commendable. She knew what was rightfully hers and she refused to take "no" for an answer. If we can be that confident and determined when dealing with unjust men, how much more should we persist, despite the devil's delays, when dealing with our faithful Father. You can trust Him to always come through for you.

AUGUST 17
RIGHTEOUSNESS IS A GIFT
LUKE 18:9-14

Luke 18:9 "And he spake this parable unto certain which trusted in themselves that they were righteous, and despised others:"

People who are self-righteous often despise others. No one can compare himself to God's perfect standard and feel good about himself. To trust in ourselves, we have to constantly compare ourselves to others. This breeds a critical attitude towards others that exalts self by debasing others.

No one can ever be righteous in the sight of God through his own righteousness. Our actions benefit us in relationships with people and prevent Satan from having an opportunity against us, but they cannot make us right (righteous) with God. We must trust in God and receive His gift of righteousness completely on the basis of faith in what Christ did for us. This is the truth that this parable is presenting.

Most people are unaware that there are two kinds of righteousness. Only one type of righteousness is acceptable to God. One form of righteousness is our own righteousness. These are the acts of holiness that we do in an attempt to fulfill the commands of the Old Testament law. This is an imperfect righteousness because human nature is imperfect and incapable of fulfilling the law.

God's righteousness is not something that we do, but something that we receive as a gift through faith in Christ. It's not possible to trust in our own righteousness and in God's righteousness simultaneously. A person who believes that he must earn God's acceptance by his holy actions must not believe in God's righteousness, which is a gift. It has to be one or the other; we cannot mix the two. Righteousness is not what Jesus has done for us plus some minimum standard of holiness that we have to accomplish. God's righteousness is perfect. Accept this gift He offers to you.

AUGUST 18
DIVORCE IS NOT GOD'S BEST
MARK 10:2-6

Mark 10:2 "And the Pharisees came to him, and asked him, Is it lawful for a man to put away his wife? tempting him."

The Pharisees didn't really want to know what Jesus taught on divorce and remarriage. They didn't value His opinion, but were tempting Him and desired to get Him mired in the big dispute of their day between liberal and conservative views on divorce. This was a very emotional issue then, just as it is today, and they thought they had Jesus in a no win situation. However, as always, Jesus proved to be more than their match and He gave them much more than what they asked for.

The Pharisees didn't question whether or not divorce was right. They took the right to divorce for granted. Instead of expounding on acceptable grounds for divorce, Jesus went to the root of the problem and showed that God never intended there to be divorce at all. If they really understood the extent of the one flesh covenant between a man and his wife, they would not be looking for an excuse to get out of marriage. This approach amazed the Pharisees and brought forth the question, "Why did Moses, in the law, make provision for divorce?"

Once a person begins to ask, "How can I get a divorce?" instead of, "How can I keep this marriage together?" indicates that there is already a serious breach in the marriage, that Jesus says is caused by a hardened heart.

Jesus answered that divorce was permitted but never intended. God allowed something that He hated because of the hardness of people's hearts. This was also true of polygamy and slavery. Jesus came to remove our stony hearts and give us hearts of flesh so that we could walk in God's best for our lives.

AUGUST 19
ONE FLESH
MATTHEW 19:3-5

Matthew 19:5 "And said, For this cause shall a man leave father and mother, and shall cleave to his wife: and they twain shall be one flesh?"

What does it mean for a man and a woman to become "one flesh"? The act of sexual intercourse between a man and a woman produces this one flesh relationship. Whether or not the man and woman ever cleave to each other in marriage, the physical act still binds them together as one flesh.

This is the reason that sexual relationships outside of marriage (whether extramarital or premarital) are so damaging. Whether or not individuals get caught, pregnant or ever hurt anyone else with their sin, they are doing a lot of damage to themselves. There is a relationship that develops through the sexual act that makes us one with that person. There is no such thing as just a night on the town or a one-night stand, and that's all there is to it. Alcoholism, child abuse, hatred, and a thousand other things that are certainly wrong, are not grounds for divorce, but fornication is. That shows us that there is something very powerful that takes place in the physical act of intercourse and explains why Satan has exploited this area so much.

Becoming one flesh with someone (sexual intercourse) is not marriage. Marriage includes, but is even beyond becoming one flesh. This can be seen clearly in John 4:17-18. Jesus said the woman He was speaking to at Jacob's well had five prior husbands and the man she was currently living with was not her husband. It is certain that this woman was having sexual relations with the man she was living with, but that didn't make him her husband. Marriage involves more than sexual relations. It is a covenant or commitment between a man and a woman that corresponds to the cleaving to each other that Jesus spoke of here.

AUGUST 20
MARRIAGE IS A COVENANT
MATTHEW 19:7-9

Matthew 19:9 "And I say unto you, Whosoever shall put away his wife, except it be for fornication, and shall marry another, committeth adultery: and whoso marrieth her which is put away doth commit adultery."

Although adultery denotes one who has unlawful intercourse with the spouse of another, in its much broader term, it means to violate or pollute. Israel violated or polluted her covenant with God. Jeremiah says, "She (Judah) defiled the land, and committed adultery" (Jer. 3:9).

Adultery in relation to marriage also reflects a violation of the covenant of companionship. Sex outside of marriage is adultery because it violates or pollutes the covenant of marriage by introducing another party and bringing that relationship into the marriage. "They two shall be one flesh" (Eph. 5:31).

Divorce also adulterates or pollutes marriage because it disrupts or denies the divorced parties the right to be faithful to their covenant of companionship. Any time one divorces his mate (except for fornication) and marries another, he is guilty of adultery. He has polluted and destroyed a relationship intended by God to be permanent and pure.

Why the "except for fornication" clause? Jesus is not saying that if fornication is involved, we must divorce, but rather when fornication is involved, that is the only time when the person getting the divorce is not guilty of adultery. That is because the partner who had an extra-marital relationship has already polluted the marriage vow. In God's original design for marriage, He intended it to be sacred, precious, pure, and permanent. The marriage covenant represents a final, irrevocable commitment where the man and the woman renounce the right to live for themselves and become "heirs together of the grace of life"(1 Pet. 3:7).

AUGUST 21
TRUST IN JESUS AS YOUR SAVIOR
MATTHEW 19:12-20

Matthew 19:16 "And, behold, one came and said unto him, Good Master, what good thing shall I do, that I may have eternal life?"

On the surface, it appears that this rich young ruler was "right on" in the way he approached Jesus and sought salvation. He ran, kneeled down to Jesus, and openly professed Him as a Good Master. What could be wrong with that?

First, he acknowledged Jesus as good, but not as God. This is a pivotal point. Every major religion of the world acknowledges that Jesus lived and will even admit that He definitely was a good man, but they won't recognize Him as God. If Jesus was only a good man, He couldn't save anybody. Jesus didn't come just to show us the way to God—He was the way, the only way unto the Father. No man can come unto the Father, but by Him (Jn. 14:6). Jesus made this point publicly many times before. This is the reason that Jesus responded to this young man's question the way He did. Jesus was saying, "God is the only one who is good. You must accept me as God or not at all." Jesus was either who He claimed to be or He was the biggest fraud that ever lived. He has to be one or the other. He cannot be both.

Second, he asked what he could do to produce salvation. He trusted in himself and believed he could accomplish whatever good work Jesus might request. This is completely opposed to the plan of salvation that Jesus came to bring. Jesus obtained salvation for us through His substitution, and He offers it to us as a free gift. All we must do is believe and receive. This rich young ruler wasn't looking for a Savior. He was trying to be his own savior. This is the reason Jesus referred him back to the commandments. He either needed to keep all of the law perfectly or he needed a Savior. Jesus desired to turn this man from trusting in himself by showing him God's perfect standard, which no one could keep, so that then he would trust in a Savior.

AUGUST 22
RECEIVE THE GIFT OF SALVATION
MARK 10:21-27

Mark 10:21 "Then Jesus beholding him loved him, and said unto him, One thing thou lackest: go thy way, sell whatsoever thou hast, and give to the poor, and thou shalt have treasure in heaven: and come, take up the cross, and follow me."

Notice that the scripture makes special mention of Jesus loving this rich young ruler. This is stated after this young man said he had kept all of God's commands, which was not the truth. Jesus was showing him that he had broken the very first commandment that states, "Thou shalt have no other gods before me" (Ex. 20:3), and also the tenth commandment that says, "Thou shalt not covet..." (Ex. 20:17). Jesus' tough answer of "sell whatsoever thou hast, and give to the poor," was not intended to hurt this young man. It was said from a heart of love and intended for his own good. This man's money had become his god and it had to be dethroned before Jesus could become his Lord.

The one thing this young man lacked was faith in Jesus as his Savior. This young ruler was trusting in his goodness and not in the salvation that Jesus offered as a gift. Millions of people are making the same mistake today. They trust in themselves instead of God.

Jesus only came to save sinners. Unless an individual acknowledges that he is a sinner, he cannot be saved. Because the whole world is guilty before God, He has provided one way of salvation for everyone. In the same way that everyone is guilty, everyone also has been justified freely by God's grace. That does not mean everyone is saved. Everyone has had the sacrificial offering of Jesus made for their sins by grace, but grace alone doesn't save. We have to put faith in what God has provided for us by grace. Although the price has been paid for the sins of the whole world, only those who receive it by faith will benefit from the salvation that Jesus offers.

AUGUST 23
IT'S NOT WHAT YOU DO
MATTHEW 20:1-16

Matthew 20:8 "So when even was come, the lord of the vineyard saith unto his steward, Call the labourers, and give them their hire, beginning from the last unto the first."

This parable begins with Jesus' statement that the kingdom of heaven is likened to a man who is a householder (owner of an estate). He goes out early in the morning to hire workers to work in his vineyard for the day. An agreed upon price was set at a penny, the normal wage paid daily for a laborer. Later, around 9:00 a.m., the landowner encouraged others, standing idle in the marketplace, to work in the vineyard, not for a set wage but for "whatsoever is right." The landowner employed more laborers at noon, at 3:00 p.m. and even some at 5:00 p.m. when there was only one hour left to work. According to Jewish law, wages must be paid each evening before the sun sets. When it came time for the steward to pay the laborers, he began with those working the shortest amount of time and paid each man a penny (a full day's wage). Those working the entire day murmured, for they supposed they would have received more. They agreed, however, to work for a penny, the stipulated wage agreed upon.

The context of this parable supports the teaching that it is impossible to earn the generosity of the Master. This is a lesson on grace. Regardless of whether our performance is better than someone else's, we all need God's grace because we all have come short of God's standard. The landowner gave freely, making all equal. Jesus is saying that the benefits of the kingdom are the same for all who have become subject to its King, regardless of what they have done. Therefore, those who are last (or least) in the sense that they have not served the Lord as long or as well as others, will truly become "first" when they share equally of the Lord's goodness with those who "have borne the burden and heat of the day" (Mt. 20:12).

AUGUST 24
SHARE IN HIS SUFFERINGS
MATTHEW 20:17-25

Matthew 20:22 "But Jesus answered and said, Ye know not what ye ask. Are ye able to drink of the cup that I shall drink of, and to be baptized with the baptism that I am baptized with? They say unto him, We are able."

The Greek word for baptize is "baptizo." This word was used by Plato (fourth century B.C.) to describe a man being "overwhelmed by philosophical arguments"; or it means sponges being "dipped" in fluid; Strabo (first century B.C.) described it as people who could not swim, being "submerged" under water. Josephus in the first century A.D. used the word to describe the city of Jerusalem as being "overwhelmed" or "plunged" into destruction by the Romans; and Plutarch (also first century A.D.) used this word to refer to a person being "immersed" in the sea. In the Septuagint (the Greek version of the O.T.), "baptizo" is used to describe Naaman dipping himself in the Jordan River (2 Ki. 5:14). From classical Greek, right down to New Testament Greek, the same basic meaning has been retained: "To immerse, submerge, dip or plunge." Jesus is stating that the disciples will indeed be plunged into the same sufferings that He will experience.

There are many forms of persecution. Having your life threatened because of your faith in Jesus is one way you can be persecuted. History shows that the church has always flourished under persecution with increased numbers and zeal. During intense, life-threatening persecution, people's priorities get straightened out and the Lord assumes His rightful place. This always works for our good, regardless of what our outward circumstances might be. It helps to recognize that it is not you that they are persecuting, but rather Christ in you. You are actually partaking in His sufferings and will share in His rewards. With this in mind, we can actually shout and leap for joy in times of persecution.

AUGUST 25
JESUS PAID THE PRICE
MARK 10:45

Mark 10:45 "For even the Son of man came not to be ministered unto, but to minister, and to give his life a ransom for many."

Jesus told His disciples many times of His death, but this is the first time He indicated the reason for His death. Now it is clear that His death would be a "ransom," defined in the Greek as a means of loosing by paying a price. The words "ransom" and "redeem" were used interchangeably in scripture.

Not only would Jesus pay the price for sin, but His death would be substitutionary. In 1 Timothy 2:6, the word "ransom" is taken from the Greek word "antilutron" which means "a redemption-price." The Greek word "anti" means "in place of." In other words, the ransom avails for all who will accept it (Jn. 3:16; Rom. 10:13).

The price paid for our redemption is the life of Jesus, that is, Jesus' blood (Col. 1:14). This redemption, according to Hebrews 9:12, is eternal and is intended to purify us from all iniquity (Ti. 2:14), and bring us to serve the living God (Heb. 9:14).

This can be illustrated by the way we use trading stamps. First, the stamps have to be purchased, then they are redeemed for the desired product. The purchase is essential, but so is the redemption. No one really wants the stamps. They want what the stamps can be redeemed for. The purchase for our total salvation has already been made with the blood of Jesus, but our bodies have not been redeemed yet. We have not received yet, all the benefits of this transaction in our physical bodies. This will take place at the second coming of the Lord when we receive our new glorified bodies. Our spirits are the only part of us that have experienced total redemption. Thank God for the redemption He has provided for you today.

AUGUST 26
PLEASE GOD NOT PEOPLE
MARK 10:43-48

Mark 10:48 "And many charged him that he should hold his peace: but he cried the more a great deal, Thou son of David, have mercy on me."

The devil will always have someone available to tell us why we shouldn't expect to get results when petitioning God. Most people would rather stay with the crowd and not do anything to draw attention to themselves even if that means not getting their needs met. They will try to make you conform as well. If this man would have listened to the crowd, he would not have received his healing. "Ye have not, because ye ask not" (Jas. 4:2).

This blind man is a good example of an active kind of faith. He was not passive in his approach toward healing. He boldly cried out to Jesus for mercy. When the crowd ridiculed him and told him to be quiet, he cried out even louder for mercy.

Many people believe that God can perform the miracle they need, but relatively few are willing to actively pursue it until they get results. They are afraid of what others will think of them. This man had his attention focused only on Jesus. Nothing else mattered and that is why he got healed.

An integral part of faith is seeking God only with your whole heart. If we are concerned about what people think so that we can gain their approval, we will never take a stand in faith for anything that we might be criticized for. This one thing has probably stopped as many people from receiving from God as anything else. You cannot be a man-pleaser and please God at the same time. Satan uses persecutions to steal away God's Word and thereby stop our faith. To see faith work, we must say with Paul, "Let God be true, but every man a liar" (Rom. 3:4).

AUGUST 27
MINISTER GOD'S LOVE
LUKE 19:1-8

Luke 19:8 "And Zacchaeus stood, and said unto the Lord; Behold, Lord, the half of my goods I give to the poor; and if I have taken any thing from any man by false accusation, I restore him fourfold."

Zacchaeus was rich, but Jesus made no demands for him to give away all his goods to the poor as He did with the rich young ruler. Zacchaeus had already repented and money was no longer his god, as was revealed by his actions. It seems that Zacchaeus was going above and beyond the requirement of restitution as stated in Mosaic law by offering to give half of his goods to the poor and to repay fourfold any theft he may have committed.

Publicans were hated by their fellow Jews. They were especially despised by the religious Jews as the epitome of sinners, and Jewish religious laws prevented devout Jews from keeping company with any publican. To eat with a publican was unthinkable as the Jews considered this actually partaking of the publican's sins. This is why the people reacted so adversely to Jesus eating with Zacchaeus.

Jesus did not eat at Zacchaeus' house to participate in his sin, but to extend mercy and forgiveness to him. This is always the criterion whereby we can judge whether we should be involved in a certain situation. We must not participate in other men's sins, but the Lord doesn't want us to retreat to monasteries either. We are the salt of the earth (Mt. 5:13), and to do any good, we have to get out of the "salt shaker." If we can be in control and minister the love of God, then we are right to associate with sinners. If we are being controlled by the ungodliness of sinners, we need to take control or withdraw.

AUGUST 28
BE FAITHFUL WITH A LITTLE
LUKE 19:12-13

Luke 19:12-13 "He said therefore, A certain nobleman went into a far country to receive for himself a kingdom, and to return. And he called his ten servants, and delivered them ten pounds, and said unto them, Occupy till I come."

The main purpose of this parable is to show that there would be a long period when Jesus would go away before returning to fulfill the prophecy about a physical kingdom on earth.

The nobleman's servants were called to give an account for what they had done with their lord's money that was delivered unto them. The servants were commanded to "occupy till I come." These servants represent the followers of Jesus. However, being a follower of Jesus is more than simply not rejecting Him. It is an active commitment to serve Him. One of the ten servants had served himself and not His master. He did nothing with what his lord had given him. This wicked servant was stripped of what he had and it was given to the servant who had used his lord's money wisely.

This illustrates that the Lord expects us to grow. This is made very clear in the parables of the kingdom which Jesus taught. In nearly every parable, growth or increase is expected. This servant who did nothing with what his lord gave him represents a believer who never grows or brings increase to God's kingdom.

What was it that this wicked servant didn't have that caused his master to take back the money he had given him? It wasn't the tangible money that he received. He had kept that laid up in a napkin and still possessed it. What he was missing, and what the other servant had that caused the lord to give this pound to him, was faithfulness. Those who are faithful with what God has given them will be given more, and those who are wasteful will have what God has given them taken away and given to another. Use wisely what God has given to you.

AUGUST 29
RELIEVE EACH OTHER'S BURDENS
LUKE 19:23

Luke 19:23 "Wherefore then gavest not thou my money into the bank, that at my coming I might have required mine own with usury?"

The Greek word for "usury" means primarily "a bringing forth, birth, or an offspring." It is used metaphorically for the profit received by a lender. The Law of Moses attempted to protect both borrower and lender. In Israel, borrowing and lending was not for big, commercial enterprises, but rather to help the poor and needy who lacked everyday necessities. In lending, the lender had the opportunity to help the poor in need. It was an act of love in which the lender actually lifted a burden by helping his fellow Israelite through a crisis, but was forbidden to charge usury. To relieve the burden of the poor, debts were released every seven years and property restored during the year of Jubilee.

In the New Testament, the practice of lending money at interest seemed to be accepted as normal business procedure. Although Jesus never condemned interest directly; in general, He was hard on the improper attitude toward riches and the oppression of the poor, just as was the Old Testament. The principle of making money from someone else's hardship is not really a godly way of doing business. It was permitted, and even encouraged in this instance, but Deuteronomy 23:19-20 makes it clear that interest was never to be charged to a fellow Israelite. Today, that would be equivalent to never loaning money with interest to a fellow Christian. Borrowing money is not condemned in scripture unless you interpret Romans 13:8 as speaking of borrowing. However, the scriptures make it clear that borrowing is not God's best. Deuteronomy 28:12 lists never having to borrow as a blessing, while Deuteronomy 28:44 lists borrowing as a part of the curse of the law. Proverbs 22:7 says, "The rich ruleth over the poor, and the borrower is servant to the lender."

AUGUST 30
RESPOND TO GOD'S DIRECTION
LUKE 19:26

Luke 19:26 "For I say unto you, That unto every one which hath shall be given; and from him that hath not, even that he hath shall be taken away from him."

What was it that this wicked servant didn't have that caused his master to take back the money he had given him? It wasn't the tangible money that he had been given. He had kept that laid up in a napkin and he still possessed it. What he was missing and what the other servant had that caused the lord to give this pound to him was faithfulness. Those who are faithful with what God has given them will be given more, and those who are wasteful will have what God has given them taken away and given to another.

Christians will one day stand before the Lord for the purpose of receiving rewards, and all our actions will be revealed, whether they were our own doings or directed by the Spirit of God. Those who were not governed by the Holy Spirit in their actions will see all their good works burned up in that day when we stand before the Lord and He tries our works. Those who acted only under the guidance of the Holy Spirit will find that their works will endure the test and they will receive a reward.

Many people choose to do good things thinking that God will be pleased. But our positive response to God's direction (faith) is what pleases God (Heb. 11:6). We were created with a purpose and every individual has a God-given plan for his life. We need to let God work in and through us and faithfully fulfill what He has called us to do.

AUGUST 31
WORSHIP FROM YOUR HEART
MARK 14:3-6

Mark 14:3 "And being in Bethany in the house of Simon the leper, as he sat at meat, there came a woman having an alabaster box of ointment of spikenard very precious; and she brake the box, and poured it on his head."

The spikenard was a fragrant plant, and its roots were used in Jesus' day to make an aromatic, costly perfume and ointment. The plant itself, grows in the Himalaya mountains at an elevation of 11,000 to 17,000 feet. For centuries, it was used by Hindus as a medicine and perfume and was an actively traded commodity. Its great cost stemmed from that it had to be transported over 6,000 miles to reach Palestine, and depending on quality, it sold for as much as 400 denarii per pound ($750 an ounce is the modern equivalent). That made it more valuable than gold. This ointment was worth at least two and one-half times more than the 30 pieces of silver that Judas received for betraying the Lord, which is why Judas was so upset. This perfume was worth two and one-half times what Judas thought Jesus was worth.

Judas didn't care about the poor. He wanted to have the money that the perfume could have been sold for in his bag (he was the treasurer for Jesus) so he could steal it. This is a very serious crime that Jesus no doubt knew about, but scripture never mentions Him confronting Judas.

Judas' reaction to this act of pure worship is typical of the reaction toward worship of many people today. Judas and some of the other disciples thought this was a waste. That was only because they didn't value Jesus as highly as Mary did. Mary had seen Jesus raise her brother from the dead and her heart was overflowing with love and worship. The disciples were looking on the outward things while Jesus was looking at Mary's heart (1 Sam. 16:7). Those who cannot see beyond the physical realm will be offended by others' displays of worship. True worship comes from the heart.

SEPTEMBER 1
THE MIRACLE OF THE DONKEY AND COLT
JOHN 12:14-15

John 12:14-15 "And Jesus, when he had found a young ass, sat thereon; as it is written, Fear not, daughter of Sion: behold, thy King cometh, sitting on an ass's colt."

This is the fulfillment of Zechariah's prophecy in Zechariah 9:9. Notice how specific Zechariah's prophecy is and how exactly it was fulfilled. Zechariah prophesied Jesus not only riding an ass, but also a colt (unbroken), the foal of an ass. Zechariah also mentioned the people rejoicing greatly and shouting which certainly came to pass on this day.

All four Gospels include a triumphal entry, but only Matthew records a donkey with a colt. A simple explanation to a so-called "contradiction" is that Jesus rode the colt while the other donkey went along. No doubt, He rode each animal part of the way.

Not only was it a miracle that Jesus knew about the ass and its colt, but also where they would be. God also worked some kind of miracle in the owner of these animals so that he would be willing to release them. It is possible that the Lord also revealed to this man that Jesus would need his animals. Perhaps he was just a devoted follower of Jesus who gladly surrendered them when he knew Jesus was the one wanting them. Either way, it was just as much a miracle that the owner was willing to surrender them as it was that Jesus knew exactly where they would be.

Jesus hadn't been in Jerusalem in quite a while and there is no indication that He had made previous arrangements with anyone there to obtain this ass and its colt. This was nothing less than supernatural knowledge imparted to Jesus through the Holy Spirit. As Jesus did, let God's gifts flow through you today.

SEPTEMBER 2
DEPEND ON GOD, NOT THE GIFT
MARK 11:1-6

Mark 11:2 "And saith unto them, Go your way into the village over against you: and as soon as ye be entered into it, ye shall find a colt tied, whereon never man sat; loose him, and bring him."

The gifts of the Spirit are not meant to be a substitute for our own faith in the Lord. We are not to depend so completely on some individual with a spiritual gift that we neglect our own spiritual growth and maturity. We can receive anything we need from the Lord without a gift of the Spirit operating through another individual, if we know how to believe. Dependence on the Lord directly is superior to dependence on the Lord indirectly through someone operating in one of the spiritual gifts.

What if there were no gifts of the Spirit and the Lord established that the only way we could receive from Him was through our own faith? There would be some individuals who would get born again who already had terminal diseases, but didn't have enough time left to mature in their faith and receive healing. They would die if it wasn't for others interceding for them or someone with the gift of healing praying for them. That's why the Lord gave these gifts—to keep us encouraged and alive so we can mature.

It is also wrong for an individual not to mature in his personal faith in the Lord and become dependent on the gifts. It is not right for someone to receive a miracle through someone with the gift of miracles and then just struggle along until the next time that gifted minister comes through town. The Lord wants us to receive His power through these gifts, but then we must mature so that we can walk in God's best on our own.

We are able to mature beyond a total dependency on the gifts to where we can hear and receive from God directly. However, none of us will ever reach such a level of maturity in the Lord where there is nothing left to learn or receive. Let Him teach you through His Word today.

SEPTEMBER 3
THE POWER OF PRAISE AND WORSHIP
LUKE 19:29-40

Luke 19:39-40 "And some of the Pharisees from among the multitude said unto him, Master, rebuke thy disciples. And he answered and said unto them, I tell you that, if these should hold their peace, the stones would immediately cry out."

There is nothing wrong with praising God. It is encouraged and commanded thousands of times in the scriptures. The reason the Pharisees were so upset was because they didn't accept Jesus as God. Indeed, it would be blasphemy for Jesus to accept worship if He wasn't God. This is another confirmation of the deity of Christ.

Only Luke records this instance of the Pharisees' objection and Jesus' answer. This was the triumphant entry of Israel's King that was prophesied and anticipated for centuries. The excitement could not be contained. If people refused to praise Him, the creation would have broken out in spontaneous praise. No rock should have to do what God created us to do.

By compiling all of the writers' accounts of what the multitudes were saying, we have this record: "Hosanna to the Son of David" (Mt. only). "Blessed is he" ("the King"- Lk.; "the King of Israel"- Jn.) "that cometh in the name of the Lord. Blessed be the kingdom of our father David that cometh in the name of the Lord" (Mk. only). "Hosanna in the highest" (Mt. and Mk. only). "Peace in heaven, and glory in the highest" (Lk. only).

Pride was what caused Satan's original sin according to Isaiah 14:12-14. He wanted to be like the most High. One thing reserved for God alone is worship, and the devil has always sought that. If he can't be the one to receive worship, then he seeks to turn others away from giving true worship to the most High God. This is the reason why praise and worship to the Lord are such powerful tools against Satan. He can't stand to see God worshiped. Worship Him with all of your heart today.

SEPTEMBER 4
GOD'S NEW CREATION
JOHN 12:20-23

John 12:23 "And Jesus answered them, saying, The hour is come,
that the Son of man should be glorified."

Philip and Andrew had just brought word to Jesus that certain Greeks or Gentiles were seeking Him at the feast. He had ministered to other Gentiles, but this is the first time that the Gentiles came specifically to seek Him instead of what He could do. Apparently, this was an added signal to Jesus that His time had come and that He could no longer confine His ministry to only the Jews. Therefore, He made statements about His death and glorification, that would break down the middle wall of partition between the Jew and the Gentile.

There was a physical wall of partition that symbolized this division in the Jerusalem temple. The Gentiles could come into a designated area of the temple known as the court of the Gentiles, but a stone wall, about five feet high, stopped them from going farther. A sign standing before the wall stated, "No man of another nation is to enter, and whosoever is caught will have himself to blame for his death!"

Many regulations and rules separated Jews and Gentiles for centuries. Christ's work on the cross abolished that separation by removing the law, thus removing the barrier between these two groups. Instead of changing the Gentiles into Jews, or the Jews into Gentiles, God made a brand new creation. It's like crossing a horse and a donkey. The result is not a horse or a donkey, but a brand new animal called a mule.

In the New Testament church there is no such thing as Jew or Gentile, bond or free; for God has created something absolutely new. It's the *"one new man, "* the new creation in Christ Jesus, the church, Christ's body, the fullness of Him, that filleth all in all (Eph. 1:23). Remember who you are "in Him."

SEPTEMBER 5
GOD'S VOICE
JOHN 12:20-28

John 12:28 "Father, glorify thy name. Then came there a voice from heaven, saying, I have both glorified it, and will glorify it again."

This is the third time recorded in the Gospels that the Father spoke in an audible voice to or about Jesus. First, at Jesus' baptism in the Jordan River and second, at the transfiguration of Jesus.

This verse makes it clear that it was a voice that the Father spoke in; however, there were different reports of the same event. Some people heard a voice and thought it was an angel who spoke. Others thought it was thunder. This illustrates "the natural man receiveth not the things of the Spirit of God: for they are foolishness unto him: neither can he know them, because they are spiritually discerned" (1 Cor. 2:14). A carnal man with a hard heart will always find some natural explanation for the supernatural, even if he heard an audible voice from God.

A hard heart keeps us from perceiving spiritual truths and stops us from understanding. When a person doesn't understand God's Word, Satan finds no resistance when he comes to steal it away. A hard heart keeps us from remembering. This isn't to say that facts or scriptures can't be recalled, it's the spiritual lessons learned that have been forgotten. Likewise, some people can quote scripture or remember what the sermon was about, but they can't perceive the spiritual life in it or retain what they did perceive, because of a hard heart.

Jesus didn't need to hear this audible voice of God because he had a more sure word of prophecy than the audible voice of God from heaven (2 Pet. 1:18-20). Jesus knew the "voice" of the Old Testament scriptures that spoke of the Christ being glorified and He could also hear the Father's voice in His heart as He had on so many other occasions. This audible voice didn't come to reassure Jesus, but it came to those who had ears to hear, so that they might believe.

SEPTEMBER 6
JESUS PAID OUR DEBT
JOHN 12:31

John 12:31 "Now is the judgment of this world: now shall the prince of this world be cast out."

There is still a future judgment of the world coming, where the wicked will be separated from the righteous and cast into the lake of fire. This verse refers to the sins of the world that were about to be placed on Jesus and that He would suffer our punishment.

Jesus suffered the punishment for our sins, so there is no reason why we should suffer for them too. The price for sin has already been paid by the only one who could fully pay it and that is Jesus. All Jesus asks of us to make His redemption ours, is faith in Him as our Lord.

Sin has a wage it must pay and no one can avoid payday without faith in Jesus. Anyone who does not receive the new birth will be held liable for all the wrong he commits as a result of his sinful nature. However, those who receive the new birth through faith in Jesus, don't have a sin nature; therefore, they will not receive the payment of death.

Physical death as well as every result of the sin nature (i.e. sickness, depression, fear, etc.) is only a by-product of the spiritual death that was already inside of us. The Lord told Adam that in the day he ate of the forbidden tree, he would surely die (Gen. 2:17). Adam didn't die physically that day, but he did die spiritually. Physical death came 930 years later for Adam (Gen. 5:5) as a by-product of his spiritual death.

Eternal life is a gift. The dictionary defines a gift as "something that is bestowed voluntarily and without compensation; a present." We have nothing to do with earning this gift. All we have to do is receive it by faith.

SEPTEMBER 7
THE POWER TO LIVE A HOLY LIFE
JOHN 12:31

John 12:31 "Now is the judgment of this world: now shall the prince of this world be cast out."

The only reason Satan ever had any right to become a prince or rule over us was because we yielded ourselves to him through sin (Rom. 6:16). Since Jesus "bore our sins in His own body on the tree" (1 Pet. 2:24), Satan no longer has power or authority over those who accept Jesus' gift of salvation. Satan has been "cast out"—stripped of any power he had. Now he can only deceive, and if we fall for his lies, we stop God's blessings from flowing in our lives.

The reason why a believer must live a holy life, is to avoid Satan's bondage. When we obey sin, we yield ourselves to Satan, the author of that sin. Yielding to sin is yielding to a person: Satan. God doesn't impute the sin to us, but the devil does. Our actions either release the power of Satan or the power of God in us.

Although God is not imputing our sins unto us, we cannot afford the luxury of sin because it allows Satan to have access to us. When a Christian does sin and gives the devil an opportunity to produce death in his life, the way to stop him is to confess the sin. God is faithful and just to take the forgiveness that is already present in our born-again spirits and release it in our flesh, thereby removing Satan and his strongholds.

A person who abandons himself to sin is actually becoming a slave to the devil while a person who obeys righteousness is yielding himself to the Lord. This is why a Christian should live a holy life.

SEPTEMBER 8
CHOOSE TO BELIEVE
JOHN 12:37-40

John 12:39-40 "Therefore they could not believe, because that Esaias said again, He hath blinded their eyes, and hardened their heart; that they should not see with their eyes, nor understand with their heart, and be converted, and I should heal them."

This could be interpreted as the ultimate teaching in predestination. That interpretation would be that these people were never given the opportunity to believe because of Isaiah's prophecies. However, the Word of God makes it clear that "whosoever shall call upon the name of the Lord shall be saved" (Rom. 10:13); "Behold, I stand at the door, and knock: if any man hear my voice, and open the door, I will come in to him, and will sup with him, and he with me" (Rev. 3:20); and "whosoever will, let him take the water of life freely" (Rev. 22:17). No one has ever been denied the opportunity to accept salvation (Ti. 2:11).

Mark 6:5 says that "he (Jesus) could there do no mighty work, save that he laid his hands upon a few sick folk, and healed them." In that instance, it is evident that the reason Jesus couldn't do any mighty work was not because He didn't possess the power, but because He chose not to use that power against a person's will. He couldn't perform the mighty works because of His decision to uphold our freedom of choice.

Likewise, these Jews could not believe because of their choice to reject Jesus. They could not believe because they chose not to believe. "They stumbled at the stumblingstone" (Rom. 9:32), which was Jesus.

Isaiah did not predestine them to this fate. Rather he saw that very few would receive the report (Isa. 53:1) about the Messiah, and therefore would be kept from the knowledge of salvation because they rejected Him in whom all the treasures of wisdom and knowledge are found (Col. 2:3). This is what Isaiah prophesied, and it came to pass. Be careful what you choose.

SEPTEMBER 9
BELIEVE THAT YOU HAVE RECEIVED
MATTHEW 21:18-19

Matthew 21:19 "And when he saw a fig tree in the way, he came to it, and found nothing thereon, but leaves only, and said unto it, Let no fruit grow on thee henceforward for ever. And presently the fig tree withered away."

The Greek word for "presently" means "instantly; immediately; soon." However, the disciples didn't realize that the fig tree had died until the next day. If the tree died instantly, why didn't they notice it until the next morning? The answer to this question is found in Mark 11:20. The tree was dead from the roots up. The tree did die instantly just as the Word declared, but what had happened to the roots wasn't visible until the next morning.

There is a spiritual lesson here that applies to us receiving things from God. When we ask, we do receive, but it may take a period of time before we perceive it in the natural realm. God's answer comes before we see the manifestation of what we have believed the Lord for when we prayed. Just as with this fig tree, the answer lies beneath the surface, and therefore we don't "see" what God is doing until the answer manifests.

Not all answers to prayer are manifested instantly. Satan can hinder God's power even after it has been released. In Daniel 10:1-13, God answered Daniel's prayer instantly, yet it took 21 days for Daniel to see God's answer manifest, because the prince of Persia (a demonic power) withheld the manifestation.

Prayer that meets the requirements outlined in God's Word is always answered. Many times we don't perceive the answer because it always comes in the spiritual realm first then is manifested in the physical realm. If we waver from our confident faith, then we abort the manifestation of our answer to prayer. But God did answer. Everyone that asks receives.

SEPTEMBER 10
OUR WORDS ARE ALIVE
MARK 11:14

Mark 11:14 "And Jesus answered and said unto it, No man eat fruit of thee hereafter for ever. And his disciples heard it."

Notice that this verse says that Jesus "answered" this fig tree. The tree had not spoken to Him verbally, but it communicated that it had figs by the leaves on it. It is a fact that a fig tree should have figs by the time the leaves are evident. A fig tree actually produces green figs before the leaves appear and if no figs are produced by that time, then the tree will not have any figs that year. This fig tree was professing something that it didn't have even though it was still too early for figs.

Not only plants, but other things can communicate with us too. Circumstances can tell you that you have failed. Your body can tell you that your prayer didn't work—the Lord didn't heal you, etc. You need to follow Jesus' example and answer these things with a positive statement of your faith.

What good could it do to talk to a tree or an inanimate object? God created the heavens, the earth, and everything that is in the earth, by His words (Heb. 11:3). The whole creation was made by and responds to words. Our words, when spoken in faith, release either life or death (Prov. 18:21). They also affect people, things, and circumstances. We can release the power that is in faith by our words.

Speaking God's Word in faith brings the Holy Spirit into action. In Luke, chapter four, when Jesus was tempted of the devil for forty days, it was the Word of God that Jesus used to defeat the enemy at His temptation. We must take advantage of God's Word by placing it in our hearts so that the Holy Spirit may bring it forth at the appropriate time to accomplish a complete and total victory. Speak to that mountain in your life.

SEPTEMBER 11
THE WORD PRODUCES FRUIT
MATTHEW 21:12-14

Matthew 21:14 "And the blind and the lame came to him in the temple; and he healed them."

When we, who are the temple of the Lord, are occupied with the cares of this life, the needs of others are not met. However, when we are cleansed (Jn. 15:3), then the Lord can accomplish His ministry through us.

Jesus tells us not to worry or be anxious about our material needs being met. It would be impossible to never think about our physical needs; even Jesus thought about His need for money to pay taxes. We are simply not to be occupied with thinking about riches or spend time worrying about our necessities. They will be added unto us as we seek first the kingdom of God.

Prosperity can be damaging to the Body of Christ. God wants to bless His children with things, but a preoccupation with these things will choke God's Word and make it unfruitful. If we follow God's formula for prosperity found in Matthew 6:19-34, then the Word will bring forth fruit and we will enjoy the physical blessings of this life too.

There are people who have received God's Word, committed themselves to it to the degree that they are able to remain faithful in persecution, but because of being occupied with the affairs of this life, the Word sown in their hearts is choked and no fruit is produced. Just as weeds in a garden will steal the nutrients and starve the plant, so the pleasures of this life, if we allow them to dominate our thinking, will stop the fruit of the Word from producing.

It takes time, effort, and diligence to be a fruitful Christian. It's quicker and easier to raise weeds than it is to raise tomatoes or corn. Let God's Word produce fruit in you.

SEPTEMBER 12
WORKS DON'T SAVE
MARK 11:16

Mark 11:16 "And would not suffer that any man should carry any vessel through the temple."
Only Mark points out that Jesus would not suffer anyone to carry any vessel through the temple. No explanation is offered by Mark as to why Jesus would not allow this. It is probable that Jesus wanted His Father's house to be dedicated completely to prayer and the ministry of God. Also, as with the Sabbath, work symbolizes our own efforts, and our own efforts will always fall short of what God demands for salvation. Therefore, anything that resembled work was inappropriate in the house of God.

What are *"works of the law?"* Any rule, command or law that a person observes in an attempt to be accepted in right standing with God is a *"work of the law."* In other words, *"works of the law"* are a righteousness produced by one's self, a righteousness belonging to one's self, offered to God as a means of meeting God's standard for acceptance.

It takes a radical revelation of the Gospel of grace to abandon faith in the works of the law. God's standard of righteousness is the RIGHTEOUSNESS OF GOD alone. God has designed salvation in such a way as to eliminate any boasting from man. If salvation was by works either partially or wholly, then man could boast. But grace and faith eliminate man's boasting altogether. Faith towards God and what He has done through Christ Jesus is the only means of receiving His free gift of salvation. Salvation by grace brings praise and glory to God. If we could save ourselves, either partially or wholly, we would take the credit for it. But that is not the case. All the glory goes to God.

SEPTEMBER 13
THE BATTLE IS IN THE MIND
MATTHEW 21:21

Matthew 21:21 "Jesus answered and said unto them, Verily I say unto you, If ye have faith, and doubt not, ye shall not only do this which is done to the fig tree, but also if ye shall say unto this mountain, Be thou removed, and be thou cast into the sea; it shall be done."
Jesus makes it very clear that we must have faith and doubt not. Every believer has faith, but most believers also have an abundance of doubt that negates their faith. It is when we purify our faith and only believe, that victory comes.

Every Christian is at war. There is a perpetual struggle against Satan and his kingdom where there are no "leaves" or "discharges." Our enemy goes about as a roaring lion, seeking whom he may devour (1 Pet. 5:8). Those who resist the devil will see him flee (Jas. 4:7). The only ones whom he devours are those who don't actively fight against him.

The mind is the battlefield where thoughts and reasonings that are contrary to God's Word, need to be captured and submitted to Christ, our Commander. Just as enemy soldiers are captured in war, so rebel thoughts must be taken captive and made to submit to Christ. Our battle against the devil takes place right between our ears. The spiritual weapons given to us are designed for the express purpose of taking EVERY thought captive and making it obedient to Christ. Keeping our minds completely stayed upon the Lord is an obtainable goal.

These weapons of ours are for the casting down of two things: Imaginations; and every high thing that exalts itself against the knowledge of God. Both of these areas are dealing with the mind. Focus on the good in every area of your life. Failure to recognize God's blessings in everyday living will cause care and anxiety. Recognizing God's hand in even the smallest thing will cause peace and keep our hearts and minds following hard after the Lord.

SEPTEMBER 14
FORGIVING OTHERS IS TO YOUR ADVANTAGE
MATTHEW 21:20-22; MARK 11:20-26

Mark 11:25 *"And when ye stand praying, forgive, if ye have ought against any: that your Father also which is in heaven may forgive you your trespasses."*

There are qualifications for believing and receiving as well as restrictions for receiving answers to prayer. Unforgiveness in our hearts will keep our prayers from being answered.

We should forgive others as quickly as it takes to make the decision to pray. The Greek word for "when" means "whenever, as soon as, or while." When we stand praying, we must forgive if we have ought ("anything at all, the least little part; whatsoever") against anyone.

When we are offended or hurt, we often feel justified in holding a grudge. The Old Testament law expressed this when it stated, "Eye for eye, tooth for tooth" (Ex. 21:23-25). Until the offense was paid, we did not feel free to forgive. However, God dealt with all men's offenses by placing sin upon the perfect Savior who was judged in place of every sinner of all time. To demand that others must earn our forgiveness is not Christlike. Jesus died for every man's sins, extending forgiveness to us while we were yet sinners. We should do the same.

It is doubtful that a person who refuses to forgive has ever experienced forgiveness himself. This is comparable to the servant who Jesus talked about in Matthew 18:23-35. He was forgiven a debt of over $3 million and yet he refused to forgive his fellow servant who owed him $3,000. The forgiveness that we have received from the Lord is infinitely greater than any forgiveness we will ever be asked to extend to others. Freely forgive as you have been forgiven.

SEPTEMBER 15
FAITH IS A MUSCLE
MATTHEW 21:23-27

Matthew 21:26 *"But if we shall say, Of men; we fear the people; for all hold John as a prophet."*

Proverbs 29:25 says, *"The fear of man bringeth a snare: but whoso putteth his trust in the Lord shall be safe."* These men were seeking to snare Jesus in His words, but they couldn't because He was safely trusting in God. It was easy for Jesus to turn the tables on them and catch them because they feared man (Jn. 5:44).

Jesus had already shown that all of their works were done so that they could be seen of men (Mt. 6:5). They were not really seeking to please God, but were doing all their religious works for the praise of men. It is totally vain for a man who is bound by the fear of man to try to intimidate a man whose trust is totally in the Lord.

When David fought Goliath (1 Sam. 17), everyone mocked him because of his belief that he could win. Goliath was a giant and David was only a small boy, but David said something important in his defense. In 1 Samuel 17:34-37, David revealed that this was not the first time he had depended on God for a victory against something bigger than himself. He had already killed a lion and a bear with his bare hands. He KNEW he could defeat Goliath with God's help. Faith must be developed much like a muscle. Those who wait until the day of the contest to start training are going to lose. That's not the way it works in the natural or the spiritual realm.

What is life all about? What is the purpose of one's existence? What is to be gained in life? What do people live for? When we say "so and so" is my life, we mean that all of our attention, our focus, and our purpose for living, is directed towards and revolves around that person. In a similar way, we need to be totally consumed with Christ and His life. True life is only found in Christ. It is not found in prestige, fortune, fame, or things, but only in the one who is life—Jesus Christ.

SEPTEMBER 16
RIGHTEOUSNESS DEPENDS ON GOD, NOT ON SELF
MATTHEW 21:23-30; MARK 11:27-33; 12:1-2; LUKE 20:1-9

Matthew 21:28-30 "But what think ye? A certain man had two sons; and he came to the first, and said, Son, go work today in my vineyard. He answered and said, I will not: but afterward he repented, and went. And he came to the second, and said likewise. And he answered and said, I go, sir: and went not."

This parable was given in response to the religious leaders rejecting Jesus' authority. Through his parable, Jesus reveals God's rejection of the Jews in response to their rejection of His Son. Jesus is showing that those who do the will of God are actually the ones invested with God's authority.

These leaders had a form of godliness like this second son, but they were not doing the will of God. The publicans and harlots had no form of godliness, but when confronted with the preaching of John, many of them repented and began to do the will of God like the first son in the story.

These religious Jews, who sat in the seat of Moses, disqualified themselves from being God's representatives here on earth, because of their hypocrisy and hard hearts. Even the publicans and harlots, who repented at John's preaching, were ahead of them. There is no sin more frequent among religious people than that of self-righteousness; that is to honor the Lord with the mouth when the heart is far from Him.

These sinners were entering the kingdom of God ahead of the very religious Jews because they knew they were sinners and they put their faith in a Savior. One of the deadliest things about religious self-righteousness is the deception that we will be saved because of our good deeds. We cannot save ourselves regardless of how good we act. Who wants to be the best sinner that ever was sent to hell?

SEPTEMBER 17
OUR RIGHTEOUSNESS IS IN CHRIST
MATTHEW 22:8-14

Matthew 22:11 "And when the king came in to see the guests, he saw there a man which had not on a wedding garment:"

In this time, it was customary for the host to provide his guests with wedding garments to wear to the wedding. It was an insult of the highest degree to refuse to wear the clothing provided since the guests were brought in directly from the highways and streets. The wedding garment speaks of the righteousness of Christ that God so graciously provides for all who accept His invitation into the kingdom. It must be put on by both good and bad (Mt. 22:10).

Right standing before a holy God is not to be achieved in keeping the law, but in humble trust in the person and work of Jesus Christ. No one who is trusting in his own righteousness can have the benefit of Christ's righteousness. The righteousness that gives men relationship with God is the RIGHTEOUSNESS OF GOD, and it comes freely through faith in Jesus Christ.

The way we obtain this righteousness is by putting faith in what Christ has done for us. When we place our faith in Christ, then the righteousness that Jesus obtained by His faith becomes ours.

Through faith in Jesus, we can receive the very righteousness of God as a gift. God's righteousness is infinitely more in quality and quantity than man's puny righteousness. No one can ever be justified in the sight of God based on his own righteousness which comes through acts of holiness. One must have God's righteousness which only comes through faith in the Lord Jesus Christ as Savior. Paul said in Philippians 3:9, *"And be found in him, not having mine own righteousness, which is of the law, but that which is through the faith of Christ, the righteousness which is of God by faith."* This is *"the righteousness of God."*

SEPTEMBER 18
YOUR LIFE BELONGS TO GOD
MATTHEW 22:20-22

Matthew 22:20-21 "And he saith unto them, Whose is this image and superscription? They say unto him, Caesar's. Then saith he unto them, Render therefore unto Caesar the things which are Caesar's; and unto God the things that are God's."

The image on the denarius, the only small silver coin acceptable for imperial tax payments, was probably that of Tiberius Caesar (reigned A.D. 14-37). The inscription upon the coin read "Tiberius Caesar Augustus, Son of the Divine Augustus" with the reverse side reading "Chief Priest." This inscription was a claim to divinity and as emperor, the right to be worshiped.

The Jews had tried many times to accuse Jesus on the basis of religious issues and had always failed. Now they approached Him about paying taxes in hopes that His answer might give them the opportunity to deliver Him to Pilate for prosecution.

These Pharisees and Herodians reasoned that any answer that Jesus gave would be wrong. If He approved of the Roman taxes, then He would lose popularity with the masses. If He spoke against the Roman taxes, then the Jews would hand Him over to the Roman government and Pilate would dispose of Him. It looked like they had Jesus trapped. Jesus, however, answered with such simple wisdom that these Pharisees and Herodians were caught in their own trap and made to look like fools.

Jesus declared, "Render (give back) to Caesar the things that are Caesar's, and to God the things that are God's" (Mk. 12:17). People are made in God's image, so they must render to God the things belonging to God (our lives) and to Caesar the things belonging to Caesar (his money and other benefits of his rule).

SEPTEMBER 19
THE RESURRECTION POWER
MATTHEW 22:23

Matthew 22:23 "The same day came to him the Sadducees, which say that there is no resurrection, and asked him,"

The Greek word used here for resurrection means "a standing or rising up." The resurrection is a major theme of New Testament teaching. Out of the 13 sermons in the book of Acts, 11 stress or imply the resurrection.

Man consists of three parts—spirit, soul, and body (1 Th. 5:23). The body is mortal while the spirit and soul are immortal. At death, man's body goes through the decomposition process and returns to its original elements. At the resurrection, man's departed soul and spirit are called forth from either heaven or hell. The material elements of the body are raised up, reassembled, and united with the spirit and soul. Thus we have the complete personality of the individual reconstituted. Everyone will be resurrected—some to life, and some to damnation.

The hope of the believer is the resurrection unto life. The natural, earthly, terrestrial, corrupt, weak, mortal, vile body is said to be raised, changed and fashioned into a spiritual, heavenly, celestial, incorrupt, glorious, powerful, and immortal body. This is the completion of everything that has been purchased for us in Christ.

Paul said in 1 Corinthians 15:12-17 that if there is no resurrection, then our faith is vain and we are yet in our sins. It is the resurrected life of Jesus that brings spiritual life into us and the resurrection of the body that brings physical regeneration, reconstituting us into the very image of God. The transformation from this physical condition to our glorified bodies will be a huge difference, but the power of God can accomplish it easily. If the Lord can work that miracle, then surely He can heal our bodies and free us from other bondages.

SEPTEMBER 20
HEAVEN
MARK 12:25

Mark 12:25 "For when they shall rise from the dead, they neither marry, nor are given in marriage; but are as the angels which are in heaven."

The word heaven comes from the Greek word meaning "the sky; heaven as the abode of God"; by implication, "happiness; power; an eternity."

Paul mentioned being caught up into "the third heaven," in 2 Corinthians 12:2. Since the third heaven exists, there must also be a first and second heaven. The first is probably the atmospheric heaven, the second, the abode of supernatural angelic beings, and the third, the place where God dwells.

God now dwells in the hearts of His people, but He also sits on His throne in heaven. The Lord's commitment to dwell in us and never leave us or forsake us, must be taken as an indication of His great love for us. Heaven has a real temple that is patterned after the Old Testament tabernacle. Saints who die go immediately into heaven and into the presence of God.

Paul had a vision of heaven that made him long to go there. Most people cling to this physical life for selfish reasons. Only when we lose our lives (die to self and live for Christ and others), do we truly find out what life is all about. If we seriously thought about what the scriptures teach us about life with Christ after this physical life, we would all think like Paul. The things prepared for us are so wonderful that we can't totally comprehend them with our finite mind. We need to value our eternal life more and our temporal life less. This would solve many problems and remove a lot of grief.

SEPTEMBER 21
MARRIAGE IS FOR THIS LIFE
LUKE 20:27-40

Luke 20:33-34 "Therefore in the resurrection whose wife of them is she? for seven had her to wife. And Jesus answering said unto them, The children of this world marry, and are given in marriage:"

It is very doubtful that the situation that the Sadducees were relating ever took place. It is more probable that they were stating a hypothetical case to complicate the understanding of the resurrection and thereby discredit it. If you accept their basic supposition (marriage continues in heaven), then their reasoning was correct. It would not be possible to administer marriage in heaven with multiple mates as their story described. Their reasoning wasn't flawed, but rather the facts that their reasoning was based on were not scriptural.

The scriptures speak of two becoming "one flesh" in marriage, and angels are not flesh. Paul said, "Flesh and blood cannot inherit the kingdom of God" (1 Cor. 15:50). Therefore, marriage is an earthly institution limited to flesh and blood mortals and will not exist in heaven. Marriage, as is death, is temporary for mortals while they are on earth. This is why a person whose mate has died, is free to remarry. Marriage pertains only to this life.

That is not to say that a couple who have loved each other deeply here on earth will love each other less in heaven. God forbid. They will love each other infinitely more, but it will be God's "agape" love (not romantic love) and it will not be limited to just one person. We can be sure that heaven will surpass any expectations that we may have so that no one will be disappointed.

Today, many people use logical reasoning to try to discredit God's Word. But Jesus said, "They err because they do not know the scriptures." Therefore, their arguments have no merit; only reasoning based on scripture has any merit.

SEPTEMBER 22
THE TWO GREATEST COMMANDS
MATTHEW 22:34-46

Matthew 22:36 "Master, which is the great commandment in the law? Jesus said unto him, Thou shalt love the Lord thy God with all thy heart, and with all thy soul, and with all thy mind. This is the first and great commandment. And the second is like unto it, Thou shalt love thy neighbour as thyself."

Jesus revealed that all of the Old Testament laws were designed to instruct us how to love God and love others. Therefore, the two commands that dealt directly with loving God and others (Lev. 19:18 and Dt. 6:5) were the most important.

The religious leaders had become so obsessed with keeping every minor detail of the law that they had lost sight of its ultimate purpose. They neither loved God nor their fellow man, yet they thought they were keeping the law. The same thing is happening today. Some of the cruelest acts of men towards their fellow men have been done in the name of the Lord by people who thought they were defending God's holy commandments. However, if we violate one of the two greatest commandments in an effort to enforce some other commandment, then we are misapplying God's Word just as these religious Jews did.

The Old Testament law and the New Testament concept of grace compels men to the same end; that is to love God and their fellowmen. However, the motivations to this end are different. The Old Testament law motivated men to love God and their fellowman through fear of punishment if they failed to comply. The New Testament concept of grace freely gives men a God-kind of love that is unconditional and tells them to love others as they are loved.

It is possible to display actions of holiness, but not love God. It is impossible for God's kind of love not to produce holiness. Holiness is a fruit and not a root of loving God.

SEPTEMBER 23
JESUS THE SERVANT
MARK 12:28-30

Mark 12:29 "And Jesus answered him, The first of all the commandments is, Hear, O Israel; The Lord our God is one Lord":

Jesus repeatedly made reference to His deity for which the Jews had sought to kill Him, yet He quotes from Deuteronomy 6:4, that *"The Lord our God is one Lord."* There are not two or three Gods, yet Jesus claimed to be God just like God the Father. This union is a great mystery that defies human understanding, but can be accepted and believed.

Jesus in His preexistent state was in the form of God. "In the beginning was the Word and the Word was with God, and the Word was God." Jesus is God manifested in the flesh (1 Tim. 3:16). However, Jesus did not demand or cling to His rights as God. He laid aside His Divine rights and privileges in order to take the form of a servant and be made in the likeness of man. He further humbled Himself by becoming obedient to the Father, even to the point of death. This was the supreme sacrifice that identified Jesus totally with humanity and enabled God to redeem mankind. By dying a criminal's death upon the cross, Jesus fulfilled the Old Testament prophecy of Deuteronomy 21:23, and bore our curse in His own body. This redeemed us from the curse, opened wide God's blessing of justification through faith in Christ, and gave us the promise of His Holy Spirit (Gal. 3:13-14).

The Creator became the creation; the Lord became the servant; the Highest became the lowest. All of this was done because of God's great love for us.

SEPTEMBER 24
UNDERSTANDING TRUTH
LUKE 20:41-44

Luke 20:44 "David therefore calleth him Lord, how is he then his son?"
Jesus took an apparent contradiction in scripture and through combining these paradoxical statements (concerning the humanity and deity of Christ), brought forth the truth that Christ is God in human flesh. Both assertions (that Jesus was David's son and David's Lord) were right at the same time.

It was correct that Christ was David's son and it was also correct that Christ was David's Lord. This meant that Christ also was God. However, Christ was not exclusively David's son nor was He exclusively David's Lord. These two truths had to be combined to arrive at the whole truth. No truth of God's Word stands independent of the other truths in God's Word.

A lack of balancing truth with truth is usually the cause of much contention among men when interpreting scriptures. Some argue that everything is by grace, while others emphatically state that without faith it is impossible to please God. The Bible teaches us that we need both grace and faith to be born again—not one without the other. The same is true of faith versus works, and many other truths in God's Word. Error can simply be truth taken to an extreme at the expense of other truths.

One of the concerns of many Christians is, "How can I know I'm thinking and acting properly?" If we seek the Lord with pure hearts and singleness of purpose, then the Lord will show us anything we need to change. In other words, all we have to do is focus on the Lord with pure hearts, and He promises to show us any errors. The only people who need to fear that they might be deceived are those who are not seeking the Lord with pure and single-minded hearts.

SEPTEMBER 25
SEEK GOD'S WISDOM
MATTHEW 23:1-9

Matthew 23:1 "Then spake Jesus to the multitude, and to his disciples,"
This rebuke by Jesus to the scribes and Pharisees for their hypocrisy was the harshest treatment that He ever gave to any group. He did this publicly before the multitude, the people the hypocrites most wanted to impress.

Jesus had faced many prior battles with the scribes and Pharisees. On this particular day, the encounter started with the chief priests and elders challenging Jesus' authority. Jesus stunned them by replying with a question that challenged their authority. He then used three parables to illustrate that the leaders of the Jews had rejected the rule of God in their lives, despite their pious religious acts. They "perceived that he spake of them."

The Pharisees countered by tempting Jesus with a question about paying taxes to the Roman government. Then the Sadducees tried to stop Jesus with a question about the resurrection, and finally, a lawyer tried to snare Him with a question about the greatest commandment. Jesus did so well in each test that "no man after that durst ask him any question." Jesus then asked the leaders who were supposed to know it all, a question that none of them could answer. These Jews, who prided themselves on having superior knowledge, were totally humiliated by a man who had never been through their religious "seminary." This resulted in them being afraid to ever try to trap Jesus again by questioning Him.

These were the events of the day that led up to Jesus' stinging public rebuke of these hypocrites. Jesus gave this rebuke knowing full well that they were planning to kill Him. Jesus was totally fearless in the face of their threats. All of these questions were intended to snare Jesus, but in His infinite superior wisdom, He evaded their traps. Ask God for His wisdom, and He will also help you evade traps.

SEPTEMBER 26
GIVE AGAPE LOVE
MATTHEW 23:10-12

Matthew 23:12 "And whosoever shall exalt himself shall be abased; and he that shall humble himself shall be exalted."

In Romans 12:10 we are admonished to desire the welfare of others more than our own; to like others better than ourselves. That is an awesome command that is only obtainable through God's supernatural love. If this simple, yet profound truth could be understood and applied, then strife would cease (Prov. 13:10). The world would see Christianity as never before, and we would discover the true joy that comes from serving someone besides ourselves.

There is much confusion today on the subject of love because we have only one English word (love) to describe a broad aspect of meanings. For example, if I said, "I love my wife, I love apple pie, and I love my dog," obviously I am not talking about love in the same degree or definition.

God's type of love; the highest kind of love, is AGAPE. This is when we seek the welfare or betterment of others even when we don't feel affection. AGAPE love does not come from one's feelings. Jesus displayed this AGAPE kind of love by going to the cross and dying for us even though He didn't feel like dying. Jesus sought the betterment of you and me, regardless of His feelings. We, too, can AGAPE love our enemies even though we don't have a warm feeling of affection for them. If they are hungry we can feed them; if they are thirsty we can give them a drink. We can choose to seek the betterment and welfare of others regardless of how we feel.

If anyone becomes a servant and humbles himself with the motive of being exalted, then he is not truly fulfilling Jesus' command. Jesus is teaching about a true, servant's heart, that loves others more than itself, and will joyfully go without so that someone else may prosper.

SEPTEMBER 27
HYPOCRISY IS AN ATTITUDE
MATTHEW 23:12

Matthew 23:12 "And whosoever shall exalt himself shall be abased; and he that shall humble himself shall be exalted."

He who thinks that he will be exalted by acting as a servant, pretending to be humble so that he will receive the promise of God's Word, is sadly mistaken. Hypocrisy is an attitude or motive.

There are two main types of hypocrisy: People who don't practice what they preach and people whose motives are wrong even though their actions are right. The second type of hypocrisy is why Jesus rebuked the scribes and Pharisees. It is more subtle than the first type and is very prevalent today in religion. They were seeking self-glory instead of seeking to glorify God. Their priorities were wrong, and their focus was on outward displays instead of on the inner condition of their hearts. Furthermore, they always persecuted the true worshipers of God.

Universally, people dislike blatant hypocrisy; although this subtle type of hypocrisy has been encouraged and even promoted by religion. Religion teaches tithing and giving for selfish motives while 1 Corinthians 13:3 and 2 Corinthians 9:7, make it clear that giving will profit us nothing unless we have the proper motive. The same thing happens when people try to achieve holiness by performing many other religious acts. It is not always the acts that are wrong, but the motives behind the acts. These wrong motives can also make you a hypocrite.

Anyone who rejects salvation because he doesn't like religious hypocrites, should remember that if he doesn't receive Jesus as his Lord, then he will spend eternity with these hypocrites in hell.

SEPTEMBER 28
GIVE CHEERFULLY, NOT OUT OF FEAR
MATTHEW 23:23

Matthew 23:23 "Woe unto you, scribes and Pharisees, hypocrites! for ye pay tithe of mint and anise and cummin, and have omitted the weightier matters of the law, judgment, mercy, and faith: these ought ye to have done, and not to leave the other undone."

Some have taught that Jesus did away with the tithe since it is not a specific part of the New Testament teaching. In this instance, Jesus made reference to the scribes and Pharisees tithing and implied that they were right in doing so. The New Covenant did not do away with the tithe, but it clarified what the motives for tithing should be.

Abram tithed over 430 years before the law was given. Jacob also tithed approximately 300 years before the time of the law. Therefore, tithing was a biblical principle that didn't begin or end with the law of Moses. However, the law of Moses did include tithing as part of its commandments and attached were stiff penalties for those who failed to comply. It was concerning these punishments for not tithing, that the New Testament differed from the Old Testament. Malachi 3:8-9 says that if a man doesn't tithe, he has robbed God and is cursed with a curse. Therefore, people gave out of the motivation of debt and obligation. Jesus redeemed us from this and all the other curses of the law, so that God will not curse us for not tithing.

The Apostle Paul also made it clear that any type of giving motivated by anything less than God's kind of love is useless. He went on to explain in 2 Corinthians 9:7, that God wants us to give, "not grudgingly, or of necessity: for God loveth a cheerful giver." The type of giving that God loves is cheerful, freewill giving. This does not mean that tithing is contrary to the New Testament. It is the "fear of punishment" motive, that the Old Testament law attached to tithing that has been done away with. Giving and tithing are still very much a part of the New Testament doctrine, and if done with the New Testament attitude, are still acceptable to God. Be a giver.

SEPTEMBER 29
GOD'S MERCY IS A GIFT
MATTHEW 23:23

Matthew 23:23 "Woe unto you, scribes and Pharisees, hypocrites! for ye pay tithe of mint and anise and cummin, and have omitted the weightier matters of the law, judgment, mercy, and faith: these ought ye to have done, and not to leave the other undone."

One of the ways that God's goodness is revealed is by His mercy. We may describe mercy as the readiness of God to relieve the misery of fallen creatures. Many times, mercy is called compassion or lovingkindness. It is expressed toward the sinner because of the misery that sin has brought upon him.

God's mercy to the believer is revealed by God taking away the misery of sin's consequences through the New Covenant of our Savior, the Lord Jesus Christ. Mercy is not something merited or earned, but a gift, as the Apostle Paul states, "Not by works of righteousness which we have done, but according to HIS MERCY He saved us" (Ti. 3:5).

Paul speaks of the heavenly Father as *"The Father of mercies."* The word "father" is used many times in scripture as an originator or as a source of something. For example, the devil is called the father of lies (Jn. 8:44), i.e. he is the author and originator of lying. Likewise, our heavenly Father is the author, originator, and source of all mercy. Each time that mankind cried out in faith, God's mercy reached out and met the need.

God is said to be rich in mercy because of His great love where with he loved us (Eph. 2:4), and to have a throne called grace whereby we may come and obtain mercy. God wasn't motivated to save us through pity or a sense of obligation as our Creator. He was motivated solely by love. God loves us.

SEPTEMBER 30
GOD RECOGNIZES OUR SACRIFICES
MARK 12:41-44

Mark 12:41-42 "And Jesus sat over against the treasury, and beheld how the people cast money into the treasury: and many that were rich cast in much. And there came a certain poor widow, and she threw in two mites, which make a farthing."

The treasury that is spoken of here is a place located in the Women's Court that was in the temple complex, but was not part of the temple itself. Women were not allowed in the temple, so the fact that this widow was casting her offering into the treasury verifies the location of the treasury.

Jesus used this instance to teach His disciples a very important lesson. He did not say these things to this widow personally. God's promises concerning giving give us an assurance that this offering was blessed back to this woman in this life, but the widow did not hear His commendation. There is no indication that this poor widow ever knew that anyone recognized the extent of her sacrifice.

Likewise, there are times when we may feel that no one knows or appreciates our sacrifices. However, just as surely as Jesus saw this woman's giving and knew of the sacrifice involved, God takes note of our smallest deeds and one day, will reward us openly.

The Lord does not judge the size of our gifts by how much we give, but rather by how much we have left over after we give. Men tend to compare themselves with each other, but the Lord doesn't judge our giving by what others give. He judges our gifts by what we have to give. The Lord looks at the heart of the giver more than at the gift. The Lord weighs the giver more than the gift. When we stand before the Lord, all of our works, not only our giving, will be tried to determine what sort—not what size they are.

OCTOBER 1
GUARD AGAINST DECEPTION
MATTHEW 24:3-5

Matthew 24:4 "And Jesus answered and said unto them, Take heed that no man deceive you."

Deception can be avoided or else Jesus would not have said, "Take heed that no man deceive you." Satan can only deceive those who allow him to do it. Ephesians 6:11 tells us to "Put on the whole armour of God, that ye may be able to stand against the wiles of the devil." Putting on the whole armour of God will protect you from the deception of the devil. Just wearing part of God's armour will not fully protect you. Many Christians have been running around with the helmet of salvation on, but nothing else. There is more to overcoming the devil than just being saved. We have to understand our righteous position in the Lord. We also must possess faith, know the Word, and understand the gospel of peace.

The Christian life is a constant struggle against Satan, who is trying to corrupt us. Most Christians are aware of the warfare, but they don't know where the warfare is occurring. The battle is in our minds. Just as the serpent didn't come against Eve with brute force, but rather used words to deceive her, likewise Satan tries to corrupt us through thoughts contrary to the Gospel. Satan's original tactic was deception and that is still his method of operation today.

One of the characteristics of children is that they are easily deceived. They are gullible. One of the things that must take place to move from childhood into sonship is spiritual discernment. This comes from being grounded in the Word of God.

The way to recognize deception is not to analyze all the false claims, but to become so familiar with what is genuine that a counterfeit will be easily recognizable. Anyone who is truly grounded in the Word of God will not be deceived.

OCTOBER 2
BASE YOUR RELATIONSHIPS ON GOD
MATTHEW 24:12

Matthew 24:12 "And because iniquity shall abound, the love of many shall wax cold."

The only reason that an abundance of iniquity would make anyone's love for the Lord wax cold, is if he were not separated from that iniquity. As with Lot, a righteous man can vex his soul from day to day by hearing and seeing the unlawful deeds of the ungodly (2 Pet. 2:8).

We have to deal with the world's system and those in it, but we need to be careful and maintain proper balance. We should shun relationships with those who influence us negatively more than we influence them positively.

Marriage is one area where this principle is especially true. There is no closer union in life than the marriage relationship. A believer who marries an unbeliever is directly violating this scripture and is toying with disaster. The Lord should be the most important person in our life. How could we possibly become "one" with a person who doesn't love our Lord?

It is folly to think that after marriage an unbelieving spouse will accept the Lord. Although that does happen, it cannot be guaranteed. In fact, statistics are overwhelmingly against this happening. Regardless of that possibility, a believer who marries an unbeliever is directly violating God's instructions here. It is not a good start to any marriage to spurn God's Word.

Being unequally yoked with unbelievers just doesn't work. Believers and unbelievers are as different as righteousness and unrighteousness; light and dark; Christ and the devil. One has faith and the other has none. One is the temple of God and the other an idol. Any Christian who doesn't see this conflict is deceived.

OCTOBER 3
YOUR NATURE IN CHRIST
MATTHEW 24:13

Matthew 24:13 "But he that shall endure unto the end, the same shall be saved."

Here, Jesus teaches that the believer must persevere to receive complete salvation. Salvation is a gift that cannot be earned or maintained by our own works. It has to be received by faith. However, there is effort on our part to maintain that faith. This is where holiness comes in.

Holiness will not produce relationship with God, nor will a lack of holiness make God turn away from us. He deals with us according to our faith in Jesus, not our performance. Holiness will keep Satan from stealing our faith, while a lack of holiness is an open invitation for the devil to do his worst. A person who wants to endure to the end cannot live a lifestyle that permits Satan free access to him.

Although God is not imputing our sins unto us, we cannot afford the luxury of sin because it allows Satan to have access to us. When a Christian does sin, and allows the devil an opportunity to produce death in his life, the way to stop this is to confess the sin. God is faithful and just to take the forgiveness that is already present in our born-again spirits and release it in our flesh, thereby removing Satan and his strongholds.

Holiness is a fruit and not a root of salvation. That is to say that holiness is a by-product of relationship with God; it does not produce relationship with God. It is the nature of a Christian to walk in the light, not in the dark. When we are rightly informed of who we are and what we have in Christ, then holiness will naturally flow out of us because it is our nature.

OCTOBER 4
YOUR HOPE IS IN ETERNITY
LUKE 21:15-22

Luke 21:18-19 "But there shall not an hair of your head perish.
In your patience possess ye your souls."

Jesus says the disciples were betrayed by parents, brothers, relatives, friends, and some disciples were even put to death. Yet, the amazing statement of Christ is that not a hair of their heads will perish. The context of this statement speaks of some of the disciples dying, so this is not a promise that no physical harm will ever come. This could only refer to the resurrection.

The Greek word for "resurrection" means "a standing or rising up." The resurrection is a major theme of New Testament teaching. Out of the 13 sermons in the book of Acts, 11 stress or imply the resurrection.

The hope of the believer is the resurrection. The natural, earthly, terrestrial, corrupt, weak, mortal, vile body is said to be raised, changed and fashioned into a spiritual, heavenly, celestial, incorrupt, glorious, powerful, and immortal body. This is the completeness that has been purchased for all of us in Christ.

The Lord views everything in the light of eternity. Man tends to view things in the context of his brief life on earth. From man's perspective, a person who dies for his faith in Jesus has lost a great deal. From Jesus' viewpoint, a martyr hasn't lost a thing. Even the very hairs on our head are numbered. The patience that Jesus is speaking of here is the calm assurance that God knows every hurt that we feel and He will abundantly recompense us in the resurrection. This knowledge enables us to control our emotions in the face of persecution (i.e. possess our souls) instead of letting our emotions of fear dominate us.

OCTOBER 5
GET READY FOR JESUS
MATTHEW 24:38-39

Matthew 24:38 "For as in the days that were before the flood they were eating and drinking,
marrying and giving in marriage, until the day that Noe entered into the ark,"

Jesus is prophesying that just as in Noah's day, people will be dominated with the temporary affairs of this life instead of eternal spiritual truths, when Jesus returns. Before our Lord's second return, there will be plenty of signs to show that the time is drawing near, but few will heed them. Preoccupation with the affairs of this life can dull us to the spiritual realm.

The Lord kindly, but seriously, points out the urgent need to be ready for His return. In the same way that a thief comes when people are the least prepared, so our Lord will return in a time when people are not looking for Him.

This is not because our Lord desires to surprise everyone and see how many He can catch unprepared. On the contrary, He is urging us to be watchful so that we will be prepared. Jesus gave us the signs of the end times to help us be prepared. He is simply prophesying that there will be a condition of apathy in the latter days that will tend to lull even the faithful to sleep if they don't take heed to His words.

Believers will not be assembled on a mountaintop somewhere waiting for the Lord's return. They will still be going about their daily routines. The Lord told us to "occupy till I come" (Lk. 19:13). We should be ready for the Lord to come back at any moment, yet work as if His return was still far off.

OCTOBER 6
FOLLOW THE LEADING OF THE HOLY SPIRIT
MATTHEW 25:14

Matthew 25:14 "For the kingdom of heaven is as a man travelling into a far country, who called his own servants, and delivered unto them his goods."
The parable of the talents continues the theme of being ready for the Lord's return, but it also makes a strong point that we are accountable to the Lord for the gifts He has given us. The Lord intends us to use these gifts to further His kingdom—not keep them hidden.

This parable also shows the Lord dealing with His servants according to their own individual gifts and abilities. The servants who doubled their Lord's money were praised equally, even though one had produced two and one-half times as much revenue for His Lord than the other. Every man's work shall be judged as to what sort it is—not what size it is.

Most people today are preoccupied with quantity of ministry instead of quality of ministry. The Lord is going to reward us based on how well we did, not on how much we did. Those who are not governed by the Holy Spirit in their actions will see all their good works burned up on the day we stand before the Lord and He tries our works. Those who acted only under the guidance of the Holy Spirit will find that their works will endure the test and they will receive a reward.

Many people choose to do good things thinking that God will be pleased. It is our positive response to God's direction (faith) that pleases God (Heb. 11:6). We were created with a purpose and every individual has a God-given plan for his life. Unless our actions are in agreement with God's plan for our lives, they will not abide the test of God's fire.

OCTOBER 7
HOW TO ESTEEM OTHERS MORE THAN SELF
MATTHEW 25:32-46

Matthew 25:40 "And the King shall answer and say unto them, Verily I say unto you, Inasmuch as ye have done it unto one of the least of these my brethren, ye have done it unto me."
When a kind act was done to someone in need, Jesus said it was done unto Him. The Lord deeply feels our hurts. When someone is neglected, Jesus says He is also being neglected. We have a high priest who is touched by the feelings of our infirmities (Heb. 4:15). When we hurt, He hurts. When we are blessed, He is blessed. The God of the universe is intricately involved with every detail of our lives.   How can we esteem others better than ourselves, when really, we think we are better than others? Some people are better athletes than others. Some are better businessmen than others. Some are better speakers than others, and so forth.

First, we need to recognize that our accomplishments don't make us better than others. There is a difference between what we do and who we are. Better performance does not make a better person. A person's character can be severely wanting even though his performance is good.

Second, to esteem someone better than ourselves simply means to value them more than we value ourselves. To some that may seem impossible, but it isn't. That is exactly what Jesus did. If Jesus, who was God in the flesh (1 Tim. 3:16), could humble Himself and value our good above His own welfare, then we should certainly be able to do the same. It can happen when we die to self and live to God.

If we think only about ourselves, we will be selfish. If we get out of self and think more about the benefit of others than the benefit of self, then we will be selfless. It's a matter of focus.

OCTOBER 8
ESCAPE CONDEMNATION
MATTHEW 26:2

Matthew 26:2 "Ye know that after two days is the feast of the passover, and the Son of man is betrayed to be crucified."

In Israel, crucifixion was a common sight. This practice was first mentioned in scripture as one used by the Egyptians (Gen. 40:19). Anyone hung upon a tree was accursed by God, according to the Mosaic law (Dt. 21:22-23).

Failure to obey the law brought on the curse. Praise God that Christ has redeemed us from the curse of the law by bearing the curse for us. Now, through Christ, we will never receive any curse from God even though we still disobey the law in some way. Justice was satisfied when Jesus died for the law that we broke, thus paying the prescribed penalty and bearing the curse. There is no condemnation awaiting us from the law; for we died in Him.

A Christian who still walks in condemnation is being condemned by the devil or himself. It's not God who condemns us (Rom. 8:34). It is the law that brought God's adverse sentence against us.

When the government condemns a building it is declared unfit for use and must be destroyed. Likewise, when Satan condemns us, he makes us feel unfit for use and ready to be destroyed. Since the Christian is no longer under the law, he should no longer be condemned or feel unfit for use. We have been accepted by the Father through Jesus.

God convicts of sin, but He doesn't condemn (Rom. 8:34). Conviction is solely for our profit with no malice, while condemnation includes punishment. Satan is the one who condemns the Christian, but the Holy Spirit has given us the power to escape that condemnation.

OCTOBER 9
RESIST THE TEMPTATION OF SIN
LUKE 22:3

Luke 22:3 "Then entered Satan into Judas surnamed Iscariot, being of the number of the twelve."

Some people have speculated that Judas betrayed Jesus in an effort to force Jesus into a confrontation with the Roman government. Then He would have to use His supernatural power in self-defense and overthrow the Romans, thereby giving independence back to the nation of Israel.

This idea is based mainly on the response of Judas when he saw that Jesus was condemned. Judas "repented himself" (Mt. 27:3), implying that the condemnation of Jesus was never his intent. However, scripture does not endow Judas with noble (even if misdirected) virtues. He was simply a thief.

This verse makes it very clear that Satan entered into Judas and was responsible for putting the betrayal of Jesus into Judas' heart. We can be assured that Satan's only purpose in motivating Judas to betray Jesus was to steal, kill, and destroy (Jn. 10:10).

Moreover, that Satan possessed Judas does not acquit Judas of the responsibility for his actions. The devil goes about seeking whom he may devour (1 Pet. 5:8). He cannot devour just anyone. We have to give place to him. By being a thief, Judas gave Satan access to him. He may have never intended to betray Jesus and therefore "repented himself" when he saw that Jesus was condemned. Once he began to willfully submit to the sin of thievery, it was hard to stop.

Sin cannot be controlled. We cannot just sin "a little." Sin, like a cancer, always grows until it brings forth death. Submitting ourselves to God and resisting the devil is our only guarantee against being devoured by the devil (Jas. 4:7). When we choose to sin, we are not submitting to God or resisting the devil.

OCTOBER 10
TEST THE GIFTS OF THE SPIRIT
LUKE 22:13

Luke 22:13 "And they went, and found as he had said unto them:
and they made ready the passover."

When a true gift of the Spirit is in operation, things will always be as the Lord has said (an exception to this is if there are conditions to meet). This is the ultimate test of whether someone's words are God-inspired (Dt. 18:22).

We cannot be led by just our own feelings concerning the gifts of the Spirit. In 1 Corinthians chapter 12, the Apostle Paul gives us direction governing the use of spiritual gifts that must supersede any urge or leading that we feel.

The first test to apply to any gift of the Spirit is to ask, "Does it glorify Jesus?" That's the point Paul is making. The Holy Spirit will never lead anyone to defame Jesus in any way. Jesus made it very clear that the Holy Spirit would only glorify Him. Any utterance or act that denies Jesus is not from the Holy Spirit.

In Paul's day, there was a transition being made from Judaism to Christianity. Some Jews were teaching that keeping the Old Testament law could produce salvation. They violently opposed Paul's teaching, that faith alone in Jesus could produce salvation. Paul considered any utterance like this as calling Jesus accursed and it definitely would not be from the Holy Spirit.

Also, the pagan religions of Paul's day believed in many gods. Anyone who tried to make Jesus just another god or "a" way to God instead of "the" way to God would be calling Him accursed. The Holy Spirit would never inspire anyone to do this. Those who are truly moved by the Holy Spirit in their utterances will always glorify Jesus.

OCTOBER 11
THE MEANING OF PASSOVER
LUKE 22:15-18

Luke 22:16 "For I say unto you, I will not any more eat thereof, until it be fulfilled in the
kingdom of God."

The Lord longed to share the passover meal with His disciples. He was less than 24 hours away from fulfilling His mission, and like anyone who can see the finish line, He must have had feelings of relief and excitement.

The passover meal commemorated the Jews' deliverance from slavery in Egypt (Ex. 13:3-10). It also had a much deeper spiritual application that, as Jesus explains here, would be fulfilled through His death. The Jewish nation as a whole had missed any future prophetic meaning of the passover.

On the night of the original passover, the Lord passed through the land of Egypt and judged the land by slaying all the firstborn men and beasts. The Jews had to slay a spotless lamb, take its blood and apply it to the door posts of their homes. They were commanded to remain indoors, under the covering of this blood until morning. When the Lord passed through the land at midnight to execute His judgment, He passed over the homes that had the lamb's blood on their doors and no one inside was hurt. This is a perfect picture of the redemption that Jesus provides for us.

Everyone deserves judgment because of his sins. However, Jesus provided Himself as a spotless, sacrificial lamb for us, so that if we apply His blood to our lives by confessing Him as Lord, God will pass over us on judgment day.

Jesus was sacrificed on the 14th day of the first month of the Jewish year—the exact day and time that the passover lambs were being slain. Truly, "Christ our passover is sacrificed for us" (1 Cor. 5:7).

OCTOBER 12
COMMUNION IS SACRED
LUKE 22:19

Luke 22:19 "And he took bread, and gave thanks, and brake it, and gave unto them, saying, This is my body which is given for you: this do in remembrance of me."

The bread of communion symbolizes the body of Jesus which was broken for us through His sufferings. He not only died for us on the cross, but also bore 39 stripes on His back by which we are healed. Partaking of communion should remind us of the emotional and physical salvation that Jesus provided for us.

The Lord's Supper comes from a part of the Passover meal that was celebrated only once a year. However, the early Christian church took communion weekly and sometimes daily. There is no specific frequency of the Lord's Supper prescribed in scripture.

As we take communion, we are solemnly proclaiming the Lord's death, and our union with Him and with others through that death. This is a profession of our faith and therefore, there are serious consequences for those who profess something they don't possess.

It is most likely that what makes a person worthy or unworthy is whether he is born again. This is also totally consistent with the doctrine of grace that Paul constantly preached. There were unbelievers among the true Christians just as Jesus prophesied, and this still exists today. It is a dangerous offense for an unbeliever to take the Lord's Supper. When taking communion, each person should examine himself to see whether he is in the faith (2 Cor. 13:5).

OCTOBER 13
LET GOD MINISTER TO YOU
JOHN 13:5-8

John 13:8 "Peter saith unto him, Thou shalt never wash my feet. Jesus answered him, If I wash thee not, thou hast no part with me."

Peter's refusal to let Jesus wash his feet came from a knowledge that he was totally unworthy to have the sinless Son of God serve him as a common servant would. Peter was correct in his assessment of his relative worth, but what he missed was that God doesn't minister to us because of our worth, but because of His love.

Even though Peter's attitude looked holy and humble, he was actually resisting God's will and committing an act of pride. Pride is not only exalting yourself above what is proper, but it can be debasing yourself below what is proper. Pride is simply self-centeredness or being self-willed instead of God-centered and submitted to God's will. Peter should have been humble enough to know that Jesus knew what He was doing and he should have submitted himself to God's will.

Likewise today, some people refuse to let God bless them, thinking they are unworthy of His favor. While it is true that our actions don't warrant God's goodness, truly humble people will receive the Lord's blessings as an expression of His love and grace toward them. Misguided humility is every bit as damaging as exaggerated pride.

Peter wanted to serve Jesus, but did not want to be served by Jesus. Jesus was telling Peter that unless he received His ministry to him, Peter would be unfit to serve Him. We cannot cleanse ourselves or others. We are totally dependent on the work of God's grace in our lives. Then and only then, are we equipped to minister to others. Before we can be the blessing that we desire to be to God or to others, we have to let God be the blessing to us that He desires to be.

OCTOBER 14
YOU ARE COMPLETE, ONLY IN HIM
MATTHEW 26:27-29

Matthew 26:28 "For this is my blood of the new testament, which is shed for many for the remission of sins."

The principle of the Old Covenant was "do" and you shall live. The principle of the New Covenant is "it is done," and includes redemption, reconciliation, righteousness, and sanctification. The work is finished! We are complete in Him!

If the Old Covenant had no defects, there would have been no attempt to institute another (Heb. 8:7). In the Old Covenant, men found themselves unable to abide in its agreement, for it was based upon a man's performance. The new agreement, however, is based totally upon God's grace. Under the Old Covenant, men approached God through a priest, while under the New Covenant, we have direct access to the Father through Jesus Christ. Under the Old Covenant, a man's sin led to his death while under the New Covenant, God is merciful to our unrighteousness. Under the Old Covenant, man could not be cleansed of a consciousness of sin while under the New Covenant, our sins and iniquities are remembered no more, and our guilty consciences are cleansed.

Prior to salvation we are incomplete and there is a constant striving in every person to satisfy his hunger. Through the new birth we are complete in Christ and our hunger now should only be for more revelation of what we already have in Christ.

In the same way that Jesus had the fullness of God in Him, we also have the fullness of Christ in us. That makes us complete or perfect in Him, that is speaking of our spiritual man. Our born-again spirits are identical in righteousness, authority, and power to Christ's spirit, because our born-again spirits are the Spirit of Christ (Rom. 8:9). It has been sent into our hearts crying, "Abba Father" (Gal. 4:6).

OCTOBER 15
A NEW REVELATION OF LOVE
JOHN 13:34

John 13:34 "A new commandment I give unto you, That ye love one another; as I have loved you, that ye also love one another."

Jesus previously stated that all the law and the prophets were dependent on loving God first, and then loving your neighbor as yourself. These truths were already in the law, but people missed them. So, this commandment was not new in the sense that it had never been given before, but it was brought to the forefront and given new meaning through the example of Jesus. Jesus not only loved His neighbor as Himself, He loved us more than Himself.

John, the apostle who wrote this Gospel, later wrote about the new commandment of love. No doubt, he received his inspiration from this teaching of Jesus. John wrote, *"Brethren, I write no new commandment unto you, but an old commandment which ye had from the beginning. The old commandment is the word which ye have heard from the beginning. Again, a new commandment I write unto you, which thing is true in him and in you: because the darkness is past, and the true light now shineth"* (1 Jn. 2:7-8). He then goes on to speak of loving one another.

This commandment, or the revelation that God gave to man through His Word, wasn't new, but was never clearly seen by men because of the darkness that separated them from God. In the light of Jesus' life, the darkness was removed and the old commandment of love became new through the example of Jesus in a way that mere words could never express.

OCTOBER 16
LOVE COMES FIRST
JOHN 13:35

John 13:35 "By this shall all men know that ye are my disciples, if ye have love one to another."

Jesus didn't say that all men would know we are His disciples by our doctrine, our rituals, our hatred for sin, or even by the way we express our love for God. He said very clearly, that the one characteristic that would cause the world to identify us as His followers, is our love, one for another.

This same night, the Lord prayed to His Father using this same thought saying, "That they all may be one; as thou, Father, art in me, and I in thee, that they also may be one in us: that the world may believe that thou hast sent me" (Jn. 17:21). The only way that Christ's body will be one as the Father and Jesus are one, is through God's kind of love.

Unity of believers, that can only come through a genuine God-kind of love, is the greatest tool for evangelism that the church has or will ever have, according to Jesus. The early church didn't have the massive organizational structures that we see today or the ability to travel anywhere in the world in just a matter of hours. They certainly did not come close to spending as much money, in proportion to us, to spread the gospel. Yet, the pagans of Thessalonica said of Paul and his companions, *"These that have turned the world upside down are come hither also"* (Acts 17:6). They had evangelized the known world in less than 30 years.

Before we can ever fulfill the great commission of Matthew 28:19-20, there must be a revival of love in the church, where doctrine and ritual take a backseat to love for one another.

OCTOBER 17
OUR SUCCESS IS IN GOD
MATTHEW 26:33

Matthew 26:33 "Peter answered and said unto him, Though all men shall be offended because of thee, yet will I never be offended."

Just like Peter, we are often more confident of ourselves than God is. Many Christians are devastated when they fail in some area that they thought they had long since grown past. We need to realize that as long as we are in this mortal body, we cannot fall asleep at our battle station against the works of the flesh. If we do, our flesh is just as capable of sin as anyone else's. If we fall, it should concern us, but not surprise us. We should simply realize with Paul, that "in my flesh dwelleth no good thing," get back into the spirit through confession and forgiveness, and go on with Jesus.

The Lord has never had anyone who was qualified working for Him. Peter wasn't qualified, and even at our best, neither are we. If we realize that we are nothing and have nothing, then we are prime candidates to be used by God.

Peter went on to become probably the best known of the twelve apostles. The Lord used him mightily, but He didn't want him, or us, to forget that it was Christ in Peter and not Peter himself who was great.

This also illustrates the extent of our Father's love and forgiveness. If God not only forgave Peter for his sin, but also reinstated and advanced him, then surely we have not pushed God's grace beyond its limit. Where sin abounds, grace abounds much more.

God doesn't see us as failures—just learners. God can redeem the worst failure and work it together for good (Rom 8:28). We need to think like God.

OCTOBER 18
TURN BACK TO GOD
LUKE 22:32

Luke 22:32 "But I have prayed for thee, that thy faith fail not: and when thou art converted, strengthen thy brethren."

The concept of "conversion" is mentioned in the Holy Scriptures at least 14 times. The basic meaning of the term is a turning or returning to God. This implies a turning away from sin and a turning to God. Repentance and putting faith in God are corresponding synonyms to conversion.

The theological basis for conversion lies in the truth of the "atonement." Although man lapses into sin, the truth of the atonement remains. When men turn to God in repentance and faith, the effects of the atonement—reconciliation and forgiveness—avail.

The Apostle Paul expresses the act of conversion in this way: "Turning to God from idols to serve the living and true God" (1 Th. 1:9). Also, "to open their eyes (the Gentiles), and to turn them from darkness to light, and from the power of Satan unto God, that they may receive forgiveness of sins, and inheritance among them which are sanctified by faith that is in me" (Jesus) (Acts 26:18).

Jesus instructed Peter to get back into ministry after he repented of his denial. If Jesus had not given Peter this command, many people might have doubted that Peter should be in a position of leadership. Indeed, Peter himself must have doubted whether he was fit. After Jesus' resurrection, the Lord again admonished Peter three times to serve Him by ministering to His sheep.

In the context of Luke 22, Peter's faith was shaken and he denied the Lord, but did not reject Him. Jesus' admonition to Peter was that when he turned back again to Him (converted), he was to strengthen the brethren.

OCTOBER 19
OUR COMFORT IS IN ETERNITY
JOHN 14:2

John 14:2 "In my Father's house are many mansions: if it were not so, I would have told you. I go to prepare a place for you."

This is Jesus' last teaching to His disciples before His crucifixion. Jesus' disciples were about to go through the greatest test of their faith that they had ever encountered. Jesus said that He was saying these things so His disciples would not be offended. Jesus was preparing them for what was to come. Why then speak of preparing them a mansion in heaven? The reason for this was to comfort the disciples and help them put things in perspective. In 1 Thessalonians 4:18, Paul tells us to comfort one another with words about being gathered unto the Lord in the air. Paul said again, "I reckon that the sufferings of this present time are not worthy to be compared with the glory which shall be revealed in us" (Rom. 8:18). Someday, all of our trials will seem like nothing and this can be a great comfort to us now.

Also, when we think about being with the Lord through all eternity, it helps us to put things in proper perspective. It is easy to get fearful about our problems and think all is lost. However, for those of us who are born again, if worse comes to worse, we still have the promise of Jesus wiping all the tears from our eyes and preparing a habitation for us where all our former sorrows will have passed away. This keeps us from despairing and makes us much stronger in our faith.

In heaven, there are many dwelling places and Jesus is preparing one for us. The thing that is going to make heaven "heaven" is that we will be with Jesus. No doubt, there will be things to see and do that will be wonderful, but nothing will compare to being with the one who loved us and died for us. A preoccupation with the details of what things will be like in heaven is missing the point.

OCTOBER 20
THERE IS ONLY ONE WAY TO THE FATHER
JOHN 14:5-6

John 14:5 "Thomas saith unto him, Lord, we know not whither thou goest; and how can we know the way?"

Thomas knew Jesus. He just didn't realize Jesus was "the way." Likewise, people today know portions of God's Word, but they don't realize that God's Word is their way to victory. Often, people cry out to God to speak to them while their Bible lays unopened on their nightstand. God has spoken to us through His Word. We just need to believe it and receive its truths as our way to victory.

Jesus didn't say: "I am a way, a truth, and a life." He claimed to be the only way, truth, and life. No man can come to the Father except through Jesus. This means that anyone who claims to honor Jesus while advocating other ways to get to God, truth, or life, besides Jesus, is deceived or is a deceiver.

Jesus' claims about Himself, of which there is only one, left no room for other means to salvation. He is either who He says He is, or He is the greatest deceiver of all time. His own statements about Himself leave no other alternatives. Therefore, other religions that recognize Jesus and His teachings as wonderful examples, but don't believe He is the only way to achieve salvation, are false.

The Word of God is a spiritual book written under the direction of the Holy Spirit. It was not written to our heads, but to the innermost part of our hearts. This is why some people find the Bible so hard to understand. They are trying to comprehend it using only their minds. The Word of God has to inspire our hearts before it can enlighten our minds.

OCTOBER 21
GOD WORKS IN THE SIMPLE THINGS
JOHN 14:7

John 14:7 "If ye had known me, ye should have known my Father also: and from henceforth ye know him, and have seen him."

Knowing Jesus is knowing the Father. This is not only because Jesus did exactly what He saw His Father do, but Jesus was God in the flesh.

The disciples didn't realize that seeing Jesus was seeing God. They were expecting something more. Many times we miss seeing God work in our lives and circumstances because we are looking for something stupendous. Although it is true that God is totally awesome, He doesn't usually choose to manifest Himself in that way.

God spoke to Elijah not in the fire, wind, or an earthquake, but in a still, small voice. Jesus didn't come to this earth in a grand way by man's standards, but was born to poor parents in a stable. Isaiah 53:2 says that Jesus had no form nor beauty that would make us think that He was anything more than a mere man.

Paul reveals in 1 Corinthians 1:27-29, that God chooses to do things this way so that no flesh will glory in His presence. The Lord wants us to focus on Him through faith and not concentrate on the physical things He uses. In the Old Testament when the Lord did use visible instruments to release His power, the Israelites made idols out of those things.

Just as the disciples saw Jesus but didn't realize that what they saw was God; likewise, God is infinitely involved in our everyday lives, but we miss Him because we are blinded by our carnal minds. The primary reason that God chooses to use those who are nothing by the world's standards is so that no one else will take the credit for the great things that are accomplished.

OCTOBER 22
GOD IS OUR COMFORT
JOHN 14:16-17

John 14:16 "And I will pray the Father, and he shall give you another Comforter,
that he may abide with you for ever;"

Remember that Jesus was saying these things to His disciples so that they would not be offended. Jesus is speaking to His disciples about the Holy Spirit, who is the Comforter. The ministry of the Holy Spirit in the life of the believer is the front line of defense against the devil and his devices of defeat. The phrase, "The God of all comfort" carries the idea of a divine comforter who encourages, refreshes, strengthens, aids, assists, and is an ever present help in the time of need. The ways that God chooses to comfort are not always the same. He may deliver you or remove the cause of the affliction, or He may comfort you with words giving you a hope for the future. He also uses people to share their faith with you by prophesying. He sends fellow-laborers to serve and strengthen you by the ministry of the Word, and uses the body of Christ as a channel to comfort you, using prayer. The point is that the source of all comfort is God, no matter what channel He chooses to use.

In 2 Corinthians 12:9, God revealed to Paul that His strength is made perfect in our weakness. Paul, who had experienced God's comfort in a way that perhaps no other man has, now reveals how the Lord accomplished this. It was through the power of the Holy Spirit. True Christianity is not the absence of trials, but the strength and comfort of Jesus through the Holy Spirit, that will bring us through to the other side.

Even a strong metal container with a vacuum inside will be crushed just by normal atmospheric pressure. But that same container, with an equal or greater amount of pressure inside, will be just fine. Likewise, an individual who is void of God's comfort inside will be crushed by the pressures of this life. But a believer who takes advantage of the comfort available to him through the Holy Spirit, can withstand anything. Victory is not dependent on the pressures without, but rather on the comfort within.

OCTOBER 23
JESUS IN THE FLESH
JOHN 14:28

John 14:28 "Ye have heard how I said unto you, I go away, and come again unto you. If ye loved me, ye
would rejoice, because I said, I go unto the Father: for my Father is greater than I."

Jesus stated His union with the Father so clearly that He was accused of blasphemy more than once. This statement about the Father being greater than Jesus must harmonize with, not contradict other claims.

A key to understanding this is given in Philippians 2:6-8, where Paul states that Jesus didn't think it was robbery to be equal with God, but humbled Himself, taking on the form of a servant (speaking of His humanity). Jesus was equal to God in His divine nature, but He made Himself inferior to the Father in regard to His humanity. Jesus didn't lose any of His deity when He became a man, but He did clothe it in flesh and submit it to the consequent limitations. In this sense, the Father was greater than Jesus.

Jesus is the pre-existent God who chose to become a man so he could redeem us by His own blood sacrifice. When He became a man, He was still 100 percent God in His spirit, but His physical body was 100 percent human. His body was sinless, but it was still flesh and subject to the natural things we all experience. The physical Jesus had to grow in wisdom and in stature.

When Jesus was born, His physical mind did not know all things. He had to be taught how to talk, walk, eat, and so forth. He had to learn that He was God in the flesh and accept that by faith. His physical mind grew in awareness of who He was. He had the witness in His spirit, but His physical mind had to "take it by faith"— the same way that we do when we believe who we are in the spiritual realm. Jesus' mental comprehension of His deity was something He learned and accepted by faith. Jesus had to become aware of His true identity through revelation and knowledge. We must do the same.

OCTOBER 24
LET GOD PRUNE YOU HIS WAY
JOHN 15:2

John 15:2 "Every branch in me that beareth not fruit he taketh away: and every branch that beareth fruit, he purgeth it, that it may bring forth more fruit."

This purging has been interpreted in many ways. The illustration that Jesus is using is one of pruning; therefore, some have said this purging is a very painful process where the Lord cuts and slashes us through things like sickness, death, poverty, and other forms of tragedy so that eventually we will bear more fruit. This teaching not only promotes problems as being good, but necessary, if we want to bear more fruit.

That thinking is not consistent with the rest of God's Word or even the context of this verse. The text makes it very clear that the purging that Jesus speaks of is done through the Word that He has spoken unto us.

Paul said in 2 Timothy 3:16-17, that God's Word was given to us "for doctrine, for reproof, for correction, and for instruction in righteousness: That the man of God may be perfect, thoroughly furnished unto all good works." That is God's method of pruning us, and He doesn't need the devil's help. His word will make us "perfect, thoroughly furnished unto all good works."

That is not to say that we cannot learn through tragedy: but God has a better way. If we mistakenly think that God is bringing tragedy into our lives to make us more fruitful, then we'll not resist the tragedies and they will not flee from us. All of us will learn by hard knocks, but the man who welcomes them with wide open arms will suffer greatly and be far behind the man who lets God's Word have His perfect work in him.

OCTOBER 25
YOUR LIFE IS IN HIM
JOHN 15:4

John 15:4 "Abide in me, and I in you. As the branch cannot bear fruit of itself, except it abide in the vine; no more can ye, except ye abide in me."

This is a profound truth that is the key to bearing fruit, but it is so easy to forget. Because the fruit is borne on the branch, it is easy to credit the branch with the fruit, but it is the vine that drew the life from the earth and channeled it through the branch.

Likewise, since we are the branch through which the life of God flows, we sometimes think that it is our own holiness that produces the fruit. The moment we think that way, we are no longer abiding (trusting in; clinging to) in the vine and we will become fruitless if we persist in this mindset.

This is actually a great relief if the believer understands this and applies it properly. It puts all the responsibility on Jesus. Our only responsibility is to respond to His ability. In the same way that you have never seen a branch travailing to bring forth fruit, so all we have to do is labor to enter into His rest (trust and depend) and completely trust Jesus as our source (Heb. 4:11). If we abide in Him, fruit will come naturally.

It's our faith in what Jesus did for us that saved us, and our faith has to continue to be in Christ, not in ourselves, to maintain salvation. Our holiness, righteousness, and justification are gifts that we receive in our spirits through Jesus.

Just like the life of a root is found in the soil, or a branch in the vine, or a fish in the sea, so the believer's true life is found in the union with Christ.

OCTOBER 26
EXPECT PERSECUTION
JOHN 15:19

John 15:19 *"If ye were of the world, the world would love his own: but because ye are not of the world, but I have chosen you out of the world, therefore the world hateth you."*

We should not think it is strange to be persecuted. *"All that will live godly in Christ Jesus shall suffer persecution"* (2 Tim. 3:12). We can actually rejoice because we are being persecuted for Jesus' sake, and the Lord will be with us in the midst of the persecution. When we stand before Him, there will be more than ample reward.

Persecution is a token that those persecuting you are under conviction. They realize that they are not living what your words or actions are advocating and in self defense, they attack you, who they perceive is the source of their conviction. If you understand this, it makes persecution much easier to take. They aren't just mad at you; they are convicted. When the Gospel is presented in the power of the Holy Spirit, there will always be either revival or riot, but not indifference.

In the midst of persecution, Satan will try to convince us that the strife is all our fault. If he succeeds, then we will back down and the pressure is taken off his followers. However, Jesus suffered continual rejection and persecution, yet we know that the problem was not with Him, but with those who rejected Him.

Jesus makes it clear that persecution is an inevitable part of living a godly life, so that we will not fall prey to introspection and self-condemnation when rejection comes. If our sinless Savior was rejected, then certainly we will be too. Don't feel guilty or condemned when persecution comes. The Word strips people of the disguises they have been hiding their sins behind, and the result is persecution.

OCTOBER 27
EMBRACE THE HOLY SPIRIT
JOHN 16:7

John 16:7 *"Nevertheless I tell you the truth; It is expedient for you that I go away: for if I go not away, the Comforter will not come unto you; but if I depart, I will send him unto you."*

The Greek word translated "expedient" means "to be an advantage; profitable." How could any situation be more advantageous or profitable than having Jesus physically with you?

When Jesus walked on this earth in His physical body, He was subject to many physical limitations. For instance, He could not always be with every one of His disciples all the time. Through the ministry of the Holy Spirit, He could. Instead of Satan getting rid of Jesus, 120 "little Christs" (that is literally what the word "Christian" means) came out of the upper room on the day of Pentecost.

Jesus taught His disciples as no teacher ever had, yet they had very little understanding because they were not born again. However, when the Holy Spirit came, He led them into all truth and even showed them things to come.

The list of advantages of having the Holy Spirit in us compared to having Jesus with us in His physical body, goes on and on. The advantages can all be summed up in that Jesus' power is now complete (Mt. 28:18) and no longer confined to one physical body.

There is no such thing as victorious Christian living without a moment by moment, hour by hour, day by day dependence upon the Spirit of God. Not only is the Christian life hard to live, but it is impossible to live without the power of God Himself.

OCTOBER 28
BE A WITNESS, NOT A JUDGE
JOHN 16:8

John 16:8 "And when he is come, he will reprove the world of sin, and of righteousness, and of judgment:"

It is the ministry of the Holy Spirit to reprove sin, righteousness, and judgment. It is not our ministry. We are simply witnesses. A witness is not the judge or the jury. A witness simply relates what he has experienced, thereby providing evidence to the truth of something. We are to witness in word and deed, to the truth of Jesus being alive in us and let God be the one who convicts. We are simply to testify to what we have seen or to what has happened to us.

Some people in their zeal, have gone beyond the witness stage and have tried to bring people under conviction themselves. This is assuming the job that belongs to the Holy Spirit alone. This not only frustrates the witness, but it drives many people away from God. We make a very poor Holy Spirit; therefore, we should stick to our job of being witnesses and let the Holy Spirit do His job.

Jesus specified an orderly progression in the way we should witness. First, we start in Jerusalem (i.e. where we are). Then we go to those nearby (Judaea). Finally, we take the Gospel to every religious and racial group (Samaria) throughout the whole world.

There are some practical reasons for becoming witnesses in this way. Jesus testified that a prophet is honored everywhere except in his home town among his family and friends. Typically, at home is the hardest place to witness. Starting with those who know us best will cause us to humble ourselves and give God all the glory. Also, if rejection comes, this tempers us and our witness, so that we will be more effective and more resilient when we go to the outer most parts of the earth.

OCTOBER 29
OVERCOME TRIBULATION
JOHN 16:33

John 16:33 "These things I have spoken unto you, that in me ye might have peace. In the world ye shall have tribulation: but be of good cheer; I have overcome the world."

Jesus said we would have tribulation. He did not say that He was the one bringing the tribulation or what the tribulation would be, but He said it would come. Then He made the amazing statement that in the midst of tribulation we were to be of good cheer.

Tribulations exist because there is a battle between the kingdom of God and the kingdom of the devil. When we operate in faith, God is able to grant us such victory that we are actually better off because of the battle. It's just like when a army goes to war. If they win, they gain spoils, but if they embrace their enemy because of the spoils they were expecting to receive, they will be killed instead of blessed. First, you have to fight and win the war, and then and only then, will the spoils be available. The enemy doesn't come to be a blessing, but a blessing can be obtained from the enemy if we are victorious.

Likewise, tribulations and adversities are not blessings from God. They are attacks from the enemy intended to steal the Word of God out of our lives. No man should say that the temptation came from God, for God is not the one who tempts any man (Jas. 1:13).

If problems were what perfected us, then most Christians would have been perfected long ago and those who experienced the greatest problems would be the greatest Christians. However, that's not the way it is. God's Word is given to us to make us perfect, and thoroughly furnished unto every good work (2 Tim. 3:17). God's Word does not need to be supplemented with problems to accomplish its work.

OCTOBER 30
REJOICE IN THE LORD—ALWAYS
JOHN 16:33

John 16:33 "These things I have spoken unto you, that in me ye might have peace. In the world ye shall have tribulation: but be of good cheer; I have overcome the world."

People in the world experience joy and happiness in direct proportion to their circumstances. Bad circumstances produce depression and sorrow, while good circumstances produce joy and peace. That's bondage, and does not have to be the case for a Christian. Our joy is not dependent on things, but rather on the person of Jesus Christ. He is our peace and joy.

The way we take advantage of this joy and peace in the midst of tribulation, is to have our minds and hearts stayed on things above and not on things of this earth. The invisible things of God are eternal while the visible problems on earth are only temporary. All the problems of this life grow very dim when we compare them to the glory of God that is ours through Jesus.

We can rejoice in the Lord always (Phil. 4:4) because rejoicing is an action, not a reaction to our environment. Joy is a gift from God that was given to us at salvation. It was placed within our born-again spirits and it doesn't fluctuate or diminish; it is constant. The Lord has put the joy inside us and we are to "work it out" by choosing to obey this command in scripture.

We are commanded to rejoice *"IN THE LORD."* Many people are not experiencing true joy because their joy is in their circumstances. That is, they are waiting to rejoice when things in their lives are going good, and that doesn't happen very often. We are suppose to *"rejoice in the Lord always."* That means we are suppose to rejoice in who the Lord is and what He has done for us. He never changes (Heb. 13:8) and His mercies and compassions are new every morning (Lam. 3:22-23).

OCTOBER 31
HOW TO EXPERIENCE ETERNAL LIFE TODAY
JOHN 17:3

John 17:3 "And this is life eternal, that they might know thee the only true God, and Jesus Christ, whom thou hast sent."

In order to fully understand what eternal life is, it is helpful to understand what it is not. Eternal life is not living forever. Everyone lives forever in either heaven or hell. Also, eternal life is not living forever in the blessings of heaven as opposed to being tormented in hell. John 3:36 and 5:24 show that eternal life is a present tense possession of the believer.

Here, Jesus defines eternal life as knowing God the Father and Jesus Christ. As we have already discussed, the word "know" is speaking of intimacy instead of mere intellectual knowledge. Therefore, eternal life is having an intimate, personal relationship with God the Father and Jesus the Son.

According to John 3:16, this intimacy with God is what salvation is all about. Forgiveness of our sins is not the point of salvation: intimacy with the Father is. Of course, Jesus did die to purchase forgiveness for our sins because unforgiven sins block us from intimacy with God. Sin was an obstacle that stood between us and God. It had to be dealt with and it was. Anyone who views salvation as only forgiveness of his sins and stops there, is missing out on eternal life.

Salvation is intended to be the way to come back into harmony with God. Instead, it is often presented as the way to escape the problems of this life and the judgment of hell later.

Most non-believers are so occupied with their "hell on earth" that they don't really think or care about their eternal future. They are fed up with religion and are looking for something that will fill the emptiness inside. Only an intimate relationship (eternal life) with our Father can do that.

NOVEMBER 1
HIS WILL IS IN THE WORD
JOHN 17:17

John 17:17 "Sanctify them through thy truth: thy word is truth."
In this prayer, Jesus prayed twice that the Father would keep His disciples from evil. Then He reveals the way that God will accomplish this—through His Word, the holy scriptures. Anyone who desires to live for God, reject the devil, and reject the world's system, must know God's Word.

We must study the scriptures, for they reveal the will of God for our actions and attitudes. To be filled with the knowledge of God's will, we must be filled with God's Word. God's Word is His will! Those who are ignorant of God's Word will be ignorant of God's will.

Knowledge of God's will is foundational in developing Christian conduct and character. There is no way we can fulfill God's will if we don't know what it is. The starting point for any Christian is understanding God's will for his life. How can a person obtain such knowledge? The first step is to desire it. Jeremiah 29:13 says, *"And ye shall seek me, and find me, when ye shall search for me with all your heart."* People ask the Lord for knowledge of His will, but don't receive it because they aren't seeking with ALL THEIR HEARTS. No one who has ever sought the Lord with all his heart has ever been disappointed.

The Holy Spirit is the dispenser of God's wisdom. It is through Him that we know the things God has revealed to us. One of the primary ministries of the Holy Spirit is to reveal God's will to us.

There is no way we can walk worthy of the Lord and please Him if we don't know His will. Furthermore, we can't be fruitful without the knowledge of His will. God has provided all that we need to be successful and victorious in this life. Believe His Word.

NOVEMBER 2
GIVE ALL THE GLORY TO GOD
JOHN 17:18

John 17:18 "As thou hast sent me into the world, even so have I also sent them into the world."
We are not from the world. Through the new birth, we come from God and should constantly remind ourselves of this. It is not good to be too "at home" in the world. We are in the world, but are not of the world. Great men and women of God have always had this attitude.

The primary reason that God chooses to use those who are nothing by the world's standards, is so no one else can take credit for the great things that are accomplished.

If the Lord used those who had it "all together" in the natural, then they would share the glory that rightfully belongs to God alone. But when the Lord works miraculously through someone who obviously has no talent or ability, then everyone says, "This must be God."

Not only does this keep others from misdirecting the glory that belongs to God, but it keeps the person who God uses from swelling up with pride. One of Satan's greatest weapons against someone who is being used by God is to tempt him to think that the Lord is using him because he possesses some superior virtue.

God uses nobodies. If we think we've become "somebody" (in our flesh), then we will cease being used. He will not share His glory with anyone else (Isa. 42:8).

NOVEMBER 3
ONE IN SPIRIT
JOHN 17:21

John 17:21 "That they all may be one; as thou, Father, art in me, and I in thee, that they also may be one in us: that the world may believe that thou hast sent me."
Jesus is praying for all believers to be one as He and the Father are one. This goes far beyond what many promote as unity today. Paul besought the Corinthians to "all speak the same thing, and that there be no divisions among you; but that ye be perfectly joined together in the same mind and in the same judgment" (1 Cor. 1:10). This is God's standard of unity.

This oneness among believers is what Jesus said would cause the world to know that Jesus is the Son of God. This is the greatest tool for evangelism that the church has. The only way that Christ's body will be one as the Father and Jesus are one is through God's kind of love. No wonder Satan tries to get believers to go at each other's throats. We spend billions of dollars a year on evangelism through television, radio, conventions and crusades, yet the world is not evangelized because the body of Christ is not united in love.

There is very little unity among believers today. This has occured over thousands of years and it probably won't be fixed over night. We must strive towards unity, but not be overwhelmed by the problem. All Christians have already been joined to each other through the body of Christ, and God the Father sees us all as His children. All divisions among Christians are made by man, not God. For a brief period of time, the church enjoyed unity on earth. Regardless of any strife and division that has occurred, all believers are still one in Christ and will live in perfect oneness throughout eternity. We are now one in Spirit. We just need to experience that unity here on earth. *"Thy kingdom come. Thy will be done in earth as it is in heaven"* (Mt. 6:10).

NOVEMBER 4
FILL UP WITH GOD
JOHN 17:23

John 17:23 "I in them, and thou in me, that they may be made perfect in one; and that the world may know that thou hast sent me, and hast loved them, as thou hast loved me."
God loves us the same as He loves Jesus. A true revelation of this will quicken our faith and allow us to walk in the fullness of God. God's love is the key that opens the door to everything that God is. *"God is love"* (1 Jn. 4:8).

God's love is not one dimensional. There is width, length, depth and height to it, that can only be comprehended through the revelation and knowledge of the Holy Spirit. Those who only have a superficial knowledge of God's love are like a person who looks at a one dimensional picture of the real thing.

In Ephesians 3:19, Paul prays for us to know the love of God which passes knowledge. How can we know the love of God if it passes knowledge? This sounds like a contradiction. The Greek word that is translated "know" in this verse is GINOSKO, which is a verb expressing experiential knowledge. The Greek word that is translated "knowledge" is GNOSIS, which is a noun denoting the act of knowledge. Simply, Paul is praying that we will experience the love of God which passes mere knowledge of it.

Since a true revelation of God's love makes us full with the fullness of God, then a lack of being full of God must mean that we lack understanding and experience of God's love. The end result of having understanding and experiential knowledge of God's love is that we will be filled with all the fullness of God.

NOVEMBER 5
CHOSEN BEFORE CREATION
JOHN 17:24

John 17:24 "Father, I will that they also, whom thou hast given me, be with me where I am; that they may behold my glory, which thou hast given me: for thou lovedst me before the foundation of the world."

God the Father had the plan of salvation worked out before He even created the world. Most of us would not have created the world and man if we knew the heartache and terrible sacrifice it would cost. But God is not man. In His judgment (which is the correct judgment) the prize was worth the cost.

We were chosen in Christ before the world began. The Lord did not choose us by our merit, but solely by our acceptance of Christ which His foreknowledge allowed Him to do before the foundation of the world. In the strictest sense, we were not personally chosen, but Christ was chosen and all those who are "in Christ" partake of His being chosen by His Father. Just as we are the beneficiaries of the covenant between God the Father and His Son Jesus, so we are chosen because we chose God's chosen, i.e. Christ. The Father would no more reject us than He would reject Jesus because we are accepted by the Father through Christ.

None of us can claim that we are without blame in the sight of men because man looks on the outward appearance (1 Sam. 16:7) and all of us have sinned (Rom. 3:23). The Lord looks on our born-again spirits which have been regenerated in Christ. He sees us holy and without blame.

If you look at any color through a red glass, that color becomes red. The same thing would happen if you looked through a green glass. Everything would become green. In a similar way, God looks at us through Christ and everything in our life becomes covered by the blood of Jesus. We are holy and without blame before Him because of His love expressed through His Son.

NOVEMBER 6
SEEK THE WILL OF GOD
LUKE 22:41-42

Luke 22:42 "Saying, Father, if thou be willing, remove this cup from me: nevertheless not my will, but thine, be done."

Jesus knew it was the Father's will for Him to be made an offering for the sins of the world. This is true because He prophesied His death and resurrection many times before. However, because of His unique relationship with God, Jesus was asking God to accomplish His will some other way, but at the same time affirming His commitment to do His Father's will and not His own.

He was not at a loss to know God's will and therefore, left this time of prayer trusting that whatever the Father deemed best for Him would happen. He knew when He began praying, what the Father's will was, and He knew at the close of His prayer that God's will could not be accomplished any other way.

For us to pray, "Lord, if it be thy will" in response to a promise that God has given us, is nothing but unbelief and is not even remotely related to what Jesus did in the Garden of Gethsemane. One of the foundational principles of answered prayer is that we must believe that we receive when we pray (Mk. 11:24). There is no way that we can fulfill that condition if we don't know God's will in that situation. Praying, "If it be thy will" takes us out of the active position of believing and puts us in the passive position of waiting and letting circumstances rule our lives. If we are seeking direction in an area where God's will is not already expressed through His Word, then we should pray James 1:5, and ask for wisdom. Then we can believe that we receive when we pray, and with that knowledge continue our prayer in faith. We should not be ignorant, but understand what the will of the Lord is (Eph. 5:17).

The only appropriate time to pray, "If it be thy will" is when we are dedicating ourselves to the service of God, regardless of where or what that may be.

NOVEMBER 7
HE IS OUR "ABBA"
MARK 14:36

Mark 14:36 "And he said, Abba, Father, all things are possible unto thee; take away this cup from me: nevertheless not what I will, but what thou wilt. "

Although God was referred to as our Father in the Old Testament, Jesus' frequent use of this title brought a whole new understanding of our relationship with God. Jesus referred to God as His Father, and He spoke of God as being our Father as well. This infuriated the religious Jews of Jesus' day who considered it blasphemy to call God their Father, because they understood that to mean they were equal with God.

We are instructed to call God our Father, revealing the kind, gentle, loving nature of our God. The term "Abba" is an affectionate term that a young child calls his father, which corresponds to our term "daddy." It is a term used to express intimacy and affectionate fondness. It removes the idea of God as a strict judge and carries the image of Him as a loving Father who cares, understands, and is our best friend. "Behold what manner of love the Father hath bestowed upon us, that we should be called the sons of God" (1 Jn. 3:1).

We are sons of God by adoption. Jesus was the Son of God by nature. As Jesus said to the Jews, ye are of your Father the devil (Jn. 8:44; Eph. 2:3). However, Jesus purchased us and made us adopted sons of God.

We are not just heirs, we are joint-heirs with Christ. To think that we share equally with the one who has inherited everything God is, and has, is beyond comprehension.

NOVEMBER 8
HIS FATHOMLESS PAIN
LUKE 22:43-44

Luke 22:44 "And being in an agony he prayed more earnestly: and his sweat was as it were great drops of blood falling down to the ground. "

It is interesting that Luke is the only one of the gospel writers to mention that Jesus' sweat was as great drops of blood. This is probably because Luke was a physician (Col. 4:14); therefore, this had special significance to him.

There have been documented cases of people actually sweating drops of blood under extreme emotional pressure. This might explain why Luke is the only writer to mention the angel strengthening Jesus. Just as when Jesus encountered Satan during His 40 days of fasting and temptation in the wilderness and the angels ministered unto Him (Mk. 1:13), so here, He needed supernatural strength to endure His sufferings.

The use of the words "as it were" might also mean that the sweat of Jesus was only comparable to blood in consistency or size, but it certainly underscores the effect Jesus' agony had on His physical body.

Jesus' sufferings for us were more than just physical. In the garden, before He suffered physically, He suffered emotionally, almost to the point of death. As Luke records, an angel had to come and give Him strength or the emotional struggle alone would have killed Him.

All that Jesus did was motivated solely by love. It was for the joy that was set before Him that He endured going to the cross. He didn't do what He did to save us out of pity or a sense of obligation as our Creator. He did it because He loves us.

NOVEMBER 9
CHOOSE TO FOCUS ON ALL THAT IS GOOD
MARK 14:38

Mark 14:38 "Watch ye and pray, lest ye enter into temptation. The spirit truly is ready, but the flesh is weak."

Temptation is linked directly to what we think upon (Heb. 11:15). Temptation has to be entered into. We can avoid temptation by avoiding thoughts that generate temptation (Prov. 23:7). Since it is impossible to not think, we cannot just try to reject the negative thoughts in this world, but we must choose to think on the positive truths of God. This is where prayer comes in.

In prayer, we have our minds stayed upon God; therefore, we are not receptive to thoughts that conceive temptation. Temptation or sin must be conceived (Jas. 1:14-15). In the physical realm, the easiest way to avoid an unwanted birth is to avoid conception, so it is in the spiritual world. It is easier to avoid being tempted by being in constant communion with God, than it is to overcome temptation once it has been conceived.

Paul admonishes the Philippian believers to reflect and meditate upon eight positive principles of thinking that will lead to a victorious Christian life (Phil. 4:8). These are things that are "true," that is: honorable, truthful and upright. Things that are "honest," that is: honorable, truthful, genuine, not characterized by deception or fraud. Things that are "just," that is: in accordance with what is right, or right conduct; any circumstance, fact or deed that is right. Things that are "pure," free from defilement or impurity.

Things that are "lovely," pleasing, agreeable, inspiring love or affection. A "good report," that is: a saying or report that is positive and constructive rather than negative and destructive. "Virtue," which is moral excellence, righteousness and goodness. "Praise," or what is praiseworthy; expressing one's esteem of a person and his virtues. We need to focus on the good in every area of our lives. Recognizing God's hand in even the smallest things will bring peace and keep our hearts and minds following hard after the Lord.

NOVEMBER 10
YOU HAVE IT ALL—IN THE SPIRIT
MATTHEW 26:41

Matthew 26:41 "Watch and pray, that ye enter not into temptation: the spirit indeed is willing, but the flesh is weak."

The Bible presents salvation as a life transforming experience. Change is one of the distinguishing characteristics of a true believer. Yet, failure to understand that this change takes place in the spirit first, and then is reflected in our outward appearance through our thoughts and actions in direct proportion to the way we renew our minds, causes much confusion.

This change has to take place in our born-again spirits first. Why is that? If you were fat before you got saved, you will be fat after you get saved, unless you go on a weight loss program. Your body doesn't instantly change and either does your soul or mind.

It is your spirit that is instantly changed at salvation. It is perfect (Heb. 12:23). It cannot sin (1 Jn. 3:9). Everything that is true of Jesus is true of our born-again spirits. Your spiritual salvation is complete. At salvation, you receive the same spirit that you will have throughout all eternity. It will not have to be changed or cleansed again. It is sealed with the Holy Spirit (Eph. 1:13); therefore, is sanctified and perfected forever (Heb. 10:10, 14; 12:23).

For the remainder of our Christian lives, we must not try to obtain faith, joy or love from God, but rather release what we already have in our spirits (Gal. 5:22-23), into our souls and bodies. Failure to understand this has caused some people to despair when they don't see sufficient change in their lives after coming to the Lord for salvation. It must be understood that the change is internal in our spirits and the outward change will take place as we renew our minds through God's Word.

NOVEMBER 11
EXERCISE YOUR SOUL
MATTHEW 26:41

Matthew 26:41 "Watch and pray, that ye enter not into temptation: the spirit indeed is willing, but the flesh is weak."

Our spirits are not our problems. The born-again Christian receives a new spirit at conversion that is just like Jesus' (1 Jn. 4:17), because it is the Spirit of Jesus. Our born-again spirits are always willing to do God's will. It's our flesh that is the problem.

The flesh, as Jesus describes it here, not only includes our physical bodies, but also describes our souls. God has given every believer everything it takes to walk in victory, but "we have this treasure in earthen vessels" (2 Cor. 4:7). That is saying that our spirits, where God has deposited all of His power and glory, are locked inside our flesh.

That does not mean that we cannot tap into this divine source. As much as we will renew our minds and act on the Word of God, we can experience this divine flow through our physical bodies. However, just as we must use our muscles to increase in strength, we must exercise ourselves (soul, mind and body) unto godliness (1 Tim. 4:7-8).

Prayer is one important way of exercising ourselves unto godliness, and is why Jesus admonished His disciples to watch and pray with Him.

NOVEMBER 12
WALK IN THE LIGHT
MATTHEW 26:41

Matthew 26:41 "Watch and pray, that ye enter not into temptation: the spirit indeed is willing, but the flesh is weak."

How do you walk in the Spirit? The way you do this is through living by, conducting your actions according to, and following the leading of the Word of God as quickened to you by the Holy Spirit. The Holy Spirit and the Word of God agree perfectly because the Holy Spirit is the one who inspired the written Word of God.

Denying the flesh will not result in walking in the Spirit. Walking in the Spirit will result in denying the flesh. This may seem like a subtle difference to some, but the difference is truly profound. As a whole, false religions teach that as we overcome our flesh, there is a noticeable increase in the presence and power of God in our lives. That was what the Pharisees of Jesus' day and the legalistic Jews of Paul's day taught. Just the opposite is true. As we experience more of the presence and power of the Spirit of God, then the influence of the flesh is diminished. Victory must come in this order. We don't walk in the Spirit as a result of overcoming the flesh, rather overcoming the flesh is the result of walking in the Spirit.

It's similar to how you fill a dark room with light. You don't shovel out the darkness and then light appears. No! You simply turn on the light and the darkness flees. Much of religion preaches to stop sinning (get rid of the darkness) and then the Holy Spirit will come and empower you (the light will come). That's not the way it works. Man can no more get rid of the power of the flesh on his own than he can get rid of the power of darkness without light. We have to receive the work of the Holy Spirit in our lives by grace and then the union with the Holy Spirit breaks the power of the flesh. The key to breaking the dominion of the flesh is to appropriate the power of the Spirit through faith, while the flesh is still causing us problems. Those who are waiting for the Spirit to manifest after they have subdued the flesh, will wait as long as the man who is trying to get rid of the darkness so the light will appear.

NOVEMBER 13
THE "OLD MAN" IS DEAD
MARK 14:41

Mark 14:41 "And he cometh the third time, and saith unto them, Sleep on now, and take your rest: it is enough, the hour is come; behold, the Son of man is betrayed into the hands of sinners."

It is not our individual acts of sin that make us a sinner. It is our sin nature that makes us commit individual acts of sin. Adam's one sin produced a sin nature in all men that in turn, caused each person to commit individual acts of sin. Jesus not only dealt with the original sin that contaminated the human race, but He also dealt with each individual act of sin.

Anyone who is trying to obtain righteousness through his actions is totally missing the point. Believers are made righteous through faith in Christ, independent of their actions. It's the same way that everyone was made a sinner: through Adam's one sin, not through our individual sins.

At salvation, our old man (Rom. 6:6) or sin nature died, but the tendency to sin remains in the thoughts and emotions that the old man left behind. No longer does the Christian have a sin nature that compels him to sin, but he must still renew his mind.

Sin ruled like a king through condemnation to bring death upon everyone. Condemnation is like the general of sin that enforces its power. Likewise, God's grace now rules like a king through righteousness to bring all who are in Christ into eternal life. Righteousness is the general of grace who defends us against all the wiles of the devil.

Remove guilt or condemnation and sin loses its strength to rule (1 Cor. 15:56). Remove the knowledge of righteousness by faith, and grace loses its power to release eternal life into our daily lives.

NOVEMBER 14
RECEIVE THE MINISTRY OF THE ANGELS
LUKE 22:43

Luke 22:43 "And there appeared an angel unto him from heaven, strengthening him."

We have angels assigned to us. Hebrews 1:14 further reveals that their purpose is to minister to us, on our behalf. In the Old Testament, Psalm 91 teaches on the ministry of angels to God's people.

Some people who have realized this truth have taken it as far as to say that we are suppose to speak to our angels and they will obey our commands. There is no instruction in scripture to do this nor is there any example of that being done. We don't have the intelligence to administer all of the angels. Many of the angels' protective duties described in Psalm 91 are preventative, and we certainly could not effectively command these activities.

Rather, these angels are dispatched exactly as this verse describes—by looking at the Father's face (Matt. 18:10). God Almighty controls them for us; however, we do have a part to play. Psalm 91 prefaces all of these promises about angels as being for those who dwell in the secret place of the most High. Verse two further instructs us to say that the Lord is our refuge and fortress and in Him we trust.

It is the combination of our faith in God and His faithfulness to us that releases the angels on our behalf. If it was solely up to God, His provision would be the same for everyone because of His mercy and grace. However, we have to receive God's grace by faith (Eph. 2:8). As you seek the Lord, become aware of His ministering spirits which were created to minister to us. Speak forth your faith in this area, and He will send forth His angels on your behalf.

NOVEMBER 15
CHOOSE TO SERVE
MATTHEW 26:51

Matthew 26:51 "And, behold, one of them which were with Jesus stretched out his hand, and drew his sword, and struck a servant of the high priest's, and smote off his ear."

In Romans chapter one, Paul calls himself a servant of Jesus Christ. Out of the six Greek words for "servant" used in the New Testament, Paul used one of the most slavish terms possible. The word used in this passage is "doulos" and comes from the root word "deo" which means "bind." Paul literally speaks of himself as a bondman or slave of Jesus Christ—a slave by free choice; yet owned and purchased by Jesus Christ.

The idea of being a love-slave by choice comes from Old Testament passages such as Exodus 21:2-6 and Deuteronomy 15:12-17. If an Israelite bought a Hebrew slave, he must set him free in the seventh year. However, if the slave loved his master and said, "I will not go away from thee," then a hole was to be bored through the lobe of his ear pronouncing him a bond-slave forever.

Jesus is the supreme example of selflessness—He puts others ahead of Himself. We see clearly from Jesus' example, that the way to exaltation in God's kingdom comes through humility and servanthood to others. Christ's humiliation, displayed in His coming to earth as a man, is not only a lesson in Christology, but also an example to all believers of what greatness in God's kingdom entails. Let this attitude of heart, taken from the example of Jesus Christ, continue to motivate all true believers in Jesus Christ.

The Creator became the creation; the Lord became the servant; the Highest became the lowest. All of this was done because of God's great love for us.

NOVEMBER 16
LEARN THE WORD BY DOING IT
MATTHEW 26:55

Matthew 26:55 "In that same hour said Jesus to the multitudes, Are ye come out as against a thief with swords and staves for to take me? I sat daily with you teaching in the temple, and ye laid no hold on me."

The four gospels refer to Jesus teaching 43 times, preaching 19 times, and preaching and teaching in the same verse, six times. This indicates that Jesus spent twice as much time teaching as He did preaching. Teaching is the basic building block for making disciples. Jesus was making disciples, not just converts.

The Greek word for "disciple" literally means "a learner," and indicates "learning by endeavor" or what we would call "on-the-job training." Jesus said in John 8:31, "If ye continue in my word, then are ye my disciples indeed." Anyone who meets this criterion is Jesus' disciple.

"Jailhouse religion," where a person is only sorry he got caught and is trying to get out of a bad situation, will not produce true discipleship. It takes a forsaking of all to be Jesus' disciple. Jesus wants us to "count the cost." It is definitely a commitment.

What the Lord has started in you, He will also continue and complete. That is not to say that your success will be automatic; you have to cooperate with what God is wanting to do in your life. Our faithfulness may always be suspect, but God's faithfulness is never in question. It is always God's will to continue and complete the good work He began in you.

NOVEMBER 17
YOUR LIFE IS NOT YOUR OWN
LUKE 22:49

Luke 22:49 "When they which were about him saw what would follow, they said unto him, Lord, shall we smite with the sword?"

The Lordship of Jesus is one of the central themes of scripture. It is clear that many times the word "Lord," when referring to Jesus, is equivalent to the divine name "Yahweh" or "Jehovah." To acknowledge Jesus as Lord is to acknowledge His deity (Jn. 20:28).

What it means to give Jesus Lordship in our lives, is to recognize His right to rule in our lives, by right of creation (Jn. 1:3) and right of redemption. *"For ye are bought with a price: therefore glorify God in your body, and in your spirit, which are God's"* (1 Cor. 6:20).

One of the most damaging attitudes of our time is the exaltation of self over others. Personal rights have been promoted at the expense of others. This is not good for society and it is certainly not the way God expects His body to operate.

As Christians, we need to develop a continual awareness that our lives are not our own. We do not have the liberty to do as we please. We should present our bodies as living sacrifices unto God, recognizing that this is just our reasonable duty to the one who gave His life for us (Rom. 12:1).

The Lordship of Jesus should be the determining factor in every action of a Christian (Rom. 14:7-10). Every thought and action should pass the test, "Is this what my *Lord* Jesus wants me to do or think?" If the answer is not a definite "yes," then it shouldn't be done. *"Whatsoever is not of faith is sin"* (Rom. 14:23).

NOVEMBER 18
HEALING IS AN EXPRESSION OF GOD'S MERCY
LUKE 22:51

Luke 22:51 "And Jesus answered and said, Suffer ye thus far. And he touched his ear, and healed him."

Jesus often healed people by touching them, and others received their healing as they touched Jesus. You can transmit the power or the anointing of God through the laying on of hands (Mk. 16:18; Heb. 6:2). The virtue of God can even be transmitted to objects and then brought to the person who needs healing or deliverance.

Jesus provided physical healing as well as forgiveness of sins. Many scriptures mention the healing of our bodies in conjunction with the forgiveness of our sins. Healing is an expression of God's love and compassion for our physical man. Healing miracles also draw men to God to get their spiritual needs met. Physical healing acts like a bell to get man's attention so that the Lord can minister to the inner man as well.

Healing has been purchased for us as part of the atonement of Christ. The Lord would no more refuse to heal us than He would refuse to forgive us. That does not mean that we deserve healing—we don't. It is a gift from God, just as salvation is a gift from God (Rom. 6:23; Eph. 2:8). We don't deserve to have our sins forgiven. We cannot demand salvation from the Lord, but we can expect it. Likewise, healing has been purchased for us through the atonement of Christ. Healing belongs to us, but it is still the mercy of God that provides healing. Every act of healing is an act of mercy.

NOVEMBER 19
GOD'S AWESOME POWER
JOHN 18:5-9

John 18:6 "As soon then as he had said unto them, I am he, they went backward, and fell to the ground."

It is evident that it was the power of God that made these 600 men fall backwards to the ground, but why did it happen when He said, "I am he"?

In this verse, and also in verse eight, the word "he" is italicized. That means that the word "he" was not in the original text, but was added by the translators to make the sentence grammatically correct. This serves a useful purpose and is very helpful in most cases. However, the translators put these additions in italics so that we could be aware of what the text literally said.

In this instance, Jesus literally said, "I am." Since Jesus was God manifest in the flesh, His statement of "I am," carried just as much weight as when He expressed it to Moses (Ex. 3:14). This is nothing less than the Almighty God releasing His glory through the powerful statement, "I AM." No wonder these men were knocked to the ground.

This graphically illustrates how Jesus could have easily defended Himself against any size army that would come to take His life. As He said in John 10:18, "No man taketh it (i.e. His life) from me, but I lay it down of myself."

There are many instances recorded in scripture where people fell to the ground as a result of being in God's presence. The same thing still happens today. Just as some people faint when they experience fear, when they experience the awesome presence of God, they become weak, and lose strength in their physical bodies.

NOVEMBER 20
FIGHT THE BATTLE IN THE SPIRIT
JOHN 18:10-11

John 18:10 "Then Simon Peter having a sword drew it, and smote the high priest's servant, and cut off his right ear. The servant's name was Malchus."

It is the Apostle John who reveals Peter as the one who cut off the servant's ear and identified the servant. It is very doubtful that Peter was aiming for Malchus' ear. It is more probable that he was making a horizontal swing at the servant's head and as the man ducked, Peter cut off his ear.

Peter was very vocal about never denying the Lord, and his actions proved that he meant what he said. There were only two swords among the disciples, yet Peter was willing to take on these 600 soldiers. This spelled certain death or imprisonment.

Peter wanted to stand with the Lord, but he was not prepared spiritually. He was still strong in his own ability. If the battle would have been in the physical realm, Peter would have fought to the death as he proved here. But when Jesus told Peter to put up his sword and not resist with his physical power, Peter was confused.

Peter only knew how to rely on the flesh. When Jesus refused to allow Peter to fight with his sword, he was defenseless. If he would have been praying with Jesus, as instructed, Peter would have been built up spiritually and able to stand with Jesus spiritually without denying Him. As the prophet Zechariah said, *"Not by might, nor by power, but by my spirit, saith the LORD of hosts"* (Zech. 4:6).

Likewise, we may sincerely desire to never deny our Lord, but it takes more than desire; it takes preparation. We all have been taught how to rely on ourselves, but we have to learn anew how to be strong in the Lord and in the power of His might (Eph. 6:10). Just as in the physical realm, where muscles have to be exercised to become strong, so we have to exercise ourselves unto godliness (1 Tim. 4:7).

NOVEMBER 21
CIRCUMCISION IS A MATTER OF THE HEART
JOHN 18:14

John 18:14 "Now Caiaphas was he, which gave counsel to the Jews, that it was expedient that one man should die for the people."

The physical nation of Israel still has a very important part to play in God's plan. It has a prominent role in end-time prophecy. However, the physical nation of Israel has been displaced in importance by the spiritual seed of Abraham: that is the church of Jesus Christ.

Christians are the true circumcised people of God. In Romans 2:28-29, Paul reveals that true circumcision is a matter of the heart, not the flesh, and that true Judaism is through new birth, not physical birth.

In Colossians 2:11, Paul says that spiritual circumcision was done by God without the hands of man. This circumcision, that was made without hands, proves that it was not done in the physical. Paul is referring to the spiritual circumcision of the heart. The sins of our heart were cut away and discarded through the sacrifice of Christ in a similar way that the foreskin is removed from a male. The physical act of circumcision is a picture of the spiritual circumcision that is now a reality in every born-again believer.

The condition of a person's flesh is not the important thing. It doesn't matter if the flesh is circumcised or holy. It is the condition of the spirit that matters with God. Those who put faith in their circumcision to save them are putting confidence in the flesh and not in God. Today, the act of circumcision is not the issue, but acts of holiness are still deemed by many as essential for receiving salvation. That is just as wrong as those in Paul's day who believed that being circumcised granted them salvation.

NOVEMBER 22
HIDE THE WORD IN YOUR HEART
MATTHEW 26:75

Matthew 26:75 "And Peter remembered the word of Jesus, which said unto him, Before the cock crow, thou shalt deny me thrice. And he went out, and wept bitterly."

There are several Greek words used for "word." The Greek word used here is RHEMA and it literally means, "a spoken word; an utterance, a saying, but specifically a spoken word appropriate for the situation." It's not the Bible lying on your coffee table that makes the enemy flee, but the Word of God hidden in your heart, activated by the power of the Holy Spirit, and spoken in the appropriate situation. It's similar to what Jesus says in John 6:63, that *"the words that I speak unto you, they are spirit and they are life."* The words that we speak from the written Word of God are empowered by the Holy Spirit. The Word by itself doesn't make us free. It is the Word we know and speak that will deliver us (Jn. 8:32).

Why is the Word so effective? Because it is the WORD of God. It has authority, because it is indeed the WORD of God. God's Word supersedes all authority of the church, of reason, of intellect, and even of Satan. That's why it is so effective.

In Luke, chapter four, when Jesus was tempted of the devil for 40 days, it was the Word of God that Jesus used to defeat the enemy at His temptation. Jesus constantly met His temptation by quoting from God's Word as He repeatedly stated the phrase, *"It is written."* Likewise, the Christian soldier must avail himself of God's Word by placing it in his heart so that the Holy Spirit may bring it forth at the appropriate time to accomplish a complete and total victory.

NOVEMBER 23
THE SILENCE OF THE SON
LUKE 22:63-64

Luke 22:63-64 "And the men that held Jesus mocked him, and smote him. And when they had blindfolded him, they struck him on the face, and asked him, saying, Prophesy, who is it that smote thee?"

Here is the account of God's own creation mocking and insulting His Son without Him intervening. The pain that this must have caused the Father defies description.

Those who struck Jesus and told Him to prophesy who it was that struck Him, must have taken Jesus' silence as proof that He was not who He claimed to be. The natural mind could not conceive that Almighty God would take this kind of abuse from His creation. But this was the plan of God.

Isaiah prophesied that, as a lamb before its shearers is dumb (Isa. 53:7), so Jesus would not open His mouth. Isaiah also mentioned that Jesus "was taken from prison and from judgment" referring to Jesus not getting a fair trial (Isa. 53:8). Isaiah went on to prophesy in Isaiah 53:9 that Jesus would make "his grave with the wicked, and with the rich in his death." This was fulfilled when Jesus was crucified between two thieves and buried in a rich man's tomb.

NOVEMBER 24
PROPHESY—TO BUILD UP THE BODY
LUKE 22:64

Luke 22:64 "And when they had blindfolded him, they struck him on the face, and asked him, saying, Prophesy, who is it that smote thee?"

Teaching and learning in the scriptures, are much more than academic. It involves being guided by God's principles in relationship to others, as well as knowing and responding to God. It calls for the learner to put the Word of God into practice, not just hear it (Jas. 1:22). It involves hearing a word from the outside and putting it on the inside, so that it may be expressed in our every action. Proverbs, chapter two, says to incline our ear unto wisdom, apply our heart to understanding, cry after knowledge, lift up our voice for understanding, seek her as silver, search for her like hidden treasures, and then we will understand and find the knowledge of God (Prov. 2:1-7). God says, "*My people are destroyed for lack of knowledge*" (Hosea 4:6), and He admonishes us to meditate on His Word day and night that we may observe to do all that is written therein.

All things should be done unto edifying. If those present cannot be taught by what is being done, then it shouldn't be done. Just as with the gift of tongues (that was spoken in the church to benefit everyone) so it is with prophecy. Those who listen will learn and be comforted.

The end result of prophecy is to comfort, encourage, edify, strengthen, exhort, stimulate and help. These should be the guidelines for prophecy within the New Testament church.

We, as believers, are given the sole responsibility in ministry to build others up. This takes place in various ways as we walk in love, promote harmony and peace, and seek the true welfare of others. We must prophesy unto the edifying of the church, and speak things that are good and beneficial to the spiritual progress of others.

NOVEMBER 25
SEEK GREATER REVELATION
JOHN 18:20

John 18:20 "Jesus answered him, I spake openly to the world; I ever taught in the synagogue, and in the temple, whither the Jews always resort; and in secret have I said nothing."

The truths of God are hidden **for** His children, not **from** them. The Holy Spirit has been instructed to teach us all things (Jn. 14:26) and has given us an unction so that we will know all things (1 Jn. 2:20). We only have to appropriate what is ours.

What God desires His New Testament saints to know, that the Old Testament saints could not know, is *"Christ in you the hope of glory."* The coming of the Messiah was predicted in the Old Testament, but the idea that He would actually dwell in us was beyond anyone's imagination. However, the New Testament is clear that Christ, by the Holy Spirit, takes up permanent residence in all believers. This is a wonderful truth that some fail to fully appreciate. Solomon said at the dedication of the temple, *"But will God indeed dwell on the earth? behold, the heaven and heaven of heavens cannot contain thee; how much less this house that I have builded?"* We could say, "How much less this physical body?" This is truly amazing!

The Lord's commitment to dwell in us and never leave us or forsake us (Heb. 13:5), must be taken as an indication of His great love for us. If we continually thought upon this, with all its implications, how could we ever be lonely or discouraged? We couldn't! Depression and self-pity would cease! Why would it matter what others thought of us if we truly understood how much Jesus thought of us?

Our attitudes and fears reveal that this revelation of "Christ in us" is not a well established revelation in most Christians. However, this verse makes it clear that our Father wants to make *"the riches of the glory of this mystery"* known unto us. We should all be seeking a greater revelation of this truth.

NOVEMBER 26
CHOOSE TO LOVE
JOHN 18:23

John 18:23 "Jesus answered him, If I have spoken evil, bear witness of the evil: but if well, why smitest thou me?"

God's kind of love is not self-serving or self-seeking. Agape love will cause a person to lay down his life for another (Jn. 15:13), because he has literally forgotten himself. Many times when heros are asked why they put themselves in jeopardy to save someone else, they reply that they didn't even think about themselves. All they thought of was the danger to the other person. That's God's kind of love.

God's type of love involves emotions many times, but it is not an emotion. It is an act of the will. We can choose to love even when we don't feel like it and we can always conduct ourselves in a godly manner, when we feel God's kind of love. God's kind of love is a choice.

God's kind of love is also the antidote to selfishness and pride. We cannot conquer self by focusing on self. The only way to win over self is to fall in love with God more than with self. It is in discovering God's love that we lose self love.

Jesus didn't feel some emotional sensation when He chose to die for us, but that was the greatest demonstration of God's kind of love that the world has ever seen. He made a choice in spite of His emotions. Because He was consumed with God's love, He acted properly, even when His emotions didn't agree. Jesus is the ultimate example of God's kind of love.

NOVEMBER 27
THE SWORD IS THE WORD
JOHN 18:33-37

John 18:36 "Jesus answered, My kingdom is not of this world: if my kingdom were of this world, then would my servants fight, that I should not be delivered to the Jews: but now is my kingdom not from hence."

Christ's kingdom is spiritual, in the hearts of men—not physical; therefore, our fight as Christians must not be with carnal weapons, but with spiritual weapons (2 Cor. 10:3-5). Spiritual forces cannot be defeated with human weapons.

When we are being attacked for being a part of Christ's kingdom, we must fight with spiritual weapons. Our warfare is not against people, but against the spiritual powers that operate behind the scenes through people. We must realize who the real enemy is and fight with the spiritual weapons the Lord has given us.

We often think that anger will put a person in his place. But *"the wrath of man does not work the righteousness of God"* (Jas. 1:20). Anger displayed against people puts us right into the hand of the devil. The way to overcome the spiritual powers that come against us through people is to turn the other cheek (Mt. 5:39). That makes the demons flee in terror.

One of the main weapons the Apostle Paul speaks of is the Gospel, which is the Sword of the Spirit, (the Word of God). It's the Word backed by God's Spirit that can pull down and crush the strongholds of Satan.

Every Christian is at war. There is a perpetual struggle against Satan and his kingdom from which there are no "leaves" or "discharges." Our enemy goes about as a roaring lion, seeking whom he may devour (1 Pet. 5:8). Those who resist the devil will see him flee (Jas. 4:7). The only ones whom he devours are those who don't actively fight against him.

NOVEMBER 28
WHAT IS A MIRACLE?
LUKE 23:8

Luke 23:8 "And when Herod saw Jesus, he was exceeding glad: for he was desirous to see him of a long season, because he had heard many things of him; and he hoped to have seen some miracle done by him."

Herod desired to see Jesus perform some kind of miracle, and some of the questions he asked Jesus made this desire obvious. However, Jesus did not use His faith to do any miracles for Herod.

Miracles are God's way of meeting the needs of those who seek Him in faith. Miracles will sometimes be used to demonstrate God's ability so that people may believe (Mk. 2:10-11), but they will not happen to skeptics who are tempting God (Lk. 4:9-12).

A miracle is a supernatural intervention of God's power over natural law. Healings occur within the boundaries of natural law while miracles are not limited to natural law. A person with a high fever who receives prayer and then begins to recover is experiencing a healing. The Lord intervened, but in natural ways. The virus, infection, or whatever was rebuked, left the body (Lk. 4:39) and then the natural healing process that the Lord built into all of us took over. When something totally supernatural happens, that's a miracle. When Jesus reattached the servant's ear and it was instantly whole after Peter cut it off (Lk. 22:51), demonstrated a miracle. It was also a healing, but it was a miraculous healing.

Feeding the five thousand (Mt. 14:19-20), walking on the water (Mt. 14:25), translating a ship and all aboard to the other side of the sea (Jn. 6:21)—all these are miracles. Miracles are usually instantaneous whereas healings are sometimes gradual.

The Lord has never had anyone who was qualified working for Him. It's by God's grace that He uses any of us. Anyone who claims to be used of God because of his great holiness is either deceived or a deceiver. It's our faith in the grace of God that allows miracles to flow through us.

NOVEMBER 29
JESUS—THE NAME ABOVE NAMES
LUKE 23:9

Luke 23:9 "Then he questioned with him in many words; but he answered him nothing."

Not only does Jesus' refusal to defend Himself show His humility, but His refraining from venting His wrath against the man who senselessly killed His friend who was the greatest of the Old Testament prophets (Mt. 11:11), also displays His humble nature.

Because of Christ's humility and obedience to the Father, God gave Him a name that is above every name in heaven, earth and under the earth. There is no exemption for anyone or anything from coming under the Lordship of Jesus. He is Lord of ALL.

Jesus has not only been exalted above every "being" that has a name, but He is also highly exalted above anything else that can be named. If you can put a name on it, Jesus is above it. Sickness, poverty, depression, anger—everything has to bow its knee to the Lordship of Jesus.

Every knee of men, angels, and demons will bow and confess that Jesus is Lord. Those who have denied His existence will bow in worship. Those who have spent their lives rebelling His authority will finally bow in submission. Every being from all ages will ultimately bow and worship Jesus. If we bow our knee to His Lordship now, we will enjoy a wonderful life here on earth, and an eternity in His blessings hereafter. Those who deny His rightful claim to the Lordship of their lives will suffer for it in this life as well as in the next. They still will have to bow their knee to His authority, so there is nothing to gain and everything to lose if they refuse to make Jesus Lord of their lives.

NOVEMBER 30
YOU'RE NOT ALONE IN PERSECUTION
LUKE 23:11

Luke 23:11 "And Herod with his men of war set him at nought, and mocked him, and arrayed him in a gorgeous robe, and sent him again to Pilate."

All of Christ's sufferings did not end when He finished His earthly ministry. He still takes the persecution of His people personally as is revealed by His statement to Saul on the road to Damascus: *"Saul, Saul, why persecutest thou me?"* He didn't ask Paul why he was persecuting His people. He said, "Why are you persecuting Me?" When we are persecuted for righteousness' sake, it is actually Christ who is being persecuted.

One of the most trying aspects of persecution is the feeling that God has forsaken you. You may think: *If God wanted to, He could stop the persecution; therefore, He doesn't care.* That's the way the devil tries to make us think; however, the Lord is with you in persecution. If you remember this, it will keep you from being discouraged when persecution comes.

True Christianity is exactly the opposite of the world's system. We are heading in a selfless direction, while the world is consumed with self. Jesus teaches us to love, while the world is full of hate. We are supposed to turn the other cheek, while the world takes opportunities to hurt us. The world and Christianity are in conflict. The only reason a Christian would not suffer persecution is if he is heading in the same direction as an unbeliever. When we go God's way, we will bump into the devil.

Christ is still suffering persecution today when His people are persecuted. He will continue to do so until the establishment of His physical kingdom.

DECEMBER 1
PILATE VIOLATES THE TRUTH
MATTHEW 27:17

Matthew 27:17 "Therefore when they were gathered together, Pilate said unto them, Whom will ye that I release unto you? Barabbas, or Jesus which is called Christ?"

Although Pilate knew that Jesus was innocent, he looked for some diplomatic way to release Jesus that would not cause him to lose popularity with the Jewish leaders. This is why he sent Jesus to Herod. He hoped that Herod would pass judgment on Jesus and save him the trouble.

When that scheme failed, Pilate drew on an old custom of releasing a prisoner to the people at the feast. He gave them a choice between Jesus, who he knew was innocent, and Barabbas, who was a murderer. Pilate thought that the crowd would certainly choose Jesus. However, through the insistence of the chief priests and scribes, the people chose Barabbas to be released.

Pilate was now out of ideas as to how to let Jesus go, and still save face with the Jews, so he condemned Jesus to death. Pilate violated what he knew to be true in his heart because of the fear of men (Prov. 29:25) and what he thought they might do to him. Without the chief priests' cooperation, he ran the risk of unrest among the Jews, and possible punishment by Caesar for failing to govern well.

As it turned out, Pilate was deposed anyway, just a few years later by Tiberius Caesar, and died in exile in Gaul in A.D. 41. At the most, Pilate gained a five-year extension of his troubled rule, and damned his soul in the process. What a person compromises to keep, he'll lose. Sin is never worth the price.

DECEMBER 2
RELIGIOUS PRIDE BRINGS DISSENSION
MARK 15:10

Mark 15:10 "For he knew that the chief priests had delivered him for envy."

The Jews were God's chosen people; therefore, God's representatives on earth. Yet, they lied and condemned an innocent man to death. Pilate could see that their real motivation for wanting Jesus dead was envy. They were doing all their religious works to be seen of men, and were upset that Jesus was getting more recognition than they were. If these Jews would have thought about what type of witness they were giving, even they would have known that their actions were not inspired by God.

We should remember that we are God's witnesses on earth, or as Paul said, *"We are epistles . . . known and read of all men"* (2 Cor. 3:2). Judging our actions in the light of, "What kind of witness will this give to others?" will help us discern whether or not we are being led of God.

The chief priests had deceived themselves and other religious people into believing that they were condemning Jesus for godly reasons, but even an ungodly ruler like Pilate could see through their lies. Religious bondage blinds people to the truth even more than sin does.

These rulers wanted to retain their power and authority, so they fought against the power and authority of Jesus. This is still the same today. Men use doctrinal issues to disguise the real issue. The truth is that, *"Only by pride cometh contention"* (Prov. 13:10). People who love to have the preeminence (3 Jn. 9) are usually the instigators of persecution.

DECEMBER 3
ONE IN SPIRIT
MATTHEW 27:18

Matthew 27:18 "For he knew that for envy they had delivered him."

Many problems arise from envy. James said, *"For where envying and strife is, there is confusion and every evil work"* (Jas. 3:16). Envy and strife go hand in hand and open the door to the devil to do anything he desires in your life. Some people would never give place to the devil through confessing the wrong things, yet through envy, they give the enemy freedom to do his worst. God's kind of love is not envious or jealous because it doesn't seek its own, but seeks the welfare of others. Envy is an indication of self-centeredness.

The Apostle Paul had some opponents who were just like many people who sow strife today. They are against everything and critical of the way those in authority handle things. They make big statements about what they would do if they were in authority, but it's all talk. They haven't proven themselves successful in managing even the smallest things, yet they want to be put in charge of big things, just based on their talk. This is not the system of advancement that Jesus advocates (Mt. 25:21; Lk. 16:11-12; 19:17).

The Lord has united every born-again Christian by baptizing us all into the body of Christ. This is already a reality. Like it or not, want it or not, every Christian is completely one in spirit with every other Christian. Failure to function as one, in our relationships with other believers means someone is not flowing in the Spirit. Our flesh is the part of us that gets in strife with other believers. As we operate in the Spirit more and more, we will come more and more into unity with our brothers and sisters in Christ.

DECEMBER 4
PILATE CONDEMNS JESUS
MATTHEW 27:24

Matthew 27:24 "When Pilate saw that he could prevail nothing, but that rather a tumult was made, he took water, and washed his hands before the multitude, saying, I am innocent of the blood of this just person: see ye to it."

This washing of the hands was not only a symbolic custom of the day that showed innocence, but was also a ritual prescribed in the Jewish law (Dt. 21:6-7; Ps. 26:6).

Matthew is the only writer to record Pilate washing his hands of guilt, just as he was the only writer to record Pilate's wife coming to him with the details of the dream she had about Jesus. Secular accounts record her name as Claudia. She is the only one who spoke for, instead of against Jesus' life during the trial.

This dream, no doubt came from God, since Claudia would have had to dreamt it before she knew of Jesus being brought to Pilate. Not only did the Lord bare witness in Pilate's heart to the innocence of Jesus, but He also gave Pilate's wife a very clear message through this dream. Pilate was not innocent in this matter. Together, these instances underscore that Pilate did not innocently condemn Jesus to death. Pilate will be trying to wash the blood of Jesus off his hands throughout eternity.

Just as God was faithful to show even Pilate the truth in this situation, we can be assured that every person who has ever rejected Jesus has done it in spite of the conviction of the Holy Spirit in his heart (Rom. 1:18-20).

DECEMBER 5
JESUS FREED US FROM SIN
LUKE 23:18

Luke 23:18 "And they cried out all at once, saying, Away with this man, and release unto us Barabbas:"

What happened to Barabbas is a picture of what happens when a person is born again. Barabbas was guilty; Jesus was innocent. Yet Jesus suffered the death that Barabbas should have experienced, and Barabbas went free.

Likewise, we were all guilty (Rom. 3:23) and condemned to death (Rom. 6:23), yet Jesus suffered our punishment so that we may go free (2 Cor. 5:21). Just as Barabbas didn't ask for this substitution, so "God commended his love toward us, in that, while we were yet sinners, Christ died for us" (Rom. 5:8).

Barabbas was freed, but he had to choose whether to accept this new start and remain free, or go back to his old ways and come under the judgment of Rome again. Likewise, we have all been freed through the substitutionary death of Jesus, but we have to choose whether to accept our freedom by putting faith in Jesus, or to reject it by denying Him.

Our death to sin and resurrection to life with Christ is already a reality in our spirits, but will only become a physical reality when we know and believe it. In the same way that Jesus died unto sin once, and death no longer has dominion over Him, the person who recognizes his death with Christ unto sin, will not allow sin to rule over him anymore. Any Christian who is struggling with sin has not recognized that he is dead unto sin.

DECEMBER 6
WHERE'S YOUR FOCUS?
MATTHEW 27:4

Matthew 27:4 "Saying, I have sinned in that I have betrayed the innocent blood. And they said, What is that to us? see thou to that."

These Jews, who had courted Judas' favor to obtain his cooperation in arresting Jesus, cared nothing for Judas. They had simply used him. The devil's crowd may flatter as long as they can use you, but you can be assured that when there is no longer anything in it for them, they will forsake you just as the chief priests did Judas.

The serpent didn't come to Eve in the garden threatening to bite her if she didn't eat of the forbidden fruit. Instead, he came with deception, presenting himself as being concerned for her welfare. Satan's greatest weapon is deceit.

Just as a football player, a boxer, or military man's success depends partly on how well he knows his opponent(s), so believers must not be ignorant of Satan's devices. Jesus stripped Satan of all his authority (Mt. 28:18). The power that Satan uses against us now, is deception. Those who ascribe other powers to him have already fallen prey to one of his lies. The devil deceives us and uses our own power and authority against us. The thing that makes deception so deadly is that those who are deceived don't know it. Once they realize they are deceived, they aren't deceived any more.

The best defense against the devil is to be so God-centered that you give no place to Satan. People who are very sensitive to the devil's presence usually are so at the expense of being sensitive to the Lord's presence. David said, *"If I make my bed in hell, behold, thou art there"* (Ps. 139:8). Anytime Satan's oppression is present, God's presence is there too (Heb. 13:5). It's just a matter of where our focus is. Focusing on the devil is a trick of the devil. Choose to focus on God.

DECEMBER 7
ACCEPT THE GIFT OF FORGIVENESS
LUKE 23:34

Luke 23:34 "Then said Jesus, Father, forgive them; for they know not what they do. And they parted his raiment, and cast lots."

Forgiveness of sins is one of the great themes of the Bible. There is so much that scripture says about it that it would take volumes of books to adequately deal with the subject. It will suffice to say that the blood of Jesus is what provided us with forgiveness of sins. That sacrifice was so great that it outweighed all our sins. It covered all the sins of the world—past, present, and future.

Most Christians have the concept that the sins they committed before they professed faith in Christ are forgiven at salvation, but any sins that are committed after that time are not forgiven until they repent and ask for forgiveness. This is not the case.

All our sins: past, present, and future were forgiven through the one offering of Jesus. If God can't forgive future sins, then none of us can be saved because Jesus only died once, nearly 2,000 years ago, before we had committed any sins. **All** our sins have been forgiven.

The forgiveness of our sins is not the ultimate goal of our salvation. It is just a necessary step. The real goal of salvation is relationship with the Father and sin is a barrier to that relationship. So, it had to be dealt with, and it was, through the blood of our Lord Jesus Christ. But those who stop with the forgiveness of sins and don't go on into eternal life are missing the heart of salvation. Our sins have been forgiven so that we may enter into intimacy with the Lord.

It is through the riches of God's grace that we have received forgiveness for our sins. There is nothing we can do to obtain forgiveness except humble ourselves and receive forgiveness as a gift through faith in Christ.

DECEMBER 8
ABRAHAM'S BOSOM
LUKE 23:43

Luke 23:43 "And Jesus said unto him, Verily I say unto thee, To day shalt thou be with me in paradise."

The paradise that Jesus spoke of must have been the same place that Jesus called "Abraham's bosom," when He told the story of the rich man and Lazarus. Jesus descended into the lower parts of the earth after His death, and John 20:17 shows that it was some time after His resurrection before Jesus ascended back to His Father. Therefore, this paradise was "Abraham's bosom," located in "sheol" in the lower parts of the earth.

The phrase *"led captivity captive"* from Ephesians 4:8, refers to Jesus liberating the Old Testament saints. When Old Testament saints died, they went to a place in the center of the earth which is called "sheol" in Hebrew. It is the Hebrew word "sheol" that is translated "hell" in Psalm 16:10, which prophesies Jesus saying, *"For thou wilt not leave my soul in hell; neither wilt thou suffer thine Holy One to see corruption"* (Acts 2:27-30).

The ungodly dead also went to "sheol," but the teaching of Jesus in Luke 16:19-31 shows that there was a great gulf fixed between the two, and those in torment (hell) envied those who were enjoying the blessings of the Lord in the part of "sheol" that was called Abraham's bosom or Paradise.

Even though these Old Testament saints were blessed, they were not able to enter into the presence of the Lord because the atonement of Christ had not been completed. So, in that sense, they were captives. When Jesus died, He descended into "sheol" and took the captives captive. He took them to heaven, into the very presence of God and vacated that part of "sheol." Now, all that's left in "sheol" is hell. In the New Testament, the Greek word that is used to refer to this area is "hades" and it is only applied to the place of torment.

DECEMBER 9
THE VEIL IS TORN
LUKE 23:45

Luke 23:45 "And the sun was darkened, and the veil of the temple was rent in the midst."
    The veil spoken of here reached from the ceiling to the floor, from wall to wall, and separated the Holy of Holies from the holy place in the temple.
    Solomon's temple was 30 cubits high (1 Ki. 6:2), but Herod increased the height to 40 cubits according to the writings of Josephus, a first century historian. Therefore, depending on what standard you use to convert cubits to feet (there is uncertainty as to exactly what a cubit equaled in feet and inches), this veil was somewhere between 60 feet and 90 feet high.
    It is significant that this veil was rent from top to bottom (Mt. 27:51; Mk. 15:38). No man could have torn the veil in this fashion. It was definitely God that rent the veil. The time when this veil was rent corresponds exactly with the moment Jesus died.
    Hebrews 9:1-9 tells us that the veil separated the Holy of Holies, where God dwelt, from the rest of the temple, where men dwelt. This signified that man was separated from God by sin (Isa. 59:1-2). Only the high priest was permitted to pass beyond this veil, and only once each year (Ex. 30:10; Heb. 9:7). This symbolized the Christ who would enter into God's presence for us and make an atonement.
    The moment that Christ died, the veil was torn in two, revealing that the sacrifice had been made and that there is no longer any separation between God and man. Jesus tore the veil, that is to say His flesh (Heb. 10:20), in two and opened up a new way unto God through Himself.

DECEMBER 10
HONOR YOUR PARENTS
JOHN 19:26

John 19:26 "When Jesus therefore saw his mother, and the disciple standing by, whom he loved, he saith unto his mother, Woman, behold thy son!"
    Children are to honor their parents, even after they become adults. However, the command to obey is temporary (Gal. 4:1-2). Honor naturally leads to obedience if nothing is asked contrary to God's laws, but honor and obedience are not synonymous. The scriptures teach that when a child marries he is to leave his father and mother and cleave unto his mate (Gen. 2:24). Parental dominance that extends into marriage is the source of many divorces and much marital strife. Yet, a child is to honor his parents all of his life.
    The definition of the word "honor" means "to esteem, respect," and the Greek word from which "honor" is translated means "to prize, i.e. to fix a valuation upon" (Strong). There are many applications of children honoring their parents. Certainly, one of the violations of this commandment today, is children esteeming and respecting the opinions of their peers above those of their parents. The idea that parents are out of date and therefore out of touch, is a devaluation of parents. Children should value the experience and wisdom of their parents more than the opinions of their peers.
    It says in Exodus 20:12 and Deuteronomy 5:16, that honoring your father and mother is the first commandment with a promise. This command is the first one of the Ten Commandments that gives a promise of blessing to those who obey it. The promised blessing is long life and things going well.
    John is the only gospel writer to give us this account of Jesus' last ministry to His mother. Even in the face of His own extreme suffering, Jesus thought of His mother and honored her by making sure that she would be taken care of after His departure.

DECEMBER 11
CHRIST IS ALIVE IN US
JOHN 19:30

John 19:30 "When Jesus therefore had received the vinegar, he said, It is finished: and he bowed his head, and gave up the ghost."

When Jesus cried, "It is finished," He was not referring to the whole plan of salvation as being completed. He still had to descend into the lower parts of the earth and lead the captives out (Eph. 4:8-9), as well as come back from the dead and ascend to the Father to make intercession for us (Heb. 7:25). Paul made it very clear in 1 Corinthians 15:14 and 17, that if Jesus did not rise from the dead, then our faith is vain and we are yet in our sins.

Why is the resurrection so important? The resurrection of Jesus makes Christianity different from religion because we are dealing with a real, live person, not just principles. **Christianity is fellowship with a real person who is alive.**

Also, forgiveness of sins is not obtained by a doctrine, but by Christ Himself. If Jesus did not rise from the dead, He can not give salvation to us. However, He did rise from the dead and now He lives forever to make intercession for us (Heb. 7:25).

It is Christ living in us that gives us power to live a victorious life. If there was no resurrection, there would be no power.

The resurrected life of Jesus is the guarantee of our physical regeneration. Because Jesus conquered death, the fear and sting of death have been removed for us. This produces great comfort for those who believe.

So, faith in the present ministry of Jesus is essential to true Christianity, and would be impossible if Jesus was not alive. Without Jesus being alive, Christianity would be just another dead religion.

DECEMBER 12
DEATH HAS LOST ITS POWER
MATTHEW 27:52

Matthew 27:52 "And the graves were opened; and many bodies of the saints which slept arose,"

This is an amazing event that only Matthew records. This earthquake apparently rolled the stones away from many of the graves in the vicinity of Jerusalem, and some of the saints buried there arose from the dead. Even at the death of Jesus, such power was released that death lost its grip on its captives.

It is uncertain whether these resurrected saints died again or were caught up to God. If they were resurrected at Christ's death, then they would have had to die again, just as Lazarus or Jairus' daughter or the widow's son at Nain or anyone else that Jesus raised from the dead during His ministry. This is because Jesus was, "the firstfruits of them that slept" (Acts 26:23; 1 Cor. 15:20). Jesus was not the first person physically raised from the dead, but He was the first person begotten from the dead to never die again.

If these people were not actually resurrected until after Jesus' resurrection, when Matthew states they came out of their graves, then they could have been resurrected with their glorified bodies to never die again.

At any rate, these saints went into Jerusalem after Jesus was resurrected and they appeared to many people. We can only guess what effect this must have had on the people.

The resurrection of Jesus puts Christianity in a class all by itself. Many people have come and gone professing some revelation from God or new way of approaching God, but only Jesus has conquered death. This makes Him unique and elevates Him above the level of any other man who has ever walked on the earth. The resurrection of Jesus is the ultimate proof of the accuracy of His doctrine.

DECEMBER 13
THE TRUE MEANING OF THE SABBATH
JOHN 19:31

John 19:31 "The Jews therefore, because it was the preparation, that the bodies should not remain upon the cross on the sabbath day, (for that sabbath day was an high day,) besought Pilate that their legs might be broken, and that they might be taken away."

The Sabbath was first mentioned in scripture in Exodus 16, when the Lord miraculously provided manna to the children of Israel in the wilderness. The Israelites were commanded to gather twice as much manna on the sixth day because God would not provide any on the seventh day (Ex. 16:5, 22-30). Shortly after this, the Lord commanded the observance of the Sabbath day in the Ten Commandments that were given to Moses on two tablets of stone on Mt. Sinai (Ex. 20:8-11). In this command, God connected the Sabbath day with the rest He took on the seventh day of creation.

According to Exodus 23:12, one of the purposes of the Sabbath was to give man and his animals one day of physical rest each week. Today's medical science has proven that our bodies need at least one day of rest each week to function at our peak. Deuteronomy 5:15 also clearly states that the Sabbath was to serve as a reminder to the Jews that they had been slaves in Egypt and were delivered from bondage, not by their own efforts, but by the supernatural power of God. However, in the New Testament, there is an even clearer purpose of the Sabbath stated. In Colossians 2:16-17, Paul reveals that the Sabbath was only a shadow of things to come and is now fulfilled in Christ. Hebrews 4:1-11 talks about a Sabbath rest that is available to all New Testament believers, but is not necessarily functional in all New Testament believers. This New Testament Sabbath rest is simply a relationship with God in which we cease from doing things by our own efforts and let God work through us. The Old Testament Sabbath is a perfect picture of the New Testament relationship.

DECEMBER 14
VALUE CHRIST HIGHER THAN SELF
MATTHEW 28:9

Matthew 28:9 "And as they went to tell his disciples, behold, Jesus met them, saying, All hail. And they came and held him by the feet, and worshipped him."

Self-denial is embraced by much of Christianity today. Historically, self-denial has always been a big part of false religion. Most religions of the world teach an abasement of self, but they do it as penitence in order to obtain salvation. This is not the denying of self that the Bible advocates.

True self-denial as the scriptures promote is not self hatred or masochism, but rather an enthroning of Christ above self. We have a new identity in Christ that replaces the old self. We don't deny self in order to obtain salvation, but it is a love response to what Christ has already done for us. He gave His all for us and we willingly give our all back to Him.

Denying self in an attempt to earn salvation is most always motivated by guilt and characterized by rigid rules. True Christianity, on the other hand, is not the observance of rituals, but a relationship that produces holiness as a fruit and not the root of salvation. Holiness doesn't come from the outside and work its way inside. When we are born again we become righteous, and we work that holiness out into our physical lives.

Trying to destroy the power of self through harsh laws actually arouses and strengthens sin. Christians must not let life become a set of rules, but rather a response to a loving relationship with Jesus Christ.

DECEMBER 15
PROOF OF THE RESURRECTION
MATTHEW 28:11

Matthew 28:11 "Now when they were going, behold, some of the watch came into the city, and showed unto the chief priests all the things that were done."

In the Jews' efforts to prevent anything from happening that would cause people to believe that Jesus was resurrected, they gave one of the most sure proofs of His resurrection. They sealed the tomb so it would be obvious if it had been opened and they obtained a guard of soldiers to protect it.

This removes all doubt that the followers of Jesus could have stolen His body. Therefore, the enemies of Jesus became a historical witness that Jesus literally rose from the dead.

The guards told the chief priests everything that happened at the tomb. This means that they had a complete account of the earthquake, the angels rolling away the stone, and the angels giving the message to the women that Jesus was alive from the dead. They may have even seen Jesus walk out of the tomb.

The very ones that the Jews had secured to guarantee there would be no rumors of Jesus being raised from the dead, became the first witnesses and heralds of the resurrection. Yet, with the testimony of impartial, non-religious eyewitnesses, they chose not to believe (Lk. 16:31).

DECEMBER 16
THE FATHER'S PLAN
LUKE 24:21

Luke 24:21 "But we trusted that it had been he which should have redeemed Israel: and beside all this, to day is the third day since these things were done."

When the right time came, God sent forth His Son from heaven in His preexistent state, into the world. He was born of a woman (virgin birth) and was made subject to the requirements of the law. Jesus was sent at a specific time. The entrance of Jesus into the physical realm was not a random thing occurring at a haphazard time. There were developments that had to take place before Christ could come to earth and redeem man. The Father sent His Son to the earth at the earliest possible time. Any time prior to the time Jesus was born of the virgin Mary, would have been premature.

His purpose for coming into the world was twofold. First, He came to *"redeem them that were under the law."* He did this by perfectly keeping the law, fulfilling it, and paying its curse (Mt. 5:17; Gal. 3:13). Thus, Christ delivered us from the entire system of the law. The Greek word for redeem means "to buy OUT OF the slave market."

Second, Christ gave us the status of sonship with all its privileges. Not only were we redeemed from the bondage of the law, but we were redeemed unto sonship. Many people stop short, only realizing what they were delivered from, not what they inherit. Sure, we need to rejoice that we are redeemed, but we also need to move on, and realize the full benefits of our inheritance.

God created us for Himself, but we sold ourselves into slavery to the devil. God bought us back through the precious blood of Jesus Christ. No amount of effort, human works, or man's own righteousness could bring the divine favor that we needed. It was the actual life of God (Lev. 17:11) that purchased our redemption.

DECEMBER 17
LET GOD'S PEACE LEAD YOU
LUKE 24:36

Luke 24:36 "And as they thus spake, Jesus himself stood in the midst of them, and saith unto them, Peace be unto you."

Just as every sport has disputes that must be settled by the officials, the peace of God is the umpire that settles all disputes as to what the will of God is for our lives. We must learn to listen to and heed the peace of God in our hearts.

God's peace is something that every born-again believer has. It's a fruit of the Spirit. That peace is always umpiring; we just don't always pay attention. How many times have you acted contrary to the peace in your heart and afterwards, you experience disaster? You say, "I never did feel good about that." That was the peace of God umpiring, but you chose to play by your own rules.

There are some things we can do to facilitate the peace of God umpiring in our hearts. First, consider ALL the options. Many wrong decisions have been made because not all the options were considered. Don't let fear rule out God's possibilities. Next, use your imagination to explore what will happen with each choice. You should be able to discern a greater peace as you consider the option the Lord would have you take. That is not to say that there will be total peace with any of the choices. In your spirit there will be total peace over the right choice, but we aren't always totally in the Spirit and it is not unusual for some turmoil to exist. Just as an umpire has to make a call, be bold enough to follow the direction that gives you the most peace.

The rudder on a ship can't go any direction until the ship is moving. The ship doesn't have to be going full steam ahead for the rudder to work, but it does have to be moving. Likewise, we have to act before the peace of God will give us perfect direction. Even if you make a mistake, you will have made it in faith, trying to follow the peace of God in your heart. The Lord can bless a wrong decision made in faith from a pure heart, more than He can bless indecision (Rom. 14:23).

DECEMBER 18
KINDS OF EVANGELISM
LUKE 24:48

Luke 24:48 "And ye are witnesses of these things."

One of the great mistakes of the modern church is thinking that evangelism is something done within the four walls of the church building. Acts 8:1-4 makes it apparent that evangelism was not done by the pastor or clergy, but by believers who went everywhere preaching the Word (Acts 8:4).

There are several methods of evangelism mentioned in the scriptures. One is house to house evangelism: *"and in every house, they ceased not to teach and preach Jesus Christ"* (Acts 5:42). Another is personal one-on-one evangelism: Philip ministered to the Ethiopian eunuch (Acts 8:26-38), Paul to Sergius Paulus (Acts 13:7), Jesus to Mary Magdalene, Nicodemus, the woman at the well, the thief on the cross, and others. There are about 35 such instances recorded in the Gospels alone. A third method is evangelism to large crowds: Peter ministered to the crowds in Jerusalem at Pentecost (Acts 2) and Paul at Lystra (Acts 14:8-18). Fourth is evangelism to entire cities: *"Then Philip went down to the city of Samaria, and preached Christ unto them"* (Acts 8:5). Also mentioned is public debate and preaching: Paul disputed in synagogues and market places (Acts 16:17); Peter and John preached in the temple (Acts 3:11-26); Paul declared, *"And how I kept back nothing that was profitable* unto you, *but have shown you, and have taught you PUBLICLY, and from HOUSE TO HOUSE, Testifying both to the Jews, and also to the Greeks, repentance toward God, and faith toward our Lord Jesus Christ"* (Acts 20:20-21). Tract evangelism is also metioned in the scriptures. The first tract evangelism with ink and pen are the Gospels. John, in his gospel stated, *"These are written, that ye might believe that Jesus is the Christ, the Son of God; and that believing ye might have life through His Name"* (Jn. 20:31).

Christians are to be wise in the way they act and speak to unbelievers. We are to make the most of every opportunity. The Christian's speech should be gracious with answers that meet the needs of each person they encounter.

DECEMBER 19
GOD POURS OUT HIS SPIRIT
LUKE 24:49

Luke 24:49 "And, behold, I send the promise of my Father upon you: but tarry ye in the city of Jerusalem, until ye be endued with power from on high."

John's baptism was a baptism with water unto repentance for the remission of sins. John preached that the Lamb of God came to take away the sins of the world (Jn. 1:29), but he didn't administer the baptism of the Holy Spirit. However, both John the Baptist and Jesus prophesied the church age, when believers would be baptized with the Holy Ghost.

The baptism of the Holy Spirit came on the day of Pentecost, but it was not only for these few individuals. Peter said in Acts 2:39, *"For the promise is unto you, and to your children, and to all that are afar off, even as many as the Lord our God shall call."* This same power is available to all believers today.

The promise of the Spirit being poured out on *"all flesh"* is speaking of all manners of flesh or mankind. It is evident that not everyone has the Holy Spirit. Rather, this reveals that the door of salvation and the filling of the Holy Spirit is opened unto Jew and Gentile, male and female, adult and child.

Many people argue whether we are in the last days. Joel prophesied that this outpouring of the Holy Ghost would take place in the last days and Peter said that was what happened here, on the day of Pentecost.

If the coming of the Holy Spirit on the day of Pentecost, which happened nearly 2,000 years ago, was the beginning of the last days, then the time must certainly be getting short for us. This should settle the argument for those who believe the Bible. Nevertheless, we can confidently say that this is **our** last generation. We need to be about our Father's work.

DECEMBER 20
BE FILLED WITH THE HOLY GHOST
LUKE 24:49

Luke 24:49 "And, behold, I send the promise of my Father upon you: but tarry ye in the city of Jerusalem, until ye be endued with power from on high."

This filling of the Holy Ghost is subsequent to the born-again experience. Paul reveals in Romans 10:9, that a person has to confess with his mouth that Jesus is Lord and believe in his heart that Jesus was raised from the dead, before he can be saved.

It is possible to be saved, yet not have what Jesus said was the baptism of the Holy Spirit. Since the Holy Spirit is now given freely and we don't have to tarry for His coming, we can receive salvation and the baptism of the Holy Spirit at the same time. However, it is not automatic. We must ask and believe for the baptism of the Holy Ghost, just as we believed for salvation.

Speaking in tongues is unique to the Church Age. This is because when a person speaks in tongues, his new born-again spirit is speaking (1 Cor. 14:14), not his mind. Before salvation, our spirit was the part of us that was, *"dead in trespasses and sins."* Until we received a new spirit (2 Cor. 5:17), the Holy Ghost could not give us this supernatural communication with the Father.

There are two kinds of speaking in tongues which are clearly spoken of in 1 Corinthians 13:1. They are called *"the tongues of men and of angels."* The tongues of men are the known languages in which the disciples spoke. The tongues of angels, or heavenly languages, are the tongues that all Spirit-filled believers can speak, and are what Paul spoke about in 1 Corinthians 12-14.

Jesus said that the Holy Spirit would lead us into all truth and teach us all things. Receiving the baptism of the Holy Ghost is the single most important key to receiving revelation knowledge from God.

DECEMBER 21
MINISTER THE GOOD NEWS
JOHN 20:21

John 20:21 "Then said Jesus to them again, Peace be unto you: as my Father hath sent me, even so send I you."

The dictionary states that to reconcile means to reestablish friendship between; to settle or resolve, as a dispute. The key to reconciliation is to effectively deal with the enmity, ill will, hatred, or hostility that caused the dispute.

The enmity between man and God was sin. God took the initiative to remove this barrier through the means and agency of Jesus Christ, thus leaving man and God as friends once again.

We have received the ministry of reconciliation. That means we are in the ministry of reconciling people to God. Much of what people call the gospel today is actually alienating man from God. True, we need to show people their need for God to get them to receive His forgiveness and reconciliation, but the angry and bitter attitude some people have when confronting the sinner, is not correct.

Imputing people's sins unto them was not the way God used Jesus to reconcile the world unto Himself. We should not focus on the problem of sin, but on the answer of God's grace (Rom. 5:20).

When you read a newspaper, you read about things that have already happened. They are not reporting prophecy. They are reporting the news. So our real job as ministers of reconciliation is to announce the good NEWS, which is an accomplished fact—that sin has already been dealt with through the person of Christ. We should say, "Now we beseech you, be ye reconciled to God. Change your mind and believe the Gospel so that you may partake of what has already been done on your behalf."

DECEMBER 22
THE EFFECTS OF SIN
JOHN 20:23

John 20:23 "Whosesoever sins ye remit, they are remitted unto them; and whosesoever sins ye retain, they are retained."

The meaning of this verse has been hotly debated for centuries. One thing is certain, it does not mean we have the power to justify a person from his sins so he can be born again; only God can do that.

Many people have taught that Jesus is saying, that if we fail to witness to others, we are retaining their sins unto them, and if we do share His love with others, then we are remitting their sins. Although there is truth in this statement, it is not what this verse is teaching. Rather, this verse deals with the temporal effects that sin has on a person's life. Not only is there a future death penalty for sin, but sin destroys us emotionally and physically in this life too. It is this present destruction that sin brings into a person's life that Jesus gave us the power to remit.

Through intercession we can remit a person's sins, so even though he has sown to the flesh and deserves to reap corruption (Gal. 6:8), he will not reap what he has sown. This is done for the purpose of loosing a person from the bondage that Satan desires to hold him in, until he sees the light and repents. This is only a temporary situation and must be continually repeated if the person we are praying for continues to live in sin.

On the other hand, there are times when it is not in the best interest of the individual to remit his sins. There are times when he needs to be made painfully aware of the consequences of his sins. In these cases, we have power to retain his sins; that is, we withdraw our intercession and he reaps what he sows in hope that this will cause him to turn back to God.

DECEMBER 23
SUPERNATURAL FAITH
JOHN 20:25

John 20:25 "The other disciples therefore said unto him, We have seen the Lord. But he said unto them, Except I shall see in his hands the print of the nails, and put my finger into the print of the nails, and thrust my hand into his side, I will not believe."

Thomas refused to believe what He couldn't see or feel. Our five senses were given to us by God and are necessary to help us function in this life, but if we do not renew our minds to acknowledge the limits of our five senses, they will keep us from believing. Faith can perceive things that the senses cannot (Heb. 11:1).

There is a human faith and a supernatural, God-kind of faith. Human faith is based on physical things that we can see, taste, hear, smell, or feel. God's kind of faith believes independently of physical circumstances. To receive God's gift of salvation, we have to use the supernatural, God-kind of faith which isn't limited by our five senses. This is because, to be saved, we must believe for things that we can't see or feel. We haven't seen God or the devil. We haven't seen heaven or hell; yet, we have to believe that these things exist. Human faith can't believe what it can't see.

Man is so destitute that he can't even believe the Gospel on his own. To receive God's gift of salvation, we have to receive the supernatural, God-kind of faith first. Where does this faith come from? How do we get it? Romans 10:17 says, *"So then faith cometh by hearing, and hearing by the word of God."* God's Word contains His faith. As we hear the Word of God about salvation, we receive God's faith so that we can believe the good news of our salvation. We actually use God's faith to get saved.

This God-kind of faith doesn't leave us after our born-again experience. God's faith becomes a fruit of the Spirit which is in our hearts. We never lose this supernatural faith. We just have to renew our minds to God's faith which is in us, and then learn how to use it.

DECEMBER 24
WE ARE ONLY COMPLETE IN CHRIST
JOHN 20:31

John 20:31 "But these are written, that ye might believe that Jesus is the Christ, the Son of God; and that believing ye might have life through his name."

Recognition of our completeness in Christ is a tremendous safeguard against deception. Prior to salvation we are incomplete and constantly strive to satisfy our hunger. Through the new birth, we are complete in Christ and our hunger should only be for more revelation of what we already have in Christ. Total satisfaction with Christ disarms Satan's lies. A big part of all temptation is dissatisfaction.

Adam and Eve would not have eaten of the forbidden fruit if they hadn't been made dissatisfied with what they had. Through Satan's lie they were led to believe that they didn't have it all (Gen. 3:5). The truth is, they did have it all. They were more like God before they ate of the fruit than after they ate the fruit. Their dissatisfaction was a preliminary step to their action of sin.

Satan tempts us in the same way he came against Adam and Eve (2 Cor. 11:3). Therefore, a full revelation of our completeness in Christ will keep us from chasing after all the things the devil has to offer. If anyone tells you that Christ isn't enough; that you need something more, then that's the devil trying to turn you away from your completeness in Christ.

In the same way that Jesus has the fullness of God in Him, we have the fullness of Christ in us. That makes us complete or perfect in Him—that is our spiritual man. Our born-again spirits are identical in righteousness, authority, and power to Christ's spirit because our born-again spirits are the Spirit of Christ (Rom. 8:9), which has been sent into our hearts crying "Abba Father" (Gal. 4:6).

DECEMBER 25
WATER BAPTISM IS A SIGN
MARK 16:16

***Mark 16:16 "He that believeth and is baptized shall be saved;
but he that believeth not shall be damned."***

Water baptism is a command of Jesus and is the initial action taken upon believing. Mark's statement could be rendered, "He who believes with saving faith (i.e. faith that produces actions) will be saved." In this sense, water baptism is very important. It is an opportunity to act on your new profession of faith. Anyone who refuses to follow Jesus' command to receive water baptism, may be suspected of not really believing.

However, there are scriptural examples of people being born again before they were baptized in water. Cornelius and his friends were filled with the Holy Ghost and spoke in tongues before they were baptized in water (Acts 10:44-48). John 14:17 records Jesus saying that an unbeliever cannot receive the Holy Ghost, so Cornelius and his friends must have been born again before their water baptism.

Water baptism is the sign of the new covenant in the same way that circumcision was the sign of the old covenant. The Apostle Paul made it clear in Romans, chapter four, that although Abraham was circumcised, his circumcision was only a sign. Abraham was justified in the sight of God before his circumcision. Paul goes on to state in Galatians 5:1-6, that anyone who trusts in circumcision has fallen from grace; Christ will profit him nothing.

It is faith in the redemptive work of Christ that produces salvation—not our actions. However, James writes that faith without works is dead (Jas. 2:20). Faith alone saves, but saving faith is never alone; it must be acted upon. This is what Mark is referring to when he speaks of baptism.

DECEMBER 26
BE SINGLE-MINDED
JOHN 21:21

John 21:21 "Peter seeing him saith to Jesus, Lord, and what shall this man do?"

Jesus had just told Peter to follow Him. However, Peter wanted to know what the Lord had planned for John. Instead of Jesus answering Peter's question, the Lord told him that what He had in store for John was none of his business.

Satan diverts many people by getting them preoccupied with what others are doing for the Lord. Comparing ourselves with others, whether we come out better or worse, is unwise (2 Cor. 10:12). We need to be so single-minded following the Lord, that we don't look to the right or to the left to see what others are doing. It doesn't matter if we are doing as much to serve the Lord as someone else. The question is, are we doing all that the Lord wants us to do?

Singleness of purpose and vision is a necessity to victorious Christian living. James said that if we try to master many things we will fail (Jas. 3:1). We have to set priorities and focus on them.

The scriptures teach that memory can be a powerful force for good in our lives. It is always good to remind ourselves that we were once apart from God's saving grace. It is an antidote against pride and self-righteousness. A person who remembers what he used to be will have a clearer understanding of who he is now. We have to cultivate our memories by meditating on the great things God has done for us and spoken to us.

DECEMBER 27
GOD IS GOOD
JOHN 21:25

John 21:25 "And there are also many other things which Jesus did, the which, if they should be written every one, I suppose that even the world itself could not contain the books that should be written. Amen."

Every detail of every man's life, who has ever walked on the earth, has not impacted the world as much as the few recorded details of Jesus' life. Jesus was not just a man; He was God manifest in the flesh (1 Tim. 3:16).

In Acts 10:38, Peter gives a very brief, yet descriptive summary of the life and ministry of Jesus. Jesus was anointed with power and with the Holy Ghost. He used this power to do good, not evil. This is one of the main characteristics of God and is one of the easiest ways to discern what is from God and what is from the devil. God is a good God and the devil is a bad devil. If it's bad, it's from the devil. If it's good, it's from God.

Tragedy can come from three sources: God, Satan, and natural law. God has used nature to bring judgment. However, the New Testament believer is exempt from this punitive judgment of God since Jesus bore it for him.

Satan is the source of much of the calamity that people ascribe to God. Many problems arise because people violate the natural laws that God put into motion. If a person drives recklessly and kills himself, it's not God or the devil that killed him. He violated natural law and thus paid the price.

It is incorrect to believe that God controls everything and therefore always has some redemptive design in tragedies. This type of thinking will lead us to ignore the devil, thereby giving him a freehand to destroy our lives. It will also cause us not to use wisdom concerning natural laws, because we will think that nothing can happen unless God wills it. We must remember that God is a good God.

DECEMBER 28
HOW TO BAPTIZE
MATTHEW 28:19

Matthew 28:19 "Go ye therefore, and teach all nations, baptizing them in the name of the Father, and of the Son, and of the Holy Ghost:"

In the same way that this commission is to every believer, not just to ministers, the command to baptize is also for every believer. It is proper for any believer to administer the ordinance of water baptism.

Jesus commands us to baptize in the name of the Father, the Son, and the Holy Ghost, yet there is no recorded instance where the believers did so. Instead, the instances of baptism that are recorded in the book of Acts show people being baptized in the name of Jesus only.

Because of this noticeable difference, doctrines have arisen that teach there is no Trinity, and that unless water baptism is administered in the name of Jesus (only), with faith in the water baptism, a person cannot be saved. This is a false teaching that has led many people astray.

Water baptism is an outward witness of the inner change that has already taken place. In Acts 10:44-48, Cornelius and his friends were filled with the Holy Ghost and spoke in tongues, proving that they were already born again before they were baptized in water.

The harmony between the commission of Jesus and the practice of the early church is simple. When we baptize people in the name of the Father, Son, and Holy Ghost, we are baptizing them in the name of Jesus because "in him (Jesus) dwelleth all the fullness of the Godhead bodily" (Col. 2:9). Therefore, baptizing in the name of either, the Father, Son, and Holy Ghost, or the name of Jesus, is correct as long as Colossians 2:9 is understood.

DECEMBER 29
WATER BAPTISM IS AN ACT OF FAITH
MARK 16:16

Mark 16:16 "He that believeth and is baptized shall be saved;
but he that believeth not shall be damned."

This scripture has led many to believe that water baptism is a part of salvation and that the born-again experience cannot be a reality without it. This same kind of thinking would make seeing Jesus a prerequisite for salvation, based on John 6:40.

It is faith in the redemptive work of Christ that produces salvation—not our actions. However, James writes that faith without works is dead (Jas. 2:20). Faith alone saves, but saving faith is never alone; it must be acted upon. This is what Mark is referring to when he speaks of baptism.

Water baptism is a command of Jesus and is the initial action taken upon believing. Mark's statement could be rendered, "He who believes with saving faith (i.e. faith that produces actions) will be saved." In this sense, water baptism is very important. It is an opportunity to act on your new profession of faith. Anyone who refuses to follow Jesus' command to receive water baptism, may be suspected of not really believing.

Water baptism is a command, but keeping this command does not produce justification. Jesus administered forgiveness of sins without any mention of water baptism.

Philip told the Ethiopian eunuch, who asked Philip to baptize him, that if he believed with all of his heart, he could be baptized (Acts 8:37). Philip used water baptism only after an individual believed. This is also how Mark used water baptism.

DECEMBER 30
USE YOUR DELEGATED AUTHORITY
MARK 16:18

Mark 16:18 "They shall take up serpents; and if they drink any deadly thing, it shall not hurt
them; they shall lay hands on the sick, and they shall recover."

This either speaks literally of supernatural protection if we pick up a snake, or symbolically of protection in our fight against the devil. Since the other four signs in this list are literal, it is most probable that this means physically taking up snakes.

The Apostle Paul experienced this supernatural protection from a viper when he was shipwrecked on the island of Melita (Acts 28:3-5). However, this is the only recorded example of this type of protection in the New Testament. There is no record of the disciples picking up snakes just to prove they were believers. That would be tempting God (Lk. 4:9-12). This, as well as drinking any deadly thing, is a promise that if we pick up snakes accidentally or are forced into that position because of our stand for Christ, we can believe for supernatural protection.

The power that is now working in believers is the same power that worked in Christ to raise Him from the dead. Everything we have as believers in Christ comes from our union with Him. Therefore, what is true of Him is true of us too. We have come to share in Christ's throne, to partake in the authority that the throne represents, and to exercise divine power and dominion. There is no place in the New Testament that tells us to ask God to do something about the devil. Rather, we, (the church) are told to do something about the devil. This is because we have been given delegated authority over the works of the enemy. God desires that the church be enlightened to this, and walk in victory.

DECEMBER 31
GOD STILL PERFORMS MIRACLES
MARK 16:20

Mark 16:20 "And they went forth, and preached every where, the Lord working with them, and confirming the word with signs following. Amen."

The Lord confirmed the preaching of His Word with miracles. If Jesus and the first century Christians needed the Word confirmed with the miraculous (Heb. 2:4), then we do too. There is no scripture that says these miraculous signs have passed away.

Some people have interpreted *"that which is perfect"* in 1 Corinthians 13:10, as being the complete Bible. This has led them to believe that the gifts of the Spirit have ceased. Although God's Word is perfect (Ps. 19:7), it is not the "perfect thing" that is referred to here. 1 Corinthians 13:8 does say that tongues shall cease, but it will not happen until *"that which is perfect is come."*

In 1 Corinthians 13:12, Paul says, *"when that which is perfect is come, we shall see face to face."* This speaks of seeing the Lord face to face, instead of vaguely, as through a dark glass, as it is now. Some might argue that this is speaking in a symbolic sense, instead of literally face to face. But the next comparison in this verse says that then, *"when that which is perfect is come,"* we shall know all things even as we are also known. There is no other way to interpret this, except as a description of when we will stand before the Lord, after this life. Then we will be face to face, and know all things even as also we are known.

Verse eight says that at the time prophecies fail and tongues cease, knowledge will vanish away. This is talking about the next life, or the new heavens and earth, because one of the signs of the end times is that knowledge shall increase (Dan. 12:4).

So the *"that which is perfect"* that Paul speaks of, cannot be the Bible. It has to be either our glorified body, or Jesus at His second coming. Either way, these verses establish that until *"that which is perfect is come,"* tongues and prophecy will remain. They are still valid gifts, and even today, it is God's will to accompany the preaching of His Word with miracles.